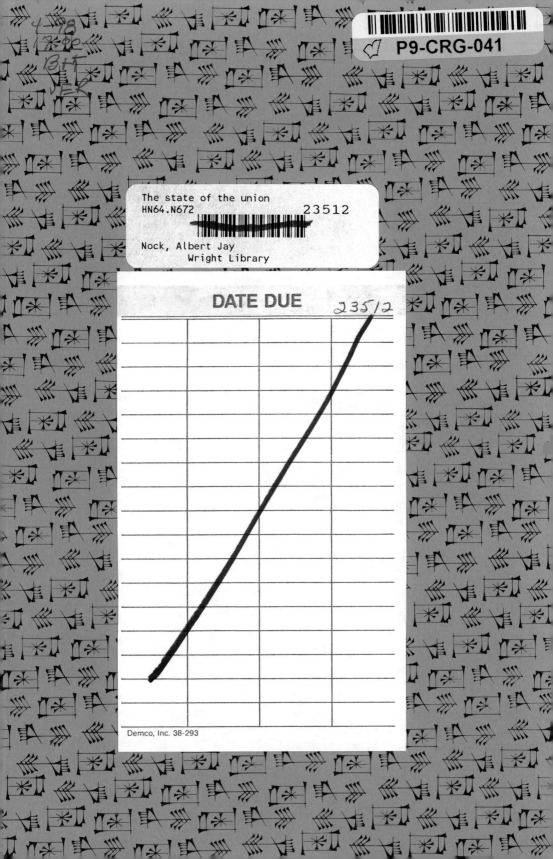

THE STATE OF THE UNION

ALBERT JAY NOCK

THE STATE OF THE UNION

Essays in Social Criticism

BY ALBERT JAY NOCK

EDITED BY

CHARLES H. HAMILTON

LibertyPress

INDIANAPOLIS

LibertyPress is a publishing imprint of Liberty Fund, Inc., a foundation established to encourage study of the ideal of a society of free and responsible individuals.

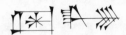

The cuneiform inscription that serves as the design motif for our endpapers is the earliest-known written appearance of the word "freedom" (*ama-gi*), or "liberty." It is taken from a clay document written about 2300 B.C. in the Sumerian city-state of Lagash.

Foreword © 1991 by Charles H. Hamilton. All rights reserved. All inquiries should be addressed to Liberty Fund, Inc., 7440 North Shadeland Avenue, Indianapolis, Indiana 46250-2028. This book was manufactured in the United States of America.

Cover and frontispiece photo from the Albert Jay Nock Collection in the Library of Congress, Washington, D.C.

Library of Congress Cataloging-in-Publication Data

Nock, Albert Jay, 1872 or 3–1945.
    The state of the union : essays in social criticism / by Albert Jay Nock ; edited by Charles H. Hamilton.
      p.   cm.
    Includes bibliographical references and index.
    ISBN 0-86597-092-0. — ISBN 0-86597-093-9 (pbk.)
    1. United States—Social conditions—1918–1932. 2. United States—Social conditions—1933–1945. 3. United States—Civilization—20th century. 4. Social problems. I. Hamilton, Charles H., 1946– . II. Title.
HN64.N63   1991
306′.0973′09042—dc20   90-22412
                                                              CIP

10 9 8 7 6 5 4 3 2 1

I think I am not wrong in ascribing the lucidity of his thought and even of his style to his profound understanding of the meaning of freedom and the wealth of its implications.
—Suzanne La Follette, Introduction to *Snoring as a Fine Art*

Contents

Foreword

"[O]ne of the most gracious but pitiless of American social analysts in our time."[1] Friends and opponents alike have described Albert Jay Nock in similar terms. One finds in Nock qualities he found in Thomas Jefferson and Viscount Falkland: "radical principles and ideals combined with Tory manners."[2] He weaved those principles and manners with an acerbic wit and profound love for the English language to write about the thing that interested him most: "the quality of civilization in the United States."[3] What he had to say often fell on deaf ears, but he contributed some powerful and lasting criticism of the state of the humane life in America.

From his first published article in 1908 until his death in 1945, Nock was the quintessential individualist as "connected critic," in Michael Walzer's phrase. His writing fits easily and uniquely into the "intellectual structure" Walzer defined as good social criticism:

> the identification of public pronouncements and respectable opinion as hypocritical, the attack upon actual behavior and institutional arrangements, the search for core values (to which hypocrisy is always a clue), the demand for an everyday life in accordance with the core. The critic begins with revulsion and ends with affirmation.[4]

Throughout his essays and books, Nock struggled to temper his revulsion at society's shabby and misdirected development with a tentative hope and affirmation.

Much of the importance of Nock's writing turns on his estimate of what the job of the critic is and on his estimate of the intended audience.

1. Bernard Iddings Bell, *Crowd Culture* (New York: Harper and Brothers, 1952), pp. 149–150.

2. Albert Jay Nock, "A Study in Manners," *On Doing the Right Thing and Other Essays* (New York: Harper and Brothers, 1928), p. 92

3. Albert Jay Nock, *On Doing the Right Thing and Other Essays,* p. ix.

4. Michael Walzer, *Interpretation and Social Criticism* (Cambridge: Harvard University Press, 1987), p. 87. Also see his interesting portraits of eleven critics in *The Company of Critics* (New York: Basic Books, 1988).

Nock understood the critic's task to be one of observation and description.

> But the true critic has his resources of joy within himself, and the motion of his joy is self-sprung. There may be ever so little hope of the human race, but that is the moralist's affair, not the critic's. The true critic takes no account of optimism or pessimism; they are both quite outside his purview; his affair is one only of joyful appraisal, assessment, and representation.[5]

He did what he believed any essayist does: he "preached publicly. Anyone who liked might listen; anyone who liked might pass by." Every society harbored a Remnant—Nock was sure—people who were capable of transcending mass culture, materialism, and political opportunism in order to seek a more humane life. Nock took up Isaiah's job—to encourage and brace up this Remnant of individuals in building a "substratum of right thinking and well-doing." These were self-selected and unknown individuals from all walks of life, "who by force of intellect are able to apprehend these principles [of the humane life], and by force of character are able, at least measurably, to cleave to them; the masses are those who are unable to do either."[6] Nock believed the critic, like all individuals in society, could do little more than articulate the principles and practice them.

Several themes run through Nock's work which set him apart from the usual company of critics. Above all, Nock continually stressed, individual freedom is the primary enabling condition for civilization and what he called "the humane life." As he often noted: "What matters is that, for life to be truly fruitful, life must be felt as a joy, and that where freedom is not, there can be no joy."[7]

Other critics might regard individual liberty of minor significance when compared to mass movements and social planning. Or they might mention freedom as a passing luxury only after the attainment of a certain moral order. Nock would have also been the first to acknowledge that freedom had potential hazards connected to it, such as temptation, shallowness, and vice. Throughout the warp and woof of his writing,

5. See "Artemus Ward" below, p. 119.
6. See "Isaiah's Job" below, pp. 129, 132, and 126.
7. See "Our Pastors and Masters" below, p. 156.

however—at his most hopeful and later at his most bitter—freedom was "the only condition under which any kind of substantial moral fibre can be developed. Everything else has been tried, world without end."[8] Nock believed that a commitment to individual liberty had to be the starting point and continual reference point for any critical enterprise.

Nock advanced as guides in living the moral, intellectual, practical, and artistic examples of what he called "the Great Tradition"—the variegated richness of Western civilization. "It is the critic's business," he wrote, "to show where and what the best is and why it is the best, to keep it continually to the front, and strictly to shape his own works and ways according to its measure."[9] He often wished that he could have written exclusively on this theme of preserving and holding up this great past. Instead, Nock was continually drawn into passing censure on the appalling state of American public affairs—in progressively strident tones.

This grounding in the Great Tradition together with a faith in freedom suffused Nock's early writings with an Enlightenment trust in human nature and progress. The humane life was possible for most people. As he got older, his Jeffersonian optimism waned. Americans had the kind of civilization they deserved, he noted, and it was a pretty poor specimen. It became clear to him that true civilization was beyond most people.

What then, Nock wondered, are the actual human and social impediments that make the humane life so elusive? "This was just what had mystified me all my life; it was the one thing above all others that I wanted to know."[10] A search for answers to that question animates the development and focus of Nock's thought throughout his career.

A large dose of human nature—what Nock in his younger days in the ministry would have called original sin—explained part of this failure of humankind. But reliance on a theological explanation for human conduct was deeply dissatisfying to the young Nock. One social factor, however, did seem to hold a key to what had reduced "the rich promise that American life had." It was that "swine in Washington

8. See "On Doing the Right Thing" below, p. 323.

9. "On Hearing Good Music Done Badly," *Atlantic Monthly,* July 1939, p. 35.

10. Albert Jay Nock, *Memoirs of a Superfluous Man* (New York: Harper and Brothers, 1943), p. 136.

invaded this life."[11] The intrusion of the political into every sphere of thought and human action received prominent attention in Nock's writing. Nock excoriated the increasing politicization · of society—a legacy of Progressivism and World War I—by which all life should be managed by politicians through the instrumentality of the State. He derided the political management of economics and morality as particular favorites for these men of little vision and faith. Nock stressed that the important elements in life are outside the political realm. For much of his career, he described himself as a philosophical anarchist; sui generis, in any case.

Nock relied on the distinction made by the German sociologist Franz Oppenheimer between the two means by which human beings satisfy their needs and desires: economic or political. When people apply their energy and ingenuity in voluntary and peaceful ways, they are using "economic means." In the marketplace, this is the free market economy. By "political means," Oppenheimer referred to the use of coercion and exploitation to transfer wealth from producers to non-producers, usually by taxation and subsidy.[12] Reliance on Statism—the political means— saps the ability of individuals, voluntary associations, and communities to devise humane and workable solutions to realize life's possibilities and challenges. Nock saw Statism's essential nature as a criminal activity—whether of the left or right, democratic or totalitarian. Only a most limited and constantly watched State would be remotely bearable.

Succumbing to political nostrums to solve problems of every variety is a perennial temptation, especially in a democracy, but it can only spell the end of useful criticism and the beginning of practical failure. As Nock pointed out: "You can't be a philosophicker and a politicker at the same time."[13]

When everything had to fit political categories—precisely what Nock railed against—even his commentary took on a political hue. Ironically, Nock contributed to this tendency. In order for him to get his non-political message across about the wellsprings of the humane life, he had to clear away a great deal of political debris. Denunciations of

11. "Pearls Before Swine," unsigned editorial by Albert Jay Nock, the *Freeman*, January 4, 1922, p. 388.

12. See *The State* by Franz Oppenheimer (New York: Free Life Editions, 1975).

13. *Selected Letters of Albert Jay Nock*, Francis J. Nock, ed. (Caldwell, Idaho: The Caxton Printers, 1962), p. 81.

politics came easily to his pen, and they were often very good. Readers saw merely the political criticism, however, and found it too negative and too sketchy as political philosophy. In dismissing Nock's as just another, albeit curmudgeonly, political perspective, they missed a critical sensibility which is beyond politics.

Nock's emphasis on the essentially non-political nature of civilization also came across as weak and incomplete because he refused to offer solutions of his own. His purpose was to get people to think. He saw defining the moral dimension of what ought to be and identifying the practical dimension of how to get there as traps that dilute the critical enterprise and blur the critic's eye for the truth. He often states in his essays that he does not urge or recommend a course of action. In part, this may have been a stylistic flourish, but it was also integral to Nock's view of the critic's role. "I was never much for evangelization. I am not sure enough that my opinions are right, and even if they were, a second-hand opinion is a poor possession."[14] Readers who wanted to be spoon-fed solutions routinely responded with outraged letters to the editor.

Nock knew the tricks of history and the vagaries of human action well enough to appreciate how even the best theories and rhetoric never translate into practice very well. Good principles could easily lead to bad outcomes and bad practice could actually have most salutary results. Nock's strictures against rationalism in politics reinforced his view of the proper role of the critic and the proper loci of positive change in any society. The critic must hope to engage in disinterested thought, and let those who are interested listen.

> Probably the only way that society can profitably progress is the way it does progress, by the long and erratic ins and outs of trial and error; and blind insistence on any theory, even a sound one, is to little purpose. One may best hang one's theory up in plain sight for any one to examine who is so disposed, and let it go at that.[15]

The only practical "programme of action" Nock proffered was the Biblical injunction, "*Get wisdom*, get understanding."[16] Right thinking

---

14. See "Anarchist's Progress" below, p. 50.
15. See "Study in Paradoxes" below, p. 123.
16. "A Programme of Action," unsigned editorial by Albert Jay Nock, the *Freeman*, April 13, 1921, p. 100.

must always come before right action. Nock concluded that salutary changes made by individuals alone make a humane life, on whatever scale, possible. The only thing one can do "to improve society is to present society with *one improved unit* . . . the method of each *one* doing his very best to improve *one*."[17]

Albert Jay Nock was an intensely private man. While he was working as editor of the *Freeman* in New York City in the 1920s, the story is told that the only way to contact him after work was to leave a message under a certain rock in Central Park. Even close friends knew little of his past or private life. Nock wanted it that way. He rankled at the perverse assumption that it is necessary to know everything about someone in biography or autobiography: "a subject's private activities, his character, and his relations of whatever kind, are insignificant except as they affect his public activities, character and relations, and . . . the sound biographer should distribute his space accordingly."[18]

Many tantalizing questions about Nock's life remain unanswered. Was he a minor league baseball player for a time? What overseas government assignments did he have from the Secretary of State before World War I? Why did he leave the ministry and quit his family? Touching on just a few dates and events in Nock's life, however, will add context to some of the themes in his writing.

Nock was born on October 13, 1870, in Scranton, Pennsylvania. He was an only child. His father, who came from a family of Dissenters, was a minister with the Protestant Episcopal Church. His mother, to whom he was very close, was a descendant of French Huguenots and of John Jay. He grew up in Brooklyn, New York, still small and rural at the end of the nineteenth century. He later moved with his parents to the northern Michigan lumber town of Alpena. Even when he matured into a cosmopolite, these small-town roots continued to replenish his beliefs in egalitarianism, individualism, self-respect, diligence, and justice. These were "the virtues that once spoke out in the Declaration of Independence. It was noticeable too, that these virtues flourished as well as they did in a state of freedom."[19]

17. *Memoirs of a Superfluous Man,* p. 307.
18. See "The Purpose of Biography" below, p. 8.
19. *Memoirs of a Superfluous Man,* p. 60.

Nock was largely self-educated until his parents sent him to a small preparatory school at the age of fourteen. He attended St. Stephen's (now Bard) College between 1887 and 1892, where he received good "preparation for life" with a "grand old fortifying classical curriculum."[20]

In 1897, Nock became an Episcopal minister and held several parish posts, which gave him considerable time to study and read. He married and he had two sons. His last church position was as rector at St. Joseph's Church in Detroit from 1907 until late 1909.

In 1908, Nock published his first article. It introduces several of the themes that were to animate his subsequent writings. Even at that early date, Nock expresses uneasiness with the small concerns of the "social practitioners." He sought to focus on the larger goal of "progress in culture," since he found the vision of religion too limiting: "Before one may hope to do much with a special mode of poetic truth like the truth of religion, at least some sense of the validity and worth of poetic truth in general must be set up."[21]

In late 1909, at the age of 39, Nock reacted to the limitations he felt and made an abrupt change in his life. He left the ministry, his wife, and children. He moved to New York City.

He joined the staff of the *American Magazine*. This was a gathering place for muckrakers and progressives intent on exploring precisely the same questions that troubled Nock: why civilization and the humane life seemed so often thwarted. For them, the remedy was exposure of the problems of social and economic injustice. In several articles, and especially in his short "Interesting People" column, Nock illustrated that men of influence could imbue political life with a new civic spirit. He profiled such men as Mayor William Jay Gaynor of New York City; E. F. Schneider, manager of the Cleveland, Southwestern & Columbus Railway; William Wirt, superintendent of schools in Gary, Indiana; and his close friend Mayor Brand Whitlock of Toledo. When his colleagues and other reformers suggested large-scale political solutions to problems, Nock demurred. Right thinking and good example alone are sufficient, he thought.

By this early period Nock had imbibed the economic analysis of Henry George, as had so many of his generation. Through the twenties,

---

20. *Memoirs of a Superfluous Man*, p. 79.
21. See "The Value to the Clergyman of Training in the Classics" below, pp. 16–17.

Nock used Georgism—with its anomalous combination of a strong free market perspective based on an analysis of the land monopoly—as a primary mode of analysis. If seemed to explain much of the injustice in the world. While he rarely advocated the practical suggestions of Henry George or especially those of his followers, the basic premises stayed with him throughout his life. In later years, Nock explained the evils of economic injustice less in Georgist terms and more in terms of the subtle influences of crass materialism, what Nock called "economism."

Nock next joined the staff of the liberal, antiwar periodical the *Nation* when Oswald Garrison Villard became editor and owner. As an associate editor from mid-1918 until nearly the end of 1919, Nock was a forceful critic and articulate voice dissenting from the modern liberal (Statist) tenor of the magazine.

World War I and the failure of Wilsonian idealism had proved as eye-opening to Nock as it had to a whole generation. Many of that generation were devastated; others embraced an extension of war collectivism. Nock, for his part, gained from the experience a heightened awareness of the destructive nature of Statism and the ways modern liberalism was exacerbating the progressive politicization of society.

Nock took up the mantle that Randolph Bourne left when he died in December 1918. "War is the health of the State" Bourne had written. Only a month before he died, Bourne wrote his mother, "Now that the war is over people can speak freely again and we can dare to think. It's like coming out of a nightmare."[22] Nock shared the same hopefulness, writing Francis Neilson (an expatriate Englishman and classical liberal) in December of 1919, "the sane radical is up for his turn at the bat and is in the right mood to make a hit."[23] But Nock also feared the nightmare would continue. As he put it in 1923: "we cannot help remembering that this was a liberal's war, a liberal's peace, and that the present state of things is the consummation of a fairly long, fairly extensive, and extremely costly experiment with liberalism in political power."[24]

---

22. Quoted in Edward Abrahams, *The Lyrical Left* (Charlottesville: University Press of Virginia, 1986), pp. 88–89.

23. *Selected Letters of Albert Jay Nock,* p. 96.

24. "Our Duty Towards Europe," unsigned editorial by Albert Jay Nock, the *Freeman,* August 8, 1923, p. 508.

Concerned that the modern era ushered in by World War I was without anchors to a past full of cultural norms and understanding of freedom, Nock set out to propound an alternative viewpoint. It would oppose the politicization of society, resurrect the true classical liberal philosophy, pursue the ideal of personal liberty, and espouse the idea of the Great Tradition. In this endeavor, Nock was joined and supported by Francis Neilson and Helen Swift Neilson (of the Swift meat-packing fortune).

The result was the *Freeman*, a weekly magazine published from March 17, 1920, until March 5, 1924. As John Chamberlain later observed in a successor magazine of the same name, the *Freeman* had a unique place in American journalism; it stood as "a great liberator . . . the great conservator of the idea of voluntarism."[25] A remarkable group of staff members and contributors joined Nock and the Neilsons to produce a periodical widely recognized as one of the best of American journalism.

In an early editorial, Nock proclaimed that the *Freeman* was "radical" and distinguished it from the liberalism that emanated from the *Nation* and the *New Republic*. It was committed to "fundamental economics," a code phrase for laissez-faire and the ideas of Henry George. The *Freeman* also believed "that the state is fundamentally anti-social and is all for improving it off the face of the earth."[26] These social, economic, and (anti)-political concerns suffused the front pages of each issue.

The *Freeman* was not all economics and politics. A wealth of erudite articles discussed other issues—manners, literature, and the "good life"—that composed the humane life. But the rhetoric attacking politicization sometimes drowned out the rest. While readers and commentators alike called the magazine brilliant, they struggled to fit the journal into a political procrustean bed. They couldn't decide if it was liberal, conservative, Bolshevik, revolutionary, anarchist, or Georgist. Lillian Symes and Travers Clement were probably closest when they placed the *Freeman* within "the main tradition of American individualism . . . individualist radicalism."[27]

25. John Chamberlain, "A. J. N.: Man of Letters," the *Freeman* 12 (November 1962), p. 59.

26. See "In the Vein of Intimacy" below, p. 216.

27. Lillian Symes and Travers Clement, *Rebel America* (New York: Harper and Brothers, 1934), p. 128.

This was an unusually productive period in Nock's life. He came into his own as an essayist, gifted editor, and social critic. One commentator has echoed the almost universal opinion that the *Freeman* "was one of the important and influential journals of this century [and] must surely constitute one of the most massive monuments of journalistic excellence ever produced in so short a period."[28] But publishing a weekly journal was exhausting. Nock wrote as much as twenty percent of the material in a twenty-four page tabloid-size issue. He edited and wrote for all but eight of the two hundred and eight issues. Even before the last issue of the *Freeman* was off the presses, Nock was on a ship to Europe. From then on, he was to divide his time between Europe (mostly Brussels) and America (usually New York City, Connecticut, or Rhode Island). While Nock was quintessentially American, he felt more and more out of step with a crassly materialistic society. He had initially criticized the expatriate urgings of Harold Stearns, but Nock now found solace in the cultures of Europe, whether visiting his twentieth century haunts or reading and studying his favorite sixteenth century French humanist, François Rabelais.

After the *Freeman*, Nock made a meager but sufficient living as an essayist. He settled into nearly twenty years of immensely productive writing. He was a regular contributor to the *Atlantic Monthly*, *American Mercury*, and *Harpers*. For Suzanne LaFollete's short-lived *new Freeman* (March 1930–March 1931), he wrote many of the editorials and the monthly "Miscellany" column. Many of those columns later appeared in *The Book of Journeyman*.

Along the way, Nock completed several longer, historical studies of aspects of the Great Tradition. In 1926, he published his still respected "study in conduct and character," *Jefferson*, and later, his loving books on Rabelais (1929 and 1934). Two collections of essays—most of which had appeared earlier as magazine articles—came out in 1928 and 1937.

Nock briefly taught American history and politics at Bard College (1931–33). In 1931, he delivered the Page-Barbour lectures at the University of Virginia which he published as *The Theory of Education in the United States* (1932). An important critique of modern education, these lectures also represent a turning point in Nock's thought. Nock

---

28. G. Thomas Tanselle, "Unsigned and Initialed Contributions to *The Freeman*," *Studies in Bibliography* 17 (1964), p. 154.

stated more clearly in this book than before that all men were not, finally, educable. Many could only be trained.

About the same time, Nock came across the views of Ralph Adams Cram, most notably in Cram's "Why We Do Not Behave Like Human Beings."[29] Cram's pseudoscientific theories (a vogue of the times) explained human evil by claiming that the vast majority of human beings were not "psychically human." Nock was quite taken by Cram's article. As he wrote in December 1934,

> I admit that Mr. Cram has shaken me up frightfully, and also that all the evidence available, every scrap of it, positive and negative, looks straight his way. Yet, perhaps because I am too old a dog to learn any new tricks, I must still put myself down, at least provisionally, as a Jeffersonian and Georgite of sorts. . . . My expectations, doubtless, run to a much more distant future than Mr. Jefferson's or Mr. George's, but I am still, perhaps quite irrationally, on their side.[30]

Nock had always struggled with a tension between the hope that human beings were perfectible and the pessimism that civilization was impossible. He had developed a number of explanations for the impediments to civilization: human nature, economics, and especially the State and the politicization of society. In a sense, Cram's view that most people were not "psychically human beings" represented, for Nock, a final, full-circle crystallization of what made civilization so difficult. He now came to accept that the evil of men's ways was quite natural—a truly secular version of original sin.

Nock cared little for the world of the 1930s and early 1940s as he lived out his sixties and entered his seventies. The work of the critic was very difficult, he felt, because "when you know a great deal about something, you have hard work to keep your knowledge from going sour.[31] It had gone sour for him.

The impact of Cram can be overdrawn, however. He certainly reinforced a bitterness that had always been in Nock's writings, becoming

29. Ralph Adams Cram, "Why We Do Not Behave Like Human Beings," *American Mercury*, September 1932, in *Convictions and Controversies* (Boston: Marshall Jones Co., 1935), pp. 137–154.

30. Albert Jay Nock, "The Quest of the Missing Link," *Free Speech and Plain Language* (New York: William Morrow and Company, 1934), p. 236.

31. See "Pantagruelism" below, p. 200.

more pronounced in later years, but Nock still held out the possibility of perfectibility for some undefined few sprinkled through every walk of life. These few were the Remnant, and they made Nock's effort worth it. For the rest, Nock said he could now accept human beings as they were:

> My change of philosophical base had one curious and wholly unforeseen effect. . . . Since then I have found myself quite unable either to hate anybody or to lose patience with anybody; whereas up to that time I had always been a pretty doughty hater, and not too patient with people. So my change of base certainly brought me into a much more philosophical temper.[32]

Cram's views, together with Nock's own inclinations, age, and experience, put a crimp in Nock's philosophical anarchism, but never affected his strong anti-Statism. Nock's writing retained its strongly anti-political flavor to the last. In 1935, he published his influential *Our Enemy, The State*. He also turned again to political journalism, writing editorials and a monthly column called "The State of the Union" from February 1936 through September 1939 for Paul Palmer's *American Mercury*. In an aside to 'A Little Conserva-tive' Nock writes, "If this be true [Cram's theory], the anarchist position would give away to the position of Spencer, that government should exist, but should abstain from any positive interventions upon the individual, confining itself strictly to negative interventions."[33] Indeed, shortly before his death, Nock criticized F. A. Hayek for not being an anti-Statist "whole-hogger" in his *The Road to Serfdom*.[34]

In 1943, Nock published his *The Memoirs of a Superfluous Man*. The book afforded Nock the opportunity to look back and summarize what he called his "philosophy of intelligent selfishness, intelligent egoism, intelligent hedonism . . . they amount merely to a philosophy of informed common sense."[35] It is full of outspoken prejudices mixed with remarkably prescient commentary on the state of contemporary society. The inconsistencies, the controlled grief, the superiority, the struggles

32. *Memoirs of a Superfluous Man,* p. 138.
33. See 'A Little Conserva-tive' below, p. 261.
34. *Economic Council Review of Books,* February 1945, p. 4.
35. *Memoirs of a Superfluous Man,* p. 304.

with hope and revulsion all combine to make this book something of a literary and critical classic in American letters. The *Memoirs* combined a summary lament about his own intellectual journey, and the lessons of how to make the most of it. Nock did not complain, for he joyfully acknowledged he had more than he deserved: "So while one must be unspeakably thankful for all the joys of existence, there comes a time when one feels that one has had enough."[36]

Albert Jay Nock died on August 19, 1945.

Nock's legacy as a social critic has often been overshadowed by the narrower political legacy claimed for him. He was, indeed, one of the founders of the renaissance of the political right in America. Conservative publisher Henry Regnery expressed the indebtedness of many when he wrote that "there can be no doubt that he contributed substantially to the development of modern conservatism."[37] He did provide a grounding for later developments in conservatism and libertarianism. In the process, a full appreciation for Nock's enduring contribution to American social criticism gets lost as factions on the right cut and paste from Nock whatever suits them.

For many readers, Nock's emphasis on individual liberty combined with his hatred of the State was certainly an important and attractive feature of his writing. But it just as easily turned others away. What interested Nock most was what remained after the political perspective was sacked. The ultimate concern was the good life, those things that made life lovely. "The final test, indeed, of any civilization—the test by which ultimately it stands or falls—is its power of attracting and permanently interesting the human spirit."[38] Nock didn't fail to make this point and develop this theme, although it is sometimes drowned out by the political harangues he indulged in so eloquently.

The shadow over Nock's critical legacy is also the result of the loss of the sharp and joyous edge so evident in his earlier writings. Even in his own eyes he became less a useful critic and more the kind of sad

36. *Memoirs of a Superfluous Man*, p. 325.

37. Henry Regnery, "A. J. N.: An Appreciation," *Modern Age* 15 (Winter 1975), p. 25.

38. Albert Jay Nock, "Prohibition and Civilization," *North American Review*, September 1916, p. 407.

curmudgeon he had earlier agreed were the likes of H. L. Mencken and Sinclair Lewis: "cheeky reporters with rather nasty minds."[39] This final bitterness can be avoided only by the best social critics; witness the literature of lamentation which includes writers as diverse as Julian Benda, Jose Ortega y Gasset, Herbert Marcuse, and Richard Weaver. This later expression of hopelessness and cynicism leads some commentators to overemphasize an elitist and negative message in Nock's writings.

Still, the themes Nock explored in his writing and which served as wedges for exposing the nature of the human experience are as prescient as ever. So too is his tentative and hopeful acceptance of the world's unknowable ways. What, then, is to be *done*? Nock reminds us that human nature requires concentration on individuals, not in an atomistic way, but as the focal point for the growth of morality, spirit, intellect, beauty, manners, and, finally, the possibility for a humane life and a lovely civilization.

> We need only remark that our place and function in it ["great and salutary social transformations"] are not apparent, and then proceed on our own way, first with the more obscure and extremely difficult work of clearing and illuminating our own minds, and second, with what occasional help we may offer to others whose faith, like our own, is set more on the regenerative power of thought than on the uncertain achievements of premature action.[40]

Artemus Ward once described the genuine critic: "They have helped the truth along *without encumbering it with themselves*"[41] At his best— and he was often at his best—Nock was able to do precisely that. Perhaps an acquaintance with Albert Jay Nock will enlist a few others in his choice company.

CHARLES H. HAMILTON

Charles H. Hamilton has edited works by Frank Chodorov, Franz Oppenheimer, and on Benjamin Tucker. He has worked for foundations and in book publishing for the last twenty years.

39. See "A Cultural Forecast" below, p. 104.
40. See "Anarchist's Progress" below, p. 51.
41. "Artemus Ward's America," *Free Speech and Plain Language*, p. 97.

Selected Bibliography

During the course of his career, Albert Jay Nock wrote hundreds of essays, editorials, and reviews. Some of the essays were assembled by Nock in four collections (*The Myth of a Guilty Nation, On Doing the Right Thing, The Book of Journeyman,* and *Free Speech and Plain Language*). One collection was assembled by friends and published posthumously (*Snoring as a Fine Art*). Nock also wrote seven books and two volumes of journals (one published after his death). He destroyed a number of manuscripts before his death.

No complete bibliography has been done for Nock's work, though I am in the process of compiling one. The dissertation by Sandor Cziraky, and the biographies by Robert Crunden and Michael Wreszin have good overlapping bibliographies.

Nock wrote many unsigned editorials for several magazines. Those contributions have been identified for the *American Magazine* (1910–1915), the *Nation* (1918–1919), and the *Freeman* (1920–1924). Still to be determined are his extensive unsigned editorial writings for the *new Freeman* (1930–1931), and the *American Mercury* (1936–1939).

There are two primary manuscript collections. The Albert Jay Nock Collection is at Yale University, in the Manuscripts and Archives Division. This collection includes the Robert M. Crunden Papers, which Crunden collected in the course of writing his biography. The Ruth Robinson Papers are also housed there. The Albert Jay Nock Papers, in the Manuscript Division of the Library of Congress, are important. A number of his manuscripts are there, as well as an extensive collection of correspondence.

I. BOOKS AND COLLECTIONS

The Myth of a Guilty Nation. New York: B. W. Huebsch, Inc., 1922.
   Originally published as ten articles in the *Freeman,* under the pseudonym "Historicus."
The Freeman Book. New York: B. W. Huebsch, Inc., 1924.
   A representative collection of articles from the complete run of the *Freeman,*

compiled by *Freeman* publisher Benjamin W. Huebsch. Many of the articles, whether originally signed or unsigned, were written by Nock and are identified in this volume.

Jefferson. New York: Harcourt, Brace and Company, 1926.

On Doing the Right Thing and Other Essays. New York: Harper and Brothers, 1928.

Francis Rabelais: The Man and His Work. New York: Harper and Brothers, 1929. Written with the research assistance of Catherine Rose Wilson. This work became an extensive introduction to the *Urquhart-Le Motteux Translation of the Works of Francis Rabelais,* published in 1931.

The Book of Journeyman: Essays from the new Freeman. New York: Publishers of the *new Freeman,* Inc., 1930.

The Theory of Education in the United States. New York: Harcourt, Brace and Company, 1932.

A Journey into Rabelais's France. New York: William Morrow & Company, 1934.

A Journal of These Days: June 1932–December 1933. New York: William Morrow & Company, 1934.

Our Enemy, The State. New York: William Morrow & Company, 1935.

Free Speech and Plain Language. New York: William Morrow & Company, 1937.

Henry George: An Essay. New York: William Morrow & Company, 1939.

Memoirs of a Superfluous Man. New York: Harper and Brothers, 1943.

II. PUBLISHED POSTHUMOUSLY

Journal of Forgotten Days: May 1934–October 1935. Hinsdale, IL: Henry Regnery Company, 1948.

Letters from Albert Jay Nock, 1924–1945, to Edmund C. Evans, Mrs. Edmund C. Evans, and Ellen Winsor. Caldwell, ID: The Caxton Printers, 1949. Edited by Frank C. Garrison.

Snoring as a Fine Art and Twelve Other Essays. Rindge, NH: Richard R. Smith, 1958.

Selected by Nock's good friends Ruth Robinson, Ellen Winsor, and Rebecca Winsor Evans.

Selected Letters of Albert Jay Nock. Caldwell, ID: The Caxton Printers, 1962.

Collected and Edited by Nock's son Francis J. Nock. Includes "Memories of Albert Jay Nock," by Ruth Robinson.

Cogitations from Albert Jay Nock. Irvington-on-Hudson, NY: The Nockian Society, 1970, revised edition, 1985.

A fine collection of aphorisms, selected and arranged by Robert M. Thornton, with a note from Jacques Barzun and "The Genial Mr. Nock" by Edmund A. Opitz.

III. INTRODUCTION AND/OR EDITED BY ALBERT JAY NOCK

Forty Years of It, by Brand Whitlock, Introduction by Albert Jay Nock. New York: D. Appleton & Company, 1914.

How Diplomats Make War, By a British Statesman [Francis Neilson], Introduction by Albert Jay Nock. New York: B. W. Huebsch, Inc., 1915.

How Diplomats Make War, 4th ed., by Francis Neilson, New Introduction by Albert Jay Nock. New York: B. W. Huebsch, Inc., 1921.

Selected Works of Artemus Ward, by Charles Farrar Browne, Edited with an Introduction by Albert Jay Nock. New York: Albert and Charles Boni, 1924.

The Urquhart-Le Motteux Translation of the Works of Francis Rabelais, 2 volumes, Edited with an Introduction and Notes by Albert Jay Nock and Catherine Rose Wilson. New York: Harcourt, Brace and Company, 1931.

Meditations in Wall Street, Anonymous [Henry Stanley Haskins], Introduction by Albert Jay Nock. New York: William Morrow & Company, 1940.

The Man Versus the State, by Herbert Spencer, Introduction by Albert Jay Nock. Caldwell, ID: The Caxton Printers, 1940.

IV. MAJOR SECONDARY SOURCES

analysis, vol. 2, no. 10 (August 1946).

A "Nock Memorial" issue, with contributions by a number of Nock's friends and acquaintances. Frank Chodorov's contribution, "The Articulate Individualist" is reprinted in *Fugitive Essays: Selected Writings of Frank Chodorov,* Charles H. Hamilton, ed. Indianapolis: Liberty Fund, 1980.

Brooks, Van Wyck. *Days of the Phoenix.* New York: E.P. Dutton, 1957. See chapter IV, "The Freeman."

Chodorov, Frank. *Out of Step.* New York: The Devin-Adain Company, 1962. See chapter XIV, "Albert Jay Nock."

Crunden, Robert M. *The Mind and Art of Albert Jay Nock.* Chicago: Henry Regnery Company, 1964.

Cziraky, J. Sandor. "The Evolution of the Social Philosophy of Albert Jay Nock," Ph.D. diss, University of Pennsylvania, 1959.

Fragments, vol. 4, no. 2 (April–June, 1966).

An issue devoted to a number of articles on Nock; the lead one by Edmund A. Opitz.

Fragments, vol. 20, no. 2 (April–June, 1982).

An issue containing a number of reconsiderations of Albert Jay Nock and his thought.

Hamilton, Charles H. *"The Freeman, 1920–1924,"* *Modern Age,* vol. 31, no. 1 (Winter 1987).

Also forthcoming in the *American Conservative Press,* Ronald Lora and William H. Longton, eds. New York: Greenwood Press, 1991.

Lora, Ronald. *Conservative Minds in America.* Chicago: Rand McNally & Company, 1971.

Neilson, Francis. "The Story of *The Freeman,"* *American Journal of Economics and Sociology,* vol. 6, supplement (October 1946).

Nitsche, Charles G. "Albert Jay Nock and Frank Chodorov: Case Studies in Recent American Individualist and Anti-Statist Thought," Ph.D. diss, University of Maryland, 1981.

Tanselle, G. Thomas. "Unsigned and Initialed Contributions to *The Freeman,"* *Studies in Bibliography,* vol. 17 (1964).

Turner, Susan J. *A History of* The Freeman: *Literary Landmark of the Early Twenties.* New York: Columbia University Press, 1963.

Wreszin, Michael. *The Superfluous Anarchist.* Providence, RI: Brown University Press, 1971.

Acknowledgments

Albert Jay Nock's books are reprinted periodically as his writing is rediscovered. Most previous volumes cover limited periods or topics. I felt there was a need for a single volume of his essays chosen from his *oeuvre*. In that way, a certain development and consistency of themes could become evident.

The articles in this volume include some of his best-known essays as well as unknown and difficult-to-find gems. They are complete (though only two of the five parts of "The State" are included here). Such a selection is my own choice and can cover only a small portion of Nock's writing. I have resisted taking excerpts from his longer books, a number of which are superb. They deserve to be read as a whole— *Memoirs of a Superfluous Man; Jefferson; Our Enemy, The State;* and *The Theory of Education in the United States*, particularly.

Certain members of the Remnant introduced me to Albert Jay Nock and have encouraged my continuing work. The volume has gained from their suggestions. A few deserve special thanks. Walter E. Grinder edited an edition of *Our Enemy, The State* which I published in 1971. He is a dear friend and supporter. Edmund A. Opitz has always been a fount of information and help in all of my work on the old right and particularly on Frank Chodorov and now AJN. Robert Crunden was un-curmudgeonly with his time and support. His suggestions and encouragement were very important. Jacques Barzun was very helpful with suggestions as well. Finally, Carol, Gregory, and Douglas provided the reason.

I would not presume to urge Nock's perspective upon the reader, but I do suspect you will see some beauty in it, may think about the world in new ways because of it, and have some fun while you are at it. I have.

Grateful acknowledgment is made to the following for permission to reprint previously published material:

The *Atlantic*, for "Peace the Aristocrat" (May 1915) and 'A Little Conservative' (October 1936).

William L. Bauhan, Publisher, for "The Purpose of Biography" and "Snoring as a Fine Art" from *Snoring as a Fine Art*, 1958.

Harper's Magazine, for "Officialism and Lawlessness" (December 1929).

Harper and Row, Publishers, for "On Doing the Right Thing," "Anarchist's Progress," "The Decline of Conversation," and "A Cultural Forecast," from *On Doing the Right Thing*, 1928, copyright renewed 1956 by Samuel A. Nock and Francis J. Nock.

William Morrow & Company, Inc., for "Thoughts From Abroad," "American Education," "Isaiah's Job," and "The Path to the River" from *Free Speech and Plain Language*, 1937, copyright renewed 1963 by Frances J. Nock and Samuel A. Nock.

The *Nation*, for "The End and the Means" (March 22, 1919) and "An Exhausted Virtue" (June 14, 1919), 1919, The Nation Company.

The Nockian Society, for "Liberalism, Properly So Called."

The *North American Review*, for "Prohibition and Civilization" (September 1916), with the permission of the University of Northern Iowa.

The *Virginia Quarterly Review*, for "The Return of the Patriots" (April 1932).

Yale University Library, for "Autobiographical Sketch" from the Albert Jay Nock Papers.

THE STATE OF THE UNION

I. A BIOGRAPHY OF IDEAS

Every person of any intellectual quality develops some sort of philosophy of existence; he acquires certain settled views of life and of human society; and if he would trace out the origin and course of the ideas contributory to that philosophy, he might find it an interesting venture. It is certainly true that whatever a man may do or say, the most significant thing about him is what he thinks; and significant also is how he came to think it, why he continued to think it, or, if he did not continue, what the influences were which caused him to change his mind.

—*Memoirs of a Superfluous Man*

Judging a man's character or philosophy by isolated acts or utterances, however well attested, instead of by the general content and tendency of his life, appears to me to be unjust and misleading. . . . One would wish the course of one's own philosopy to be traced by the direction of its sincere current, rather than of its occasional eddy or backwater: so it is fair, surely, to apply the same canon of criticism to others.

—"Concerning Matthew 23: 13–26,"
unpublished manuscript

The Purpose of Biography

What is biography for? What useful purpose does it serve? Why should one write it? What is its actual importance in the field of literature? Above all, what is autobiography for, and what proper motive might one have for writing it?

I put these questions to one of my literary acquaintances the other day, in the hope of clearing my own mind. It has once or twice been suggested to me (as I suppose it has been suggested to everybody who has ever published anything) that I should write the biography of this-or-that eminent person. My instinct promptly jibbed at the suggestion; and in each case, after dallying with the idea awhile, I threw it over. Then latterly, while looking into one or two current biographies, I was moved to wonder what prompted my instinct. Was it the consciousness of incapacity or of laziness or of both? Probably both, to a degree; yet I thought there must be a little more to it than that, because I had already caught myself pondering the question why these biographies had been written. I could not see that they served any purpose worth serving; they seemed to me to be addressed mostly to a vulgar and prying inquisitiveness; and this in turn led me to raise the questions which I subsequently put to my literary friend.

We finally agreed, my friend and I, that the legitimate function of modern biography (and *a fortiori* of autobiography) is to help the historian. We recalled the fact that biography, as now understood, is comparatively a new thing in our literature. Neither of us could put our finger on an example of it earlier than the seventeenth century. In principle, modern biography is an objective account of the life of one man. It begins with his birth, ends with his death, and includes every item of detail which has any actual or probable historical significance. All collateral matter which goes in by way of "setting" should be cut down to what is in distinct and direct relation to that one man. In principle, above all, modern biography admits of nothing tendentious, nor does it admit of the puffing out or slighting of detail to any degree beyond what the author, in all good faith and conscience, believes the historical importance of that detail would warrant.

If biographical practice followed principle, obviously, fewer biographies would be written, far fewer autobiographies, and far fewer of either would be generally read; the only person likely to profit by them would be the historian. Things being as they are, however, commercial considerations intervene between principle and practice, as they always do. Publishers look with a jaundiced eye on a biography which in their view is not "readable"; and their view of what is readable is set by what experience has shown to be the terms of popular demand. The author, under a double pressure to produce a readable book—for most authors are not above some little thought of profit—sees that the satisfaction of these terms is quite incompatible with a devotion to principle, and proceeds accordingly.

Hence, as a rule, the actual practice of modern biography is heavily sophisticated in response to the extremely unwholesome terms of a lively popular demand for that type of literature. Like our practice of fiction, it aims to hit the lowest common denominator of taste and intelligence among its potential public. This procedure is bad. For the writer, it is bad in two ways. First, because it tempts him to pick subjects which, from the historical point of view, are not worth a biography; and this category, as I shall presently show, includes some of the most eminent names. Second, the current low conception of what makes a book readable tempts him continually to a culpable misplacement of emphasis among the various orders of fact with which he deals. To cite an extreme instance, some time ago I read a wretched misshapen sketch of a great musician's life. All I got out of it which I did not already know was that this musician had the habit of using very filthy language. Evidences of this habit were scattered so over-liberally throughout the volume as to make one think the thing had been written expressly to air them.

For the reader as well as the writer, the sophistication of biography is bad; and this also in two ways. First, because it acquaints the public, often with great overemphasis, with a variety of matters which not only are devoid of historical significance, but also are preëminently none of the public's business. This stiffens the reader in his congenital resentment of privacy, his share in the vulgar assumption, so odiously overdeveloped in the United States and so powerfully encouraged by the dominant influences in our public life—the assumption that anybody's doings are everybody's business by full right and title. I do not speak of matters which might be thought questionable, but of those in general which are in their nature one's own concern, and none other's. If the subject "wore a checked shirt and a number-nine shoe, and had a pink wart on his nose," he was within his rights; it was nobody's business, the fact has no historical value whatever, and a disquisition on it, however "readable," has no place in a biography.

Second, the vogue of commercial biography is bad for the reader because it fosters the erroneous notion that knowing something *about* a subject, or even knowing a great deal about him, is the same thing, or just as good, as knowing the subject himself; and here comes in the case of those biographers whose subject is simply not worth a biography, and will not support one. To know Thoreau, for example, is an inestimable privilege, and anyone may have it; it is got in the most direct and simplest possible way by reading his works, and it cannot be got in any other way. All that is worth anyone's knowing *about* Thoreau can be got in five minutes out of any good encyclopædia. Reading the biographical portions of Mr. Canby's recent book, therefore, if I may say so, makes one feel like Mr. Weller's charity-boy at the end of the alphabet. Among other matters, for instance, Mr. Canby has dredged up evidence tending to show that Thoreau was not indifferent to female society; well, what of it? The fact, if it be a fact, has no historical importance; and either in liking the ladies or in disliking them he was quite within his rights, and it is none of the public's business. It may be said that the curiosity stirred by this order of research will egg people on to reading Thoreau, and thus put them in the way of actually knowing him. This seems to me highly improbable; they are far more likely to rest on an *Ersatz*-knowledge vamped up out of what Mr. Canby tells them, and let it go at that. In fact, I suspect that the popular appetite for "readable" biography is symptomatic not only of a low and prurient curiosity, but also, when this motive is not dominant, of a wish to live exclusively on predigested cultural food, which no one can do. A passive and workless *Ersatz*-knowledge of illustrious men seems to me to reflect our national ideals of a passive and workless *Ersatz*-education, a passive and workless *Ersatz*-culture; ideals which we are beginning to see are illusory.

In the case of any subject, no matter how eminent, most of the minutiæ of his day-to-day existence are of no earthly importance to the historian. Even at this early date Lord Morley's biography of

Gladstone, a classical example, free from any taint of commercialism, reminds us that Time is a great winnower, and we are driven to wonder whether some other literary form might in general be more serviceable; or whether, as a compromise measure, an alternative might be found in amending our practice by laying down the rule that a subject's private activities, his character, and his relations of whatever kind, are insignificant except as they affect his public activities, character and relations, and that the sound biographer should distribute his space accordingly.

Matters which are in themselves minutiæ may take on an adventitious importance to the historian by reason of consequences accruing from them to the public. There can be no doubt of that. Disregard of it is what has vitiated a great deal of earlier biography, and has led to the vogue of debunking, now happily on the wane. Unless the subject is contemporary, however, or nearly so, the biographer is in as good a position as the historian to understand this and to make all proper discriminations. A sound biographer of Priam's son, for example, would anticipate the historian of Ilium with a pretty full account of his dallyings with the skittish Helen; so, *mutatis mutandis,* would a sound biographer of Louis XV, or of Napoleon III. On the other hand, none of the first Napoleon's adventures in Mrs. Chikno's "roving and uncertificated line," though they seem to have been both enterprising and extensive, is worth a button to history, and therefore the sound biographer would finish off the whole assortment in about three agate lines. That George Washington was a man of sin—that he swore, drank whiskey, gambled, went to dances, infested the theatre, chased the light-o'-loves, smoked cigarettes, or whatever it was that the debunkers lay to his charge—this seems to have had no bearing on his public activities, and is therefore nothing for the sound biographer to waste space on. That he was a land-speculator and land-jobber did bear heavily on his public activities, and a sound biographer would take all due notice of it.

Matthew Arnold left an explicit request that he should not be the subject of a biography. No doubt his unfailing critical sense told him that there was nothing in the circumstances of his life to make a biography worth the paper it was written on. A recent effort made in disregard of his wish—and made, one must say, in execrably bad taste—shows clearly that this may well have been the case. Like Thoreau, he was a public figure in but one capacity, that of a man of letters. One may know him intimately and profitably through his works—there is no other way—but what one may know or not know *about* him is of no importance. Joseph Butler, the great bishop of Durham, took extraordinary care to baffle what we who are bred on the ideals of journalism and the cinema call "personal publicity." All that is known *about* him is that he rode around his diocese on a black pony, rode very fast, and was scandalously imposed upon by beggars. Yet one may know Butler intimately, say through the *Rolls Sermons,* and thereby make a valuable acquaintance, even for these days of so much supposititious enlightenment on religious matters. I have often thought it is unfortunate that so many of us are contemptuous of "the old religion" without knowing the best that the old religion could do. Knowing the Goethe of the *Conversations* is an imperishable benefit, but how much is there to know about Goethe that is worth knowing or is anyone's business to know? I think very little. Recent publications have settled me in the firm belief that one who knows Ruskin, Emerson, Coleridge, intimately, but knows nothing about them, is far ahead of one who knows all about them, but does not know them. Knowing Homer and Shakespeare is certainly something; but all that anyone actually knows about Shakespeare can be written on a postcard, and nobody knows even where or when Homer was born.

All I have been saying about biography bears with even greater force on autobiography because it is harder to assess the actual importance of one's own doings and adventures in life than it is to deal in the same disinterested fashion with those of others. There is greater difficulty in drawing the line firmly between matters of legitimate private interest and those of legitimate public interest. My friend Mr. Villard's recent book called *Fighting Years* is of great value to the historian of his period—I know of none more valuable—but only after Mr. Villard does finally get around to talking about his fighting years. What precedes this (counting in a few later lapses from objectivity) comes roughly to a fourth of the book; it deals with matters which are of highly justifiable interest to Mr. Villard and his family, to me and the rest of his friends, but which are of no legitimate interest to the public—they are indeed none of the public's business. One wishes that Mr. Villard had resolutely forgone all notion of an autobiography, struck into his subject at the point where his fighting years began, and cast his book in the form of

memoirs. As an inveterate reformer, if he had wished—as I think he
might well have done—to show "how he got that way," he could have
done it easily in an introductory paragraph.

I have seen in my time—a rather long time, as man's life goes—only
one specimen of this type of literature which seemed to me flawless.
One could do no better than let it serve as a structural model for both
biography and autobiography, and I therefore feel justified in speaking
of it somewhat at length as such. I came on it only lately, about six
months ago. It is not the work of a writer, a man of letters, or even
one of more than moderate literary attainments. It is the work of a
Russian musician.

Rimsky-Korsakov, Nikolai Andreyevitch, commenced his autobiography
in 1876, when he was thirty-two years old. He ended it in 1906, two
years before his death. He worked at it at long intervals; ten years
elapsed between the first and second chapters, six between the second
and third, eleven between the seventh and eighth. He died in 1908; his
widow brought out the book in 1909, suppressing certain passages,
and a second edition came out in 1910. An English translation, said to
be excellent, was made by Mr. Joffe from this second edition, and was
published, I think in 1923, by Mr. A. A. Knopf. I have not seen it. A
third Russian edition appeared in 1928, edited by the composer's son,
Andrei Nikolaivitch, who restored the passages which had been cut out
of the two editions preceding.

Like Thoreau, Rimsky-Korsakov was in one capacity, and one only,
a public figure. In all other respects his life, like Thoreau's, had not a
single feature of legitimate interest to the public. The first signal merit
of his book lies in its clear, consistent consciousness that the public
was entitled to the fullest information about everything which bore
directly or indirectly on the author's character and activities as a
musician, and was not entitled to any information about anything which
had any other bearing. The book's fidelity to this sound principle is
amazing. My copy of it runs to three hundred closely-printed pages,
and I have scanned it line by line for some sign of departure or
wavering, but I have not found one.

The domestic "setting" of the author's birth and infancy is a matter
of ten lines. His father played the piano (an old one) by ear; so did an

uncle, who could not read music, but was "very musical," though the father seems to have had the better musical memory. The author's mother habitually slowed down the tempo of the songs she sang to him in his childhood; this was an "odd trait," and the author has the notion that he may have inherited this tendency from her. This is all we are told of either parent's biography. He does not mention the name of his father or mother, or say a word about their families or forebears. In the second chapter he gives his father a paragraph of praise, but it is only by way of showing that, in spite of their *ancien régime* distaste for a musical career, his parents disinterestedly did their best for him.

The author had a wife, "an excellent musician," and has nothing to say about her in any other capacity. He does mention her name, but he had to do that in order to distinguish her from a sister who was a singer; she was a pianiste, and they often appeared together. He had children; the birth of a son gets half a line. They are brought into the narrative only as some incident—for example, the illness of a son or the death of a daughter—had this-or-that effect on some musical project which was under way. The incident itself gets bare mention; we do not know what ailed the boy or what carried off the girl. The author's own indispositions are brought in vaguely to account for some difficulty with his music; "pain in the head, a feeling of pressure," worried him at the Marinsky's rehearsal of his fairy-ballet *Mlada*. There is collateral evidence that the author was genuinely fond of the four friends and comrades who had valiantly weathered through the terrible *Sturm und Drang* period of Russian music in the last quarter of the century; yet see how the book takes the death of the one perhaps closest to him:

> On the sixteenth of February, 1887, very early in the morning, I was taken by surprise when V. V. Stassov came to my door in a great state of agitation, saying "Borodin is dead!" . . . I shall not describe the emotion of us all. What would become of *Prince Igor* and his other incomplete or unpublished works? Stassov and I went at once to the dead man's apartment, and carried off all his manuscripts to my house.

Twice, in going through the book, the reader may think he has caught the author napping, but he will be wrong. In the first chapter Rimsky-Korsakov has a bit to say about his love for the sea, and about an older brother who is a lieutenant in the navy. This seems irrelevant, but in the next chapter we find the author himself in the Naval College, on his way to becoming an officer; and this in turn is introductory to the account of sixteen years of effort to drive the two careers in double harness, and of the one's reactions upon the other. Again, in the sixteenth chapter he waxes lyrical to the extent of nine lines, praising rural joys of the truly old-fashioned Russian village of Stelovo, where he spent the summer of 1880; but you see the point when you turn a page and discover that in those two-and-a-half months he composed the whole of *Snegourotchka*. Writing in the period 1894–1896, almost at the end of his life, he says that "up to this present time I have never finished off any work so easily and rapidly." He recalled the delights of Stelovo because they had a conspicuous bearing on music. The trees, the river, fruits, flowers, the incessant song of birds—"all this was in some sort of harmony with my leanings toward pantheism, and my love for the subject of *Snegourotchka*."

Another merit of the book, as great as the first, is born of the author's clear understanding that its sole function is that of helping the historian of Russian music. Everything that would help the historian is there, and nothing is there which would confuse him, waste his eyesight, or arouse his distrust. To show that this is so would take more space than I can afford. I can only suggest that those who are thinking of doing something with biography should get a copy of the book and make a careful study of it from this point of view.

But to help the historian, the biographer must be objective; he must resolutely keep prepossession from laying traps for the historian's feet. The third great merit of Rimsky-Korsakov's book is that it perfectly meets this requirement; one does not see how objectivity could be carried further. This is the more remarkable, perhaps, because the book, like Mr. Villard's, is a record of "fighting years." It deals with a violent æsthetic rebellion which Mr. Ernest Newman, in his superb *Musical Critic's Holiday,* admirably compares with the great Florentine revolt against musical orthodoxy in 1600; yet nowhere in the book can I find the trace of a single biased judgment, a single prepossession. I would have the intending biographer go through it once more, and study it carefully from this point of view.

A fourth signal merit is that Rimsky-Korsakov always "comes across." He never butters up a person or a situation, and on the other hand, he never exaggerates anything unfavorable to either. He says exactly all that should be said, but never a word more. In this respect his work stands in vivid and gratifying contrast to all the attempts at autobiography that I have seen in recent years; they do not quite come across. The five Russian rebels were very young, going on for thirty; being young, they were ardent, irrepressible, aggressive. The leading spirit, Balakirev, was the only one who could pretend to anything like a professional knowledge of music, and he had next to none. Let the reader notice Rimsky-Korsakov's treatment of Balakirev throughout, and especially the marvelous summing-up of his influence on his comrades. The others were rank amateurs; two of them were notable, however, in their proper professions. The half-French Cui was a distinguished engineer-officer in the army, and Borodin was a distinguished physician and chemist. Moussorgsky was an officer in the Preobrazhensky regiment, but presently left the army, and became a functionary in the civil service, in the Department of Forests.[1] Not one of them was a trained musician. They really did not know what they wanted, what they were driving at, and knew even less of how to drive at it. To deal disinterestedly with matters like these is something of an achievement— let the reader observe how Rimsky-Korsakov deals with them. Not a word is said about anyone's personal character, qualities or habits, except as bearing on music; then what is said is said in full, and with complete objectivity. Balakirev went to pieces, Moussorgsky drank too much, Borodin's household was in continual disorder; well, that was that, and its effect upon their productivity was such-and-such. Alone among critics, Stassov gave the rebels enthusiastic support; its effect was this-and-that. He had certain critical defects; the outcome of them was so-and-so.

Is it perhaps possible that our writers are overdoing biography a little? Is not autobiography, coarsened and discolored by commercialism as it is, being rather recklessly overdone among us? I fear so. I have before me now a letter from someone who proposes to write a biography of a personage whom I used to know slightly. The prospect depresses me,

---

1. Mr. Virgil Thomson, in his recent book, *The State of Music,* says that Cui was a chemist and Moussorgsky a customs official. This is a curious error, but trivial, hardly worth noticing, because the only point is that neither man was a professional musician, and Mr. Thomson makes this point clearly.

for to my certain knowledge that personage, like Thoreau, will simply not support a biography. The utmost that can be expected is that this intending biographer will produce, *Gott soll hüten,* one more "readable" book, one more windfall for the book clubs or a likely bid for the Pulitzer prize; and this, as Rabelais says of an enterprise essentially similar, is a terrible thing to think upon.

All the more so because meanwhile other literary forms, quite as respectable and far more appropriate, go begging. If some aspect of a subject's public career strikes you as possibly fruitful, why not write an essay about it, as Mr. Brooks did in his *Ordeal of Mark Twain?* The essay-form is greatly neglected; yet a critical essay on Thoreau, for example, one such as Matthew Arnold wrote on Gray and on Wordsworth, would be worth a dozen inevitably abortive attempts at a biography. There are innumerable great essays to be written about great American figures as seen in the light of the present time. At this point in the course of our public affairs, for example, what would more powerfully conduce to a competent understanding of our political selves and our political condition than such an essay on John Adams as Walter Bagehot would write; or what more to a salutary sense of our spiritual decrepitude than an essay on Emerson such as Ernest Renan, Scherer or Sainte-Beuve would write—or, indeed, an essay on that same Thoreau?

If, again, you are interested in a subject's standards of personal character and conduct, write a study of them. If you have been a close observer of great affairs, or of affairs which if not great are amusing, unusual, interesting, picaresque, write memoirs. The best and most useful book of memoirs that I ever saw was anonymous; the author almost never spoke of himself. It came out in 1892, entitled *An Englishman in Paris.* I wish Mr. Villard had done something like that; it would have had the ingratiating and persuasive literary quality which, owing to the autobiographical form, his work now falls just short of having. If your observations and reflections seem worth printing, print your diary; it is the best literary form for the purpose—Blunt's diary and the Goncourts' are gold mines for the historian. All these literary forms seem to me as sorely neglected by us as the biographical form seems sorely overworked.

But people will not read essays, memoirs, studies, diaries, and therefore publishers will not touch them, especially if offered by obscure or unpopular authors; people want biography. It may be a little indelicate to say so, but on this point it seems to me that the testimony of an author who is both obscure and unpopular might be worth something. All I have ever written has been in one or another of these forms, and I have somehow managed to get it published; and there is evidence that many more people read it than I would have dared think were likely to do so. Hence I am far from sure that this prejudice of public and publishers is as strong as it is supposed to be. I have sometimes wondered whether the book market would actually collapse if authors and publishers declared a general strike on the biographical form. I doubt it. I know a pampered cat named Thomas, who turns his back on any kind of food but liver, and will have none of it—for a while— but when he finds his choice dealt down to fish or nothing, he takes fish and likes it. On a similar choice, the pampered public might take something besides biography and get it down without too much retching. However that may be, publishers and authors might at least unite on the less radical measure of tightening up the practice of biography a little. If an author must write biography, let him write it on something like correct principles. If it is positively decreed in the council of the gods that he shall write an autobiography, let him write one like Rimsky-Korsakov's.

This essay first appeared in the March 1940 issue of the *Atlantic Monthly* and was later reprinted in the posthumously published *Snoring as a Fine Art and Twelve Other Essays,* collected by Ruth Robinson, Ellen Winsor, and Rebecca Winsor Evans.

The Value to the Clergyman of Training in the Classics

The other night, in company with an eminent expert in social problems, I had the privilege of hearing Mr. Post lecture on the witch's work that the railroads are making with our political institutions. As we left the building, the first unmistakable breath of spring in the air brought with it a sudden, disquieting flood of recollections of my home in the Virginia mountains, and there occurred to me at once the pensive and graceful lines from Virgil's *Georgics:* "O for the fields, and the streams of Spercheios, and the hills animated by the romping of the Lacaenian girls, the hills of Taygetus!" The social practitioner, who regards my favorite pursuits with an eye of gentle toleration—thinking them a harmless means of keeping inefficient and sentimental persons from meddling underfoot of those like himself who are bearing the burden and heat of the day—took my arm and said, "I suppose now, your way out of all these troubles with the railroads would be to put Mr. Harriman and Mr. Pierpont Morgan to reading Virgil's *Georgics.*" I had considerable satisfaction in telling him that he was not much more than half wrong.

The reply was not dictated solely by my own prepossessions. The function of the Christian minister is to recommend religion as the principal means of making the will of God prevail in all the relations of human society. He promotes the practice of the discipline of Jesus as the highest mode of spiritual exercise looking toward human perfection. But religion is an inward motion, a distinct form of purely spiritual activity; not an intellectual process, an external behavior, or a series of formal observances. The final truth of religion is poetic truth, not scientific truth; in fact, with sheer scientific truth religion has very little vital concern. The Christian minister, then, has his chief interest in recommending a special mode of spiritual activity, in interpreting a special mode of poetic truth. But his experience bears witness that the general must precede the special. Before one may hope to do much with a special mode of spiritual activity like religion, at least some notion of spiritual activity in general must have made its way. Before

16

one may hope to do much with a special mode of poetic truth like the truth of religion, at least some sense of the validity and worth of poetic truth in general must be set up. Here it may be seen how distinctly progress in religion is related to progress in culture—I do not say progress in education, for the recent changes in educational aims and ideals make of education a very different thing from culture; the recent revolution in educational processes compels us to differentiate these very sharply from the works and ways of culture. Education, at present, is chiefly a process of acquiring and using instrumental knowledge. Its highest concern is with scientific truth, and its ends are the ends of scientific truth. Culture, on the other hand, is chiefly a process of acquiring and using formative knowledge; and while culture is, of course, concerned with scientific truth, its highest concern is with poetic truth. Culture prizes scientific truth, it respects instrumental knowledge; it seeks to promote these, where necessary, as indispensable and appointed means to a great end; but culture resolutely puts aside every temptation to rest upon these as ends in themselves. Culture looks steadily onward from instrumental knowledge to formative knowledge, from scientific truth to poetic truth. The end of culture is the establishment of right views of life and right demands on life, or in a word, *civilization,* by which we mean the humane life, lived to the highest power by as many persons as possible.

Because material well-being is the indispensable basis of civilization, the more thoughtless among us are apt to use the word civilization only in a very restricted and artificial sense. Our newspapers especially appear to think that the quality of civilization is determined by being very rich, having plenty of physical luxuries, comforts, and conveniences, doing a very great volume of business, maintaining ample facilities for education, and having everyone able to read and write. The civilization of a community, however, is determined by no such things as these, but rather by the power and volume of the humane life existing there—the humane life, having its roots struck deep in material well-being, indeed, but proceeding as largely and as faithfully as possible under the guidance of poetic truth, and increasingly characterized by profound and disinterested spiritual activity. Thus it is possible for a community to enjoy ample well-being, and yet precisely the right criticism upon its pretensions to be that it is really not half civilized—that not half its people are leading a kind of life that in any reason or conscience can be called humane. Let us imagine, say, a community whose educational institutions deal in nothing but instrumental knowledge and recognize no truth that is not scientific truth; with all its people able to read and write indeed, yet with a very small proportion of what they read worth reading and of what they write worth writing; with its social life heavily overspread with the blight of hardness and hideousness; with those who have had most experience of the beneficence of material well-being displaying no mark of quickened spiritual activity, but rather everywhere the outward and visible sign of an inward and spiritual dullness, enervation, and vulgarity; to apply the term civilization to anything as alien to the humane life, as remote from the ideal of human perfection, as this, seems to us unnatural and shocking. In such a community, no doubt, all manner of philanthropic and humanitarian enterprise may abound; what we nowadays call social Christianity, practical Christianity, may abound there. We do not underestimate these; their value is great, their rewards are great; but the assumption so regularly made, that these in themselves are sufficient indication of a chaste and vigorous spiritual activity on the part of those who originate and promote them is, in the view of culture, manifestly unsound. There is much room just now, we believe, for a searching exposition of Article XIII, "Of Good Works Done before Justification." We of the ministry, therefore, must keep insisting that as our concern is purely with the processes and activities of the spirit, only so far forth as these things represent the fruit of the spirit can we give them our interest.

The Christian minister, then, is interested in civilization, in the humane life; because the special form of spiritual activity which he recommends is related to the humane life much as the humane life is related to material well-being. He is interested in the humane life for himself, because he must live this life if he hopes to prepossess others in its favor. And here comes in the ground of our plea that Greek and Latin literature may be restored and popularized. One makes progress in the humane life by the only way that one can make progress in anything—by attending to it, by thinking about it, by having continually before one the most notable models of the humane life. And of these available models, we find so large a proportion furnished to us in the literature of Greece and Rome as to force upon us the conviction that in our efforts to exemplify and promote the humane life we simply cannot do without this literature. The friends of education as it now is keep insisting that citizens should be trained to be useful men of their time, men who do things, men who can develop our natural and commercial resources, carry our material well-being on to a yet higher degree of abundance and security, and play a winning game at politics. For these purposes, they tell us, instrumental knowledge and scientific truth are the only things worth knowing. We content ourselves with remarking simply, It may be so; but with all this we, at any rate, can do nothing. The worst of such justifications is that, like Mr. Roosevelt's specious and fantastic plea for the strenuous life, they are addressed to a public that needs them least. There is small danger that interest in anything making for material well-being, for the development of our commerce and industrial pursuits, will fail for a long time to come. As for politics, statesmen trained on instrumental knowledge may well be instrumental statesmen, such as ours are; and these, too, appear to be for ever and ever. Our interest is in knowing whether education as it now is will give us citizens who can accomplish anything worth talking about in the practice of the humane life. The friends of education tell us that men trained as they would and do train them will turn out shrewd, resourceful business men, competent investigators, analysts, and reporters in the professions, clever, practical men in public life. Again we reply, It may be so; but will they turn out business men of the type, say, of Mr. Stedman, professional men of the type of Dr. Weir Mitchell (if we may venture to bring forward these gentlemen by name), public men and politicians of the type of Mr. Hay or Governor Long? When these questions are satisfactorily answered, we will cheerfully reconsider what we say in behalf of Greek and Latin literature; but unless and until they are so answered, we must continue to point out as in our view the cardinal defect in education, that it does next to nothing for the humane life, next to nothing for poetic truth, next to nothing for spiritual activity; and its failure in these directions being what it is, that our civilization is retarded and vulgarized to correspond.

For the sake of civilization, therefore, we of the ministry venture our plea in behalf of culture. We beg that some of the stress now laid upon purely instrumental knowledge be relieved. How can we even be understood when, for the sake of the great end of our calling, we praise and recommend culture and all the elements and processes that enter into culture, if the whole bent of secular training is against these, and

serves but to confirm the current belief that the only real knowledge
is instrumental knowledge, the only real truth is scientific truth, the
only real life is a life far short of what life might be and what it ought
to be? We ask that Greek and Latin literature be restored. We do not
pretend to argue for the disciplinary worth of Greek and Latin studies,
their value as a memory-exercise, as furnishing a *corpus vile* for our
practice in analysis, or as a basis for the acquisition of modern languages.
We argue solely for their moral value; we ask that they be restored,
understood, and taught as an indispensable and powerful factor in the
work of humanizing society. As these subjects are now taught (if an
unprofessional opinion may be offered without offense) their gram-
matical, philological, and textual interests predominate. Mr. Weir
Smyth's excellent anthology, for instance, is probably an example of
the very best textbook writing of its kind, and a glance at this—
comparing it, if one likes, with the editorial work of Professor Tyrrell,
in the same series—shows at once that Mr. Weir Smyth's purposes,
admirable as they are, are not our purposes. We would be the very last
to disparage Mr. Weir Smyth's labours or to fail in unfeigned praise of
the brilliant, accurate, and painstaking scholarship which he brings to
bear on all matters that he sees fit to include within the scope of his
work. But *sat patriae Priamoque datum;* again we say it is not likely that
instrumental knowledge, even in our dealings with the classics, will
ever be neglected. Let us now have these subjects presented to us in
such a way as to keep their literary and historical interests consistently
foremost. Let the study of Greek and Latin literature be recommended
to us as Mr. Arnold, for example, recommends it; let the Greek and
Latin authors be introduced to us as Mr. Mackail introduces them; let
them be edited for us as Professor Tyrrell edits them; let them be
interpreted to us as Professor Jebb or Professor Jowett interprets them.
Or, if the current superstition demands that we continue to receive the
Greek and Latin authors at the hands of the Germans, or at second-
hand from the Germans, we make no objection; we stipulate only that
our editorial work be done for us not by the German philologists,
textual critics, grammarians, or by American students trained in their
schools, but by Germans of the type of Lessing, Herder, and Goethe—
men who are themselves docile under the guidance of poetic truth,
who are themselves eminent in the understanding and practice of the

humane life; men, therefore, who can happily interpret this truth and freely communicate this life to us.

The consideration of Greek and Latin studies in view of the active pastorate usually, we believe, takes shape in the question whether or not it is worth while for a minister to be able to read the New Testament and the Fathers in the original. Into this controversy we have never seen our way to enter; nor have we been able to attach to it the importance that it probably deserves. What interests us in Greek and Latin studies is the unique and profitable part these play in the promotion of the humane life. Nor do we argue with the friends of education as to the possibility of generating and serving the humane life by means of the discipline of science; we affirm simply that the humane life is most largely generated and most efficiently served by keeping before one the models of those in whom the humane life most abounds; and that of these models, the best and largest part is presented to us in the literature of Greece and Rome. The men in undergraduate work with us, back in the times of ignorance before natural science had come fully into its own, knew little of the wonders of the new chemistry. Little enough did they know of such principles of botany, physics, geology, astronomy, zoölogy, and so on, as one of our children in the high school will now pretend to rattle you off without notice. But they knew their Homer, their Plato, their Sophocles, by heart; they knew what these great spirits asked of life, they knew their views of life. And with that knowledge there also insensibly grew the conviction that their own views and askings had best conform, as Aristotle finely says, "to the determination of the judicious." This was the best, perhaps the only, fruit of their training; they became steadied, less superficial, capricious, and fantastic. Living more and more under the empire of reality, they saw things as they are, and experienced a profound and enthusiastic inward motion toward the humane life, the life for which the idea is once and forever the fact. This life is the material upon which religion may have its finished work. Chateaubriand gives Joubert the highest praise that can be bestowed upon a human character, when, speaking of Joubert's death as defeating his purpose of making a visit to Rome, he says, "It pleased God, however, to open to M. Joubert a heavenly Rome, better fitted still to his Platonist and Christian soul." It is in behalf of the humane life, therefore, that we of the active pastorate place our present valuation upon the literature of Greece and Rome: for the first step in Christianity is the humanization of life, and the finished product of Christianity is but the humane life irradiated and transfigured by the practice of the discipline of Jesus.

This was Nock's first published essay, printed in the June 1908 issue of the *School Review*. It developed from a paper Nock contributed to a symposium on classical studies at the University of Michigan at Ann Arbor. His byline read "Rev. A. J. Nock, St. Joseph's Church, Detroit." Many of the issues raised here were to occupy him for the rest of his life.

Autobiographical Sketch

I was born at Scranton, Pennsylvania, on the thirteenth of October, sometime in the early 'seventies. I do not know the exact date, but it could hardly have been earlier than 1874. When required to produce a date in order to get passports, etc., I have put it down as 1873. I am sure of the day, however, for my mother's birthday came ten days earlier, so we always held a joint celebration on the third of October. I was born at Scranton because my grandparents lived there then, and my mother went home for the occasion, as women often did at that time. I understand they are less sentimental about such matters now, and bear their young in hospitals.

My mother's name was Emma Sheldon Jay. My father's name was Joseph Albert. He was a clergyman of the Protestant Episcopal Church; so was his youngest brother, Edwin Gaines. I have mentioned elsewhere that their father, a steelmaker in Staffordshire, was a licensed lay preacher of the Methodist persuasion; so the interest in religion seems to have been more or less hereditary in the family. For a brief while I have held a license and had an unimportant position in the Church. This being virtually a sinecure, it gave me time to pursue some advanced studies in history and philosophy. In my *Memoirs* I have told everything of any consequence about my paternal ancestry; indeed, I believe I have told all I know about it, except that my grandparents lived successively at Windsor Locks, Connecticut; at Ramapo (I believe, or perhaps Sloatsburg) in Rockland County, New York; and at what is now Erastina, on Staten Island, where my grandfather built a rather fine house, for those days. This was before the industry in heavy chemicals on the opposite shore in New Jersey ruined the region with its vapours. My grandfather was superintendent of steelworkers in all three places. His oldest son Thomas Gill (my grandmother's name was Maria Gill) was president of the Rome Locomotive Works, at Rome, N.Y. He built the miniature locomotives in use on the Elevated before electrification. I saw one of these a few years ago, hooked up to some work-cars on a switch below Eighth St. on the Sixth Avenue line, so I fancy some still may exist. The brother next older, George Franklin, was superintendent of a rolling-mill for the Union Pacific Railway. I think he and my father were both born in Rockland County, but I am not sure; perhaps at Windsor Locks; perhaps one at the one place, the other at the other; I really have no idea.

My mother's ancestry were from New York. Relatives have told me that I am somewhere in the family line of Chief Justice Jay, but I know nothing about this, and was never enough interested to look it up. I suppose it might be by way of his brother James, but I have actually no idea. All I know about James is that he invented the invisible ink which Washington gave his spies on John Jay's recommendation (which I have seen) for use in writing their reports. This ink appears to have been something quite remarkable, and Washington had a good deal of trouble, for some reason, to get enough of it. Chief Justice Jay was truly great and in every way admirable. I have always regarded him as, next to John Adams, the most profound and far-sighted statesman of his time. I should be much more concerned with finding myself in his spiritual line than in his family line, though it is true, as Ernest Renan said, that "man does not improvise himself," and ancestry does count, even as it does with dogs and horses.

As might be supposed, my parents were quite poor, but we somehow never seemed to lack anything we needed, and I never saw a trace of discontent or a failure in cheerfulness over their lot in life, as indeed over anything. We always lived well. I have often wondered how any amount of money would have improved our condition or would have caused the springs of happiness within ourselves to run any clearer; and I do not even now see how it would. In point of wealth the social life around us in my childhood and youth was remarkably undifferentiated. Some were richer than others; but the rich lived without ostentation, mostly by preference, but largely in conformity to the rather crude and superficial spirit of equality which prevailed at the time. This was especially true of the social life in our Michigan lumbertown when I was eight or ten years old. The millionaires of the industry went about in their shirt-sleeves all summer, and their families put on no airs whatever. A drummer getting off the steamboat from Detroit one hot night saw a dilapidated-looking figure in shirt-sleeves standing on the wharf, and offered him a quarter to carry his satchel to the hotel, which the man cheerfully agreed to do and did, never letting on that he was by far the richest man in town, perhaps as rich as anyone in Michigan. He was a Yankee from Maine; he said afterwards simply that he was not above earning a quarter so easily, and hoped he never would be, because a quarter was always a good thing to have, and you could never tell what it might grow up to.

This social atmosphere agreed with my temperament, with the result of fixing in me a pretty clear idea of what money will buy and what it will not buy; also that if a person works to gain either one he must make up his mind to gain it largely at the expense of the other. I learned to want little that money could bring me, and I have had all I wanted. If I had ever so much money I would still choose to live exactly as I do, for I regard the accumulation of purchaseable goods as a mere burden—*impedimenta,* as the Romans called it—something that acted *in pedes,* slowing down the progress of one's feet in the direction one wanted them to take. But I say this entirely without prejudice to those who choose otherwise, for I see no moral quality in my preference for making life's journey with light baggage; I simply do not envy them. I have all along been clearly aware that my rich acquaintances would have a great horror of living as I do, quite as I should be lost and distracted in living as they do; and I have no doubt that theirs is the better way for them, as mine is the better for me.

This preference probably has its root in the fierce resentful hatred of responsibility with which I was born and which is one of my leading characteristics; the cause no doubt, that did most to make me an easy prey for the philosophy and individualism as expounded by Spencer. Responsibility to myself and for myself, yes. I am, as I have always been proud to accept that, proud to assert it in the face of God, man, beast, or devil. But responsibility for anything beyond that I accept only on the strength of the most searching evidence; and I have a peculiarly resolute resentment against the impositions by State, Church or social conventions of responsibilities which are purely artificial in substance and fraudulent in intention.

In looking over my writings I see that this disposition has given them a uniform temper. If they were done by another hand, and I were examining them with a critical eye, I should say that they were clearly the work of a man with an acute sense of responsibility, for truth of fact and logic, but none whatever for his effect or lack of effect on the reader; in short, a man who was, in his own view, responsible only to and for himself. That this is so seems evident from the fact that although I am well known as an exponent of individualism's philosophy, I have never made a single personal disciple. The reason is, as my writings plainly show by their temper—for every writer's temper pervades his writings and can neither possibly be concealed nor counterfeited—I have not only never tried, but never even wished, to make one. If my writings have led anyone to broaden the scope of his mind or to contract it, that is his affair, not mine. The spirit of Rabbinism, the disposition by ever so little to invade another person's consciousness and take possession of it, is utterly hateful to me as being, in my judgement, an impudent intrusion. That it is so, I think, is pointedly suggested by the quality of those who pursue this practice; they are politicians, propagandists, quidnuncs, adepts in "social science," uplifters, sectarian crusaders. One says of such what Virgil said to Dante of some minor malefactors in the outskirts of hell: "Look, and pass them by."

One may see from this how easily the temper of individualism incurs the charge of arrogance. I have always had to face this charge; I think unjustly. As far as I know, I have no pride of opinion. The question of who is right and who is wrong has seemed to me always too small to be worth a moment's thought, while the question of what is right and what is wrong has seemed all-important. I am by far more grateful for correction of thought or belief than for any other service, and I am sure that those who have corrected me will say that I have been quick and happy to acknowledge it. I feel that the true individualist is bound by his philosophy to hold his opinions under correction from any one at any time; to state them freely and in full, on any proper occasion; to discuss them objectively, but never to hold a brief for them or dispute an opposing opinion in the manner of an attorney, even though the opinion be absurd. If a person believes the earth is flat, the individualist will not dispute his belief or enter into any argument about it; and this not only, or not nearly so much, because the belief is absurd, as because the individualist is conscious that the person holding it is within his rights, and he must respect them. I speak only of course, concerning honest opinions, honestly held.

The individualist temper, however, was not originally mine, but in so far as I have any claim to it now, it was a rather early acquisition.

In childhood and youth my temper was quick, very violent, easily stirred into explosions of impatience and anger, subsiding again as quickly, leaving me ashamed and regretful, ready to go any distance to make up for the outburst. I was never tempted to be vindictive or malicious, but quite the contrary. The discipline I applied to my temper is worth mentioning because I have applied it as successfully to other irregularities. Mark Twain said he had often sworn off smoking and could never keep to it, but when he swore off wanting to smoke he found he had no trouble at all. I seem to have anticipated him, in principle, for though I tried hard to quit losing my temper I was unable to do it, but when at the age of twenty-five or so I deliberately tried to quit wanting to lose my temper, I had no difficulty worth speaking of, nor have I had any since that time.

My likes and dislikes have always been extremely strong and positive, not in any way determined by convention or any other superficial considerations such as those of family, social standing, wealth, class, creed, or even of humanity, as rated by zoölogical definition. In this as elsewhere I am strictly an individualist. Someone asked me years ago if it were true that I disliked Jews, and I replied that it was certainly true, not at all because they are Jews but because they are folks, and I don't like folks. All differentiations of this kind are foreign to me. My disposition toward mankind has been greatly modified of late, however, since R. A. Cram made hash of the possibilist theory of man's place in nature on which I had been stumbling along so many years. I have explained this in my *Memoirs*. Nevertheless, I should still say that my principal faults and failings are those of temper, as they have always been, especially in the way of impatience and disregard of the weakness or incapacity of men. I have never been able to "suffer fools gladly," as the Apostle says one should, and this has blinded me to the sterling good qualities of a great many people, which is most unjust. I try to overcome this bad disposition, but with poor success.

Hence it is not surprising that I have no power of attraction or any faculty of attaching people to myself. I am said to be difficult of acquaintance, unwilling to meet any one half way, and showing a social manner which is easy, not diffident, but formal and unresponsive, tending constantly to hold people off. I am aware of this and regret it as a serious fault, and one which gives rise to much unfortunate

misunderstanding; and yet it is one which is extremely hard to deal
with for several reasons, most of these running back to a root in the
individualist philosophy.

In a society like ours, bitterly resentful of privacy, the integrity of
one's personality is constantly under attack from all sides; not only
under direct frontal attack, but, which is worse, it is always exposed
to insidious influences which will infect it and rot it down. To the
individualist, the integrity thus menaced is the most precious thing on
earth; and the dangers to it being what they are, they beget a
corresponding extreme of sensitiveness and caution which in time
becomes a sort of secondary instinct. "Hide thy life," said Epicurus,
and the individualist is the one who most diligently lays that invaluable
advice to heart.

Like Prince von Bismarck in diplomacy, I have no secrets. There is
nothing in my history that for precautionary reasons I should have any
wish to cover up. I am not at all shy, diffident, self-conscious, and no
one could care less than I for what might be thought or said of him.
Yet all the information I have ever given out about myself is what
appears in my *Memoirs* and what I am putting down here. In the
Atlantic of March, 1940, I published a brief essay setting forth a rule
for biographical writing, and my *Memoirs* were an experiment in keeping
to that rule. The purpose of the book (which no reviewer seemed to
discern, though it was stated plainly in the Preface) was to trace the
growth of a philosophy of life. I think that anyone who had read my
essay would give me credit for keeping to my own rule reasonably well.
There is not much in the book but what bears pretty directly on its
purpose.

The boarding-school I attended was in Pekin, Illinois, near Peoria. My
undergraduate work was done at St. Stephen's College, Annandale,
New York, about twenty miles above Poughkeepsie. Both institutions
were under auspices of the Protestant Episcopal Church, which is the
American agency of the Established Church of England. The college
was modelled after one of the Oxford colleges—in spirit as well as in
all other respects. I have given a full account of my education in my
Memoirs, and I can think of nothing more to say about it. The lumbertown in Michigan, where we lived, was Alpena, at the head of Thunder

Bay. My father built a very good stone church there, which I imagine must still be standing, much as it was.

I have had sound good health always. I escaped all children's diseases except measles, which gave me a hard run at the age of thirty-five. Curiously, in spite of excellent health, I cannot remember a day when I was wholly free from pain of some kind. There must have been such days, of course, probably many, but I do not recall one. I never had a headache, and with all my rough seafaring on the North Atlantic I was never sea sick. Seeing how severely others suffer from these two disabilities, I have sometimes wished I might have one go at them, so that I might sympathise properly, for their attacks must be really dreadful. My mother was subject to both, but latterly the headache left her; my father had occasional headaches. My nervous system is so highly organized that I am uncommonly sensitive to pain, though I bear it rather stoically, nor does it affect my disposition; in fact, I am somewhat less irritable under pain than when free of it.

I am less sensitive to heat and cold than most people, though my mind is more active in summer. I dress lightly in winter, and sleep under unusually light bed-covering. Like Goethe, when the barometer is low, I am inert. The thought of action becomes formidable, and I have to put on a great deal of extra steam to get anything done. A thunderstorm retards my circulation, making me suffer the distress of slow suffocation; the pressure and constriction begin to lighten when the storm is about half over. My constitution is of the spring-steel type, flexible, always bending, but so far not breaking, though I have never been careful of myself. I have great power of resistance to certain impacts; to others almost none, as for instance, sudden loud noises or the motion of crowds. A walk of ten blocks on Fifth Avenue at noon or across Times Square in the evening, uses me up. A lively dinner party guarantees me a sleepless night, and a serious sustained conversation at lunch puts me out of action for the whole afternoon. I sleep soundly at full length prone, apparently as a rule motionless, for the bed-covering seems hardly disturbed at all and only perhaps twice a year do I wake with any consciousness of having dreamed, virtually never remembering a single item of what the dream was. I wake invariably in low spirits, the fit lasting usually less than an hour.

I notice the deterioration due to advancing age in only two directions. My memory for names was always weak, and has now become markedly weaker; and the same is true of my sense of direction, which was always poor. In New York, for example, I find myself confused oftener than formerly, and obliged to note which way is east or west, uptown or downtown; especially when coming out of a subway or getting off a bus. My sense of hearing, taste and smell, always very acute, seem unimpaired, and my eyes still stand hard usage as well as ever; and I notice no weakening of my appetites or digestive functions. Something of this is probably due to my having lived always on the abstemious side, especially in the matter of drink and simple diet. I have done this purely by taste and preference, never tempted to any excess, so I can claim no credit for it.

Persistence of reproductive power interests me on account of its apparent relation to longevity. It seems that as long as you can reproduce your kind, nature will stand by and give you a lift in emergency of illness. This is most noticeable in the convalescence of children, when the full development of reproductive power is as yet in prospect. But when that power fails, nature cares nothing for you and will not keep you, but leaves you unaided to the ministrations of the quacks and *schochetim*.

Probably in my case this power, always strong, has lasted as well as it has by reason of its having been relatively but little used. No women's attraction for me has ever been primarily libidinous, nor ever remained purely so. The interest stirred by what we commonly call sex-appeal never affected me. I am a great admirer of women's physical beauty, as I am of the objects in a jeweller's window; I look at both in the spirit of a delighted connoisseurship, with not the least desire of possession; indeed the free offer of possession would be most embarrassing. What attracts me to women in the first instance is the display of psychical qualities combined with a force of intellect sufficient to carry them and make them effective. This combination is not often found, especially in our American society; and when it exists it is too often vitiated by sex-consciousness. As a rule, American and English women seem to me morbidly conscious of their sex.

Where it is found at its free best, however, as I have explained in my *Memoirs,* the ensuing relationship simply reduces physical possession to what seems to me to be its proper level in the scale of importance, as something to be undertaken or not as the progress of the relationship shall determine. Thus I have enjoyed the very extreme of what might be called a eunuch's intimacy with admirable and charming women who were no more interested than I in importing the element of physical possession into our relationship; and again in other and much fewer instances, it was clear that the intimacy would be greatly improved and strengthened by admitting their importation, so it was accordingly admitted. The aim of a free association between men and women is the enhancement of psychical values and the conservation of romance, beauty and poetry in human existence. I think the view set forth in my *Memoirs* is the correct one, that association in marriage is inimical to this, as involving a radical confusion of function.

I have no more faculty for making myself interesting to women than to men; still less making myself loved or even much cared for. On the other hand, I have known only two men and one woman in my life to whom I could present myself unreservedly; that is to say, leaving no area of consciousness which they were not free to enter and to explore as they chose.

If I were asked what my life has been worth to the world, I should say actually nothing but potentially perhaps a good deal. My few achievements will never be accepted, but if they were I think society might profit by them. What, then, have I done?

Everyone knows that all attempts at a large-scale incorporation of mankind in any field of enterprise have failed, and in the long run broken down. I believe I am the first to show not only why they have failed, but why they must fail. I have shown why political nationalism will be forever impracticable, and all forms of political organisation beyond the simplest and smallest; also the large-scale organisation of religion, education, labour, and other activities. In short, I have pointed out that as long as the disintegrating forces of these great material laws, acting in concert, is what it is, human societies must hereafter present the same pattern of rise and fall which they have hitherto presented, and with approximately the same periodicity. I have also been the first, I think, to show some of the tremendous implications of R. A. Cram's thesis of man's place in nature, when carried out to its logical length, which for some reason Cram did not do. By the terms of his own thesis his succeeding book, *The End of Democracy,* had no point whatever and I cannot understand his writing it. I have not worked out these matters in full, but I have written enough to show clearly the line of approach which an exhaustive treatise should take.

For a person of almost unlimited leisure, I have written very little and fitfully. My inclination has always been towards literary criticism, with which I have done virtually nothing. My reasons for this were the dearth of eligible subjects, and the non-existence of any periodical in which serious criticism could appear. Aside from my work on Rabelais, Thomas Jefferson and Henry George, with two or three short essays, my dealings with literature have been in the way of reviewing, which I like to do. My brief essay on "Artemus Ward," and one equally brief on "The Misuses of Adversity," both reprinted from the *Atlantic* in the volume called *Free Speech and Plain Language,* would be perhaps enough to suggest the kind of thing I should most enjoy doing and would have done diligently if I had lived in an earlier period. So much of my casual writing has had to do with public affairs that I suppose I am put down as a journalist or publicist, neither of which I could possibly be.

My literary style has been well spoken of, as showing due respect for my native tongue. I am pleased to hear it called distinctively American. One critic remarked that it forms a perfect bridge between the Classical English prose of the eighteenth century and the American vernacular; and that the transitions were invariably made in the very best of good taste. Nothing could have been more pleasing to me than this. The essay on "The Misuses of Adversity" has many instances of the kind of thing referred to, so if my critic's opinion holds good there it would probably hold good throughout my work.

On reading this over I see that I must add a word or two to what I have said about my indifference to the physical lure of women. This trait, I believe, is due to, or I might say is part of, my almost abnormal hatred for any loss of self-control however slight or momentary. The sight of anything like self-abandonment, for instance the sight of a drunken person, fills me with aversion amounting to dread. So, going back to Mark Twain's rule, the thought of the reaction from yielding to an unwarranted sensuous appetite reduces one to an *ad hoc* impotence. The point is not that desire is repressed; the desire is simply not there. If affectional associations warrant the desire, which in my case has not often happened, that is another matter. If they do not, you might keep me abed with any Helen or Cleopatra until doomsday, and she would get nothing out of it. By count half a dozen times in my life some circumstance has caused me to sleep with some woman with whom I had what I called a eunuch's relationship of absolute freedom from conventional restraint. We were fond of each other and thoroughly enjoyed the intimacies of being abed together, and the fact that we carried them no further than we did was due to nothing but disinclination.

My only failure in emotional self-control which so far has seemed unconquerable is brought about by my hearing a certain order of music or by reading prose or verse that is composed in the grand style. Not even as a child have I ever shed tears for grief or pain, but a suite of Bach or certain quartettes of Haydn will put them beyond my control. So also will choruses of Aeschylus and Sophocles, as passages from English prose writers such as Bishop Butler, William Law, the Cambridge Platonists. The more grandiose order of music, the later symphonies of Beethoven, the operas of Wagner, Berlioz, Ernest Reyer—nothing of this disturbs my emotional balance in the least.

I may mention one or two characteristic traits as having no virtue whatever, because they are mine by birth, not by acquisition. I have always been singularly free of envy, jealousy, covetousness; I but vaguely understand them. Having no ambition, I have always preferred the success of others to my own, and had more pleasure in it. I never had the least desire for place or prominence, least of all for power; and this was fortunate for me because the true individualist must regard power over others as preeminently something to be loathed and shunned.

Nock wrote this sketch for Paul Palmer, who requested some biographical background for a volume of Nock's letters he was planning to edit. It was probably written in 1944 or very early in 1945. It is published here for the first time.

Palmer was editor of the *American Mercury* from 1935 to 1939 and considered himself one of Nock's close friends. During that time, Nock wrote his "The State of the Union" column and a great many of the unsigned editorials in the *American Mercury*.

Anarchist's Progress

When I was seven years old, playing in front of our house on the outskirts of Brooklyn one morning, a policeman stopped and chatted with me for a few moments. He was a kindly man, of a Scandinavian blonde type with pleasant blue eyes, and I took to him at once. He sealed our acquaintance permanently by telling me a story that I thought was immensely funny; I laughed over it at intervals all day. I do not remember what it was, but it had to do with the antics of a drove of geese in our neighbourhood. He impressed me as the most entertaining and delightful person that I had seen in a long time, and I spoke of him to my parents with great pride.

At this time I did not know what policemen were. No doubt I had seen them, but not to notice them. Now, naturally, after meeting this highly prepossessing specimen, I wished to find out all I could about them, so I took the matter up with our old colored cook. I learned from her that my fine new friend represented something that was called the law; that the law was very good and great, and that everyone should obey and respect it. This was reasonable; if it were so, then my admirable friend just fitted his place, and was even more highly to be thought of, if possible. I asked where the law came from, and it was explained to me that men all over the country got together on what was called election day, and chose certain persons to make the law and others to see that it was carried out; and that the sum-total of all this mechanism was called our government. This again was as it should be; the men I knew, such as my father, my uncle George, and Messrs. So-and-so among the neighbours (running them over rapidly in my mind), could do this sort of thing handsomely, and there was probably a good deal in the idea. But what was it all for? Why did we have law and government, anyway? Then I learned that there were persons called criminals; some of them stole, some hurt or killed people or set fire to houses; and it was the duty of men like my friend the policeman to protect us from them. If he saw any he would catch them and lock them up, and they would be punished according to the law.

A year or so later we moved to another house in the same neighbourhood, only a short distance away. On the corner of the block—rather a long block—behind our house stood a large one-story wooden building, very dirty and shabby, called the Wigwam. While getting the lie of my new surroundings, I considered this structure and remarked with disfavour the kind of people who seemed to be making themselves at home there. Some one told me it was a "political headquarters," but I did not know what that meant, and therefore did not connect it with my recent researches into law and government. I had little curiosity about the Wigwam. My parents never forbade my going there, but my mother once casually told me that it was a pretty good place to keep away from, and I agreed with her.

Two months later I heard someone say that election day was shortly coming on, and I sparked up at once; this, then, was the day when the lawmakers were to be chosen. There had been great doings at the Wigwam lately; in the evenings, too, I had seen noisy processions of drunken loafers passing our house, carrying transparencies and tin torches that sent up clouds of kerosene-smoke. When I had asked what these meant, I was answered in one word, "politics," uttered in a disparaging tone, but this signified nothing to me. The fact is that my attention had been attracted by a steam-calliope that went along with one of the first of these processions, and I took it to mean that there was a circus going on; and when I found that there was no circus, I was disappointed and did not care what else might be taking place.

On hearing of election day, however, the light broke in on me. I was really witnessing the august performances that I had heard of from our cook. All these processions of yelling hoodlums who sweat and stank in the parboiling humidity of the Indian-summer evenings—all the squalid goings-on in the Wigwam—all these, it seemed, were part and parcel of an election. I noticed that the men whom I knew in the neighbourhood were not prominent in this election; my uncle George voted, I remember, and when he dropped in at our house that evening, I overheard him say that going to the polls was a filthy business. I could not make it out. Nothing could be clearer than that the leading spirits in the whole affair were most dreadful swine; and I wondered by what kind of magic they could bring forth anything so majestic, good and venerable as the law. But I kept my questionings to myself for some reason, though, as a rule, I was quite a hand for pestering older people about matters that seemed anomalous. Finally, I gave it up as hopeless, and thought no more about the subject for three years.

An incident of that election night, however, stuck in my memory. Some devoted brother, very far gone in whisky, fell by the wayside in a vacant lot just back of our house, on his way to the Wigwam to await the returns. He lay there all night, mostly in a comatose state. At intervals of something like half an hour he roused himself up in the darkness, apparently aware that he was not doing his duty by the occasion, and tried to sing the chorus of "Marching Through Georgia," but he could never get quite through three measures of the first bar before relapsing into somnolence. It was very funny; he always began so bravely and earnestly, and always petered out so lamentably. I often think of him. His general sense of political duty, I must say, still seems to me as intelligent and as competent as that of any man I have met in the many, many years that have gone by since then, and his mode of expressing it still seems about as effective as any I could suggest.

When I was just past my tenth birthday we left Brooklyn and went to live in a pleasant town of ten thousand population. An orphaned cousin made her home with us, a pretty girl, who soon began to cut a fair swath among the young men of the town. One of these was an extraordinary person, difficult to describe. My father, a great tease, at once detected his resemblance to a chimpanzee, and bored my cousin abominably by always speaking of him as Chim. The young man was not a popular idol by any means, yet no one thought badly of him. He was accepted everywhere as a source of legitimate diversion, and in the graduated, popular scale of local speech was invariably designated as a fool—a born fool, for which there was no help. When I heard he was a lawyer, I was so astonished that I actually went into the chicken-court one day to hear him plead some trifling case, out of sheer curiosity to see him in action; and I must say I got my money's worth. Presently the word went around that he was going to run for Congress, and stood a good chance of being elected; and what amazed me above all was that no one seemed to see anything out of the way about it.

My tottering faith in law and government got a hard jolt from this. Here was a man, a very good fellow indeed—he had nothing in common with the crew who herded around the Wigwam—who was regarded by the unanimous judgment of the community, without doubt, peradventure, or exception, as having barely sense enough to come in when it rained; and this was the man whom his party was sending to Washington as contentedly as if he were some Draco or Solon. At this point my sense of humour forged to the front and took permanent charge of the situation, which was fortunate for me, since otherwise my education would have been aborted, and I would perhaps, like so many who have missed this great blessing, have gone in with the reformers and uplifters; and such a close shave as this, in the words of Rabelais, is a terrible thing to think upon. How many reformers there have been in my day; how nobly and absurdly busy they were, and how dismally unhumorous! I can dimly remember Pingree and Altgeld in the Middle West, and Godkin, Strong, and Seth Low in New York. During the 'nineties, the goodly fellowship of the prophets buzzed about the whole country like flies around a tar-barrel—and, Lord! where be they now?

It will easily be seen, I think, that the only unusual thing about all this was that my mind was perfectly unprepossessed and blank throughout. My experiences were surely not uncommon, and my reasonings and inferences were no more than any child, who was more than half-witted, could have made without trouble. But my mind had never been perverted or sophisticated; it was left to itself. I never went to school, so I was never indoctrinated with pseudo-patriotic fustian of any kind, and the plain, natural truth of such matters as I have been describing, therefore, found its way to my mind without encountering any artificial obstacle.

This freedom continued, happily, until my mind had matured and toughened. When I went to college I had the great good luck to hit on probably the only one in the country (there certainly is none now) where all such subjects were so remote and unconsidered that one would not know they existed. I had Greek, Latin, and mathematics, and nothing else, but I had these until the cows came home; then I had them all over again (or so it seemed) to make sure nothing was left out; then I was given a bachelor's degree in the liberal arts, and turned adrift. The idea was that if one wished to go in for some special branch of learning, one should do it afterward, on the foundation laid at college. The college's business was to lay the foundation, and the authorities saw to it that we were kept plentifully busy with the job. Therefore, all such subjects as political history, political science, and political economy were closed to me throughout my youth and early manhood; and when the time came that I wished to look into them, I did it on my own, without the interference of instructors, as any person who has gone through a course of training similar to mine at college is quite competent to do.

That time, however, came much later, and meanwhile I thought little about law and government, as I had other fish to fry; I was living more or less out of the world, occupied with literary studies. Occasionally some incident happened that set my mind perhaps a little farther along in the old sequences, but not often. Once, I remember, I ran across the case of a boy who had been sentenced to prison, a poor, scared little brat, who had intended something no worse than mischief, and it turned out to be a crime. The judge said he disliked to sentence the lad; it seemed the wrong thing to do; but the law left him no option. I was struck by this. The judge, then, was doing something as an official that he would not dream of doing as a man; and he could do it without any sense of responsibility, or discomfort, simply because he was acting as an official and not as a man. On this principle of action, it seemed to me that one could commit almost any kind of crime without getting into trouble with one's conscience. Clearly, a great crime had been committed against this boy; yet nobody who had had a hand in it— the judge, the jury, the prosecutor, the complaining witness, the policemen and jailers—felt any responsibility about it, because they were not acting as men, but as officials. Clearly, too, the public did not regard them as criminals, but rather as upright and conscientious men.

The idea came to me then, vaguely but unmistakably, that if the primary intention of government was not to abolish crime but merely to monopolize crime, no better device could be found for doing it than the inculcation of precisely this frame of mind in the officials and in the public; for the effect of this was to exempt both from any allegiance to those sanctions of humanity or decency which anyone of either class, acting as an individual, would have felt himself bound to respect—nay, would have wished to respect. This idea was vague at the moment, as I say, and I did not work it out for some years, but I think I never quite lost track of it from that time.

Presently I got acquainted in a casual way with some officeholders, becoming quite friendly with one in particular, who held a high elective office. One day he happened to ask me how I would reply to a letter that bothered him; it was a query about the fitness of a certain man for an appointive job. His recommendation would have weight; he liked the man, and really wanted to recommend him—moreover, he was under great political pressure to recommend him—but he did not think the man was qualified. Well, then, I suggested offhand, why not put it just that way?—it seemed all fair and straightforward. "Ah yes," he said, "but if I wrote such a letter as that, you see, I wouldn't be reëlected." This took me aback a bit, and I demurred somewhat. "That's all very well," he kept insisting, "but I wouldn't be reëlected." Thinking to give the discussion a semi-humorous turn, I told him that the public, after all, had rights in the matter; he was their hired servant, and if he were not reëlected it would mean merely that the public did not want him to work for them any more, which was quite within their competence. Moreover, if they threw him out on any such issue as this, he ought to take it as a compliment; indeed, if he were reëlected, would it not tend to show in some measure that he and the people did not fully understand each other? He did not like my tone of levity, and dismissed the subject with the remark that I knew nothing of practical politics, which was no doubt true.

Perhaps a year after this I had my first view of a legislative body in action. I visited the capital of a certain country, and listened attentively to the legislative proceedings. What I wished to observe, first of all, was the kind of business that was mostly under discussion; and next, I wished to get as good a general idea as I could of the kind of men who were entrusted with this business. I had a friend on the spot, formerly a newspaper reporter who had been in the press gallery for years; he guided me over the government buildings, taking me everywhere and showing me everything I asked to see.

As we walked through some corridors in the basement of the Capitol, I remarked the resonance of the stonework. "Yes," he said, thoughtfully, "these walls, in their time, have echoed to the uncertain footsteps of many a drunken statesman." His words were made good in a few moments when we heard a spirited commotion ahead, which we found to proceed from a good-sized room, perhaps a committee room, opening off the corridor. The door being open, we stopped, and looked in on a strange sight.

In the centre of the room, a florid, square-built, portly man was dancing an extraordinary kind of break-down, or *kazák* dance. He leaped straight up to an incredible height, spun around like a teetotum, stamped his feet, then suddenly squatted and hopped through several measures in a squatting position, his hands on his knees, and then leaped up in the air and spun around again. He blew like a turkey-cock, and occasionally uttered hoarse cries; his protruding and fiery eyes were suffused with blood, and the veins stood out on his neck and forehead like the strings of a bass-viol. He was drunk.

About a dozen others, also very drunk, stood around him in crouching postures, some clapping their hands and some slapping their knees, keeping time to the dance. One of them caught sight of us in the doorway, came up, and began to talk to me in a maundering fashion about his constituents. He was a loathsome human being; I have seldom seen one so repulsive. I could make nothing of what he said; he was almost inarticulate; and in pronouncing certain syllables he would slaver and spit, so that I was more occupied with keeping out of his range than with listening to him. He kept trying to buttonhole me, and I kept moving backward; he had backed me thirty feet down the corridor when my friend came along and disengaged me; and as we resumed our way, my friend observed for my consolation that "you pretty well need a mackintosh when X talks to you, even when he is sober."

This man, I learned, was interested in the looting of certain valuable public lands; nobody had heard of his ever being interested in any other legislative measures. The florid man who was dancing was interested in nothing but a high tariff on certain manufactures; he shortly became a Cabinet officer. Throughout my stay I was struck by seeing how much of the real business of legislation was in this category— how much, that is, had to do with putting unearned money in the pockets of beneficiaries—and what fitful and perfunctory attention the legislators gave to any other kind of business. I was even more impressed by the prevalent air of cynicism; by the frankness with which everyone seemed to acquiesce in the view of Voltaire, that government is merely a device for taking money out of one person's pocket and putting it into another's.

These experiences, commonplace as they were, prepared me to pause over and question certain sayings of famous men, when subsequently I ran across them, which otherwise I would perhaps have passed by without thinking about them. When I came upon the saying of Lincoln, that the way of the politician is "a long step removed from common honesty," it set a problem for me. I wondered just why this should be generally true, if it were true. When I read the remark of Mr. Jefferson, that "whenever a man has cast a longing eye on office, a rottenness begins in his conduct," I remembered the judge who had sentenced the boy, and my officeholding acquaintance who was so worried about reëlection. I tried to reëxamine their position, as far as possible putting myself in their place, and made a great effort to understand it favorably. My first view of a parliamentary body came back to me vividly when I read the despondent observation of John Bright, that he had sometimes known the British Parliament to do a good thing, but never just because it was a good thing. In the meantime I had observed many legislatures, and their principal occupations and preoccupations seemed to me precisely like those of the first one I ever saw; and while their personnel was not by any means composed throughout of noisy and disgusting scoundrels (neither, I hasten to say, was the first one), it was so unimaginably inept that it would really have to be seen to be believed. I cannot think of a more powerful stimulus to one's intellectual curiosity, for instance, than to sit in the galleries of the last Congress, contemplate its general run of membership, and then recall these sayings of Lincoln, Mr. Jefferson, and John Bright.[1]

1. As indicating the impression made on a more sophisticated mind, I may mention an amusing incident that happened to me in London two years ago. Having an engagement with a member of the House of Commons, I filled out a card and gave it to an attendant. By mistake I had written my name where the member's should be, and his where mine should be. The attendant handed the card back, saying, "I'm afraid this will 'ardly do, sir. I see you've been making yourself a member. It doesn't go quite as easy as that, sir—though from some of what you see around 'ere, I wouldn't say as 'ow you mightn't think so."

It struck me as strange that these phenomena seemed never to stir any intellectual curiosity in anybody. As far as I know, there is no record of its ever having occurred to Lincoln that the fact he had remarked was striking enough to need accounting for; nor yet to Mr. Jefferson, whose intellectual curiosity was almost boundless; nor yet to John Bright. As for the people around me, their attitudes seemed strangest of all. They all disparaged politics. Their common saying, "Oh, that's politics," always pointed to something that in any other sphere of action they would call shabby and disreputable. But they never asked themselves why it was that in this one sphere of action alone they took shabby and disreputable conduct as a matter of course. It was all the more strange because these same people still somehow assumed that politics existed for the promotion of the highest social purposes. They assumed that the State's primary purpose was to promote through appropriate institutions the general welfare of its members. This assumption, whatever it amounted to, furnished the rationale of their patriotism, and they held to it with a tenacity that on slight provocation became vindictive and fanatical. Yet all of them were aware, and if pressed, could not help acknowledging, that more than 90 per cent of the State's energy was employed directly against the general welfare. Thus one might say that they seemed to have one set of credenda for week-days and another for Sundays, and never to ask themselves what actual reasons they had for holding either.

I did not know how to take this, nor do I now. Let me draw a rough parallel. Suppose vast numbers of people to be contemplating a machine that they had been told was a plough, and very valuable—indeed, that they could not get on without it—some even saying that its design came down in some way from on high. They have great feelings of pride and jealousy about this machine, and will give up their lives for it if they are told it is in danger. Yet they all see that it will not plough well, no matter what hands are put to manage it, and in fact does hardly any ploughing at all; sometimes only with enormous difficulty and continual tinkering and adjustment can it be got to scratch a sort of furrow, very poor and short, hardly practicable, and ludicrously disproportionate to the cost and pains of cutting it. On the other hand, the machine harrows perfectly, almost automatically. It looks like a harrow, has the history of a harrow, and even when the most enlightened effort is expended on it to make it act like a plough, it persists, except for an occasional six or eight per cent of efficiency, in acting like a harrow.

Surely such a spectacle would make an intelligent being raise some enquiry about the nature and original intention of that machine. Was it really a plough? Was it ever meant to plough with? Was it not designed and constructed for harrowing? Yet none of the anomalies that I had been observing ever raised any enquiry about the nature and original intention of the State. They were merely acquiesced in. At most, they were put down feebly to the imperfections of human nature which render mismanagement and perversion of every good institution to some extent inevitable; and this is absurd, for these anomalies do not appear in the conduct of any other human institution. It is no matter of opinion, but of open and notorious fact, that they do not. There are anomalies in the church and in the family that are significantly analogous; they will bear investigation, and are getting it; but the analogies are by no means complete, and are mostly due to the historical connection of these two institutions with the State.

Everyone knows that the State claims and exercises the monopoly of crime that I spoke of a moment ago, and that it makes this monopoly as strict as it can. It forbids private murder, but itself organizes murder on a colossal scale. It punishes private theft, but itself lays unscrupulous hands on anything it wants, whether the property of citizen or of alien. There is, for example, no human right, natural or Constitutional, that we have not seen nullified by the United States Government. Of all the crimes that are committed for gain or revenge, there is not one that we have not seen it commit—murder, mayhem, arson, robbery, fraud, criminal collusion and connivance. On the other hand, we have all remarked the enormous relative difficulty of getting the State to effect any measure for the general welfare. Compare the difficulty of securing conviction in cases of notorious malfeasance, and in cases of petty private crime. Compare the smooth and easy going of the Teapot Dome transactions with the obstructionist behaviour of the State toward a national child-labour law. Suppose one should try to get the State to put the same safeguards (no stronger) around service-income that with no pressure at all it puts around capital-income: what chance would one have? It must not be understood that I bring these matters forward to complain of them. I am not concerned with complaints or reforms, but only with the exhibition of anomalies that seem to me to need accounting for.

In the course of some desultory reading I noticed that the historian Parkman, at the outset of his volume on the conspiracy of Pontiac, dwells with some puzzlement, apparently, upon the fact that the Indians had not formed a State. Mr. Jefferson, also, who knew the Indians well, remarked the same fact—that they lived in a rather highly organized society, but had never formed a State. Bicknell, the historian of Rhode Island, has some interesting passages that bear upon the same point, hinting that the collisions between the Indians and the whites may have been largely due to a misunderstanding about the nature of land-tenure; that the Indians, knowing nothing of the British system of land-tenure, understood their land-sales and land-grants as merely an admission of the whites to the same communal use of land that they themselves enjoyed. I noticed, too, that Marx devotes a good deal of space in *Das Kapital* to proving that economic exploitation cannot take place in any society until the exploited class has been expropriated from the land. These observations attracted my attention as possibly throwing a strong side light upon the nature of the State and the primary purpose of government, and I made note of them accordingly.

At this time I was a good deal in Europe. I was in England and Germany during the Tangier incident, studying the circumstances and conditions that led up to the late war. My facilities for this were exceptional, and I used them diligently. Here I saw the State behaving just as I had seen it behave at home. Moreover, remembering the political theories of the eighteenth century, and the expectations put upon them, I was struck with the fact that the republican, constitutional-monarchical and autocratic States behaved exactly alike. This has never been sufficiently remarked. There was no practical distinction to be drawn among England, France, Germany, and Russia; in all these countries the State acted with unvarying consistency and unfailing regularity against the interests of the immense, the overwhelming majority of its people. So flagrant and flagitious, indeed, was the action of the State in all these countries, that its administrative officials, especially its diplomats, would immediately, in any other sphere of action, be put down as a professional-criminal class; just as would the corresponding officials in my own country, as I had already remarked. It is a noteworthy fact, indeed, concerning all that has happened since then, that if in any given circumstances one went on the assumption that they were a professional-criminal class, one could predict with accuracy what they would do and what would happen; while on any other assumption one could predict almost nothing. The accuracy of my own predictions during the war and throughout the Peace Conference was due to nothing but their being based on this assumption.

The Liberal party was in power in England in 1911, and my attention became attracted to its tenets. I had already seen something of Liberalism in America as a kind of glorified mugwumpery. The Cleveland Administration had long before proved what everybody already knew, that there was no essential difference between the Republican and Democratic parties; an election meant merely that one was in office and wished to stay in, and the other was out and wished to get in. I saw precisely the same relation prevailing between the two major parties in England, and I was to see later the same relation sustained by the Labour Administration of Mr. Ramsay MacDonald. All these political permutations resulted only in what John Adams admirably called "a change of impostors." But I was chiefly interested in the basic theory of Liberalism. This seemed to be that the State is no worse than a degenerate or perverted institution, beneficent in its original intention, and susceptible of restoration by the simple expedient of "putting good men in office."

I had already seen this experiment tried on several scales of magnitude, and observed that it came to nothing commensurate with the expectations put upon it or the enormous difficulty of arranging it. Later I was to see it tried on an unprecedented scale, for almost all the Governments engaged in the war were Liberal, notably the English and our own. Its disastrous results in the case of the Wilson Administration are too well known to need comment; though I do not wish to escape the responsibility of saying that of all forms of political impostorship, Liberalism always seemed to me the most vicious, because the most pretentious and specious. The general upshot of my observations, however, was to show me that whether in the hands of Liberal or Conservative, Republican or Democrat, and whether under nominal constitutionalism, republicanism or autocracy, the mechanism of the State would work freely and naturally in but one direction, namely, against the general welfare of the people.

So I set about finding out what I could about the origin of the State, to see whether its mechanism was ever really meant to work in any other direction; and here I came upon a very odd fact. All the current popular assumptions about the origin of the State rest upon sheer guesswork; none of them upon actual investigation. The treatises and textbooks that came into my hands were also based, finally, upon guesswork. Some authorities guessed that the State was originally formed by this-or-that mode of social agreement; others, by a kind of muddling empiricism; others, by the will of God; and so on. Apparently none of these, however, had taken the plain course of going back upon the record as far as possible to ascertain how it actually had been formed, and for what purpose. It seemed that enough information must be available; the formation of the State in America, for example, was a matter of relatively recent history, and one must be able to find out a great deal about it. Consequently I began to look around to see whether anyone had ever anywhere made any such investigation, and if so, what it amounted to.

I then discovered that the matter had, indeed, been investigated by scientific methods, and that all the scholars of the Continent knew about it, not as something new or startling, but as a sheer commonplace. The State did not originate in any form of social agreement, or with any disinterested view of promoting order and justice. Far otherwise. The State originated in conquest and confiscation, as a device for maintaining the stratification of society permanently into two classes— an owning and exploiting class, relatively small, and a propertyless dependent class. Such measures of order and justice as it established were incidental and ancillary to this purpose; it was not interested in any that did not serve this purpose; and it resisted the establishment of any that were contrary to it. No State known to history originated in any other manner, or for any other purpose than to enable the continuous economic exploitation of one class by another.[2]

2. There is a considerable literature on this subject, largely untranslated. As a

This at once cleared up all the anomalies which I had found so troublesome. One could see immediately, for instance, why the hunting tribes and primitive peasants never formed a State. Primitive peasants never made enough of an economic accumulation to be worth stealing; they lived from hand to mouth. The hunting tribes of North America never formed a State, because the hunter was not exploitable. There was no way to make another man hunt for you; he would go off in the woods and forget to come back; and if he were expropriated from certain hunting-grounds, he would merely move on beyond them, the territory being so large and the population so sparse. Similarly, since the State's own primary intention was essentially criminal, one could see why it cares only to monopolize crime, and not to suppress it; this explained the anomalous behaviour of officials, and showed why it is that in their public capacity, whatever their private character, they appear necessarily as a professional-criminal class; and it further accounted for the fact that the State never moves disinterestedly for the general welfare, except grudgingly and under great pressure.

Again, one could perceive at once the basic misapprehension which forever nullifies the labors of Liberalism and Reform. It was once quite seriously suggested to me by some neighbours that I should go to Congress. I asked them why they wished me to do that, and they replied with some complimentary phrases about the satisfaction of having some one of a somewhat different type "amongst those damned rascals down there." "Yes, but," I said, "don't you see that it would be only a matter of a month or so—a very short time, anyway—before I should be a damned rascal, too?" No, they did not see this; they were rather taken aback; would I explain? "Suppose," I said, "that you put in a Sunday-school superintendent or a Y.M.C.A. secretary to run an assignation-house on Broadway. He might trim off some of the coarser fringes of the job, such as the badger game and the panel game, and put things in what Mayor Gaynor used to call a state of 'outward order and decency,' but he *must* run an assignation-house, or he would

---

beginning, the reader may be conveniently referred to Mr. Charles A. Beard's *Rise of American Civilization* and his work on the Constitution of the United States. After these he should study closely—for it is hard reading—a small volume called *The State* by Professor Franz Oppenheimer, of the University of Frankfort. It has been well translated and is easily available.

promptly hear from the owners." This was a new view to them, and they went away thoughtful.

Finally, one could perceive the reason for the matter that most puzzled me when I first observed a legislature in action, namely, the almost exclusive concern of legislative bodies with such measures as tend to take money out of one set of pockets and put it into another— the preoccupation with converting labour-made property into law-made property, and redistributing its ownership. The moment one becomes aware that just this, over and above a purely legal distribution of the ownership of natural resources, is what the State came into being for, and what it yet exists for, one immediately sees that the legislative bodies are acting altogether in character, and otherwise one cannot possibly give oneself an intelligent account of their behaviour.[3]

Speaking for a moment in the technical terms of economics, there are two general means whereby human beings can satisfy their needs and desires. One is by work—i.e., by applying labour and capital to natural resources for the production of wealth, or to facilitating the exchange of labour-products. This is called the economic means. The other is by robbery—i.e., the appropriation of the labour-products of others without compensation. This is called the political means. The State, considered functionally, may be described as *the organization of the political means,* enabling a comparatively small class of beneficiaries to satisfy their needs and desires through various delegations of the taxing power, which have no vestige of support in natural right, such as private land-ownership, tariffs, franchises, and the like.

It is a primary instinct of human nature to satisfy one's needs and desires with the least possible exertion; everyone tends by instinctive preference to use the political means rather than the economic means, if he can do so. The great desideratum in a tariff, for instance, is its license to rob the domestic consumer of the difference between the

3. When the Republican convention which nominated Mr. Harding was almost over, one of the party leaders met a man who was managing a kind of dark-horse, or one-horse, candidate, and said to him, "You can pack up that candidate of yours, and take him home now. I can't tell you who the next President will be; it will be one of three men, and I don't just yet know which. But I can tell you who the next Secretary of the Interior will be, and that is the important question, because there are still a few little things lying around loose that the boys want." I had this from a United States Senator, a Republican, who told it to me merely as a good story.

price of an article in a competitive and a non-competitive market. Every manufacturer would like this privilege of robbery if he could get it, and he takes steps to get it if he can, thus illustrating the powerful instinctive tendency to climb out of the exploited class, which lives by the economic means (exploited, because the cost of this privilege must finally come out of production, there being nowhere else for it to come from), and into the class which lives, wholly or partially, by the political means.

This instinct—and this alone—is what gives the State its almost impregnable strength. The moment one discerns this, one understands the almost universal disposition to glorify and magnify the State, and to insist upon the pretence that it is something which it is not— something, in fact, the direct opposite of what it is. One understands the complacent acceptance of one set of standards for the State's conduct, and another for private organizations; of one set for officials, and another for private persons. One understands at once the attitude of the press, the Church and educational institutions, their careful inculcations of a specious patriotism, their nervous and vindictive proscriptions of opinion, doubt or even of question. One sees why purely fictitious theories of the State and its activities are strongly, often fiercely and violently, insisted on; why the simple fundamentals of the very simply science of economics are shirked or veiled; and why, finally, those who really know what kind of thing they are promulgating, are loth to say so.

The outbreak of the war in 1914 found me entertaining the convictions that I have here outlined. In the succeeding decade nothing has taken place to attenuate them, but quite the contrary. Having set out only to tell the story of how I came by them, and not to expound them or indulge in any polemic for them, I may now bring this narrative to an end, with a word about their practical outcome.

It has sometimes been remarked as strange that I never joined in any agitation, or took the part of a propagandist for any movement against the State, especially at a time when I had an unexampled opportunity to do so. To do anything of the sort successfully, one must have more faith in such processes than I have, and one must also have a certain dogmatic turn of temperament, which I do not possess. To be quite candid, I was never much for evangelization; I am not sure enough that my opinions are right, and even if they were, a second-hand opinion is a poor possession. Reason and experience, I repeat, are all that determine our true beliefs. So I never greatly cared that people should think my way, or tried much to get them to do so. I should be glad if they *thought*—if their general turn, that is, were a little more for disinterested thinking, and a little less for impetuous action motivated by mere unconsidered prepossession; and what little I could ever do to promote disinterested thinking has, I believe, been done.

According to my observations (for which I claim nothing but that they are all I have to go by) inaction is better than wrong action or premature right action, and effective right action can only follow right thinking. "If a great change is to take place," said Edmund Burke, in his last words on the French Revolution, "the minds of men *will be fitted to it*." Otherwise the thing does not turn out well; and the processes by which men's minds are fitted seem to me untraceable and imponderable, the only certainty about them being that the share of any one person, or any one movement, in determining them is extremely small. Various social superstitions, such as magic, the divine right of kings, the Calvinist teleology, and so on, have stood out against many a vigorous frontal attack, and thrived on it; and when they finally disappeared, it was not under attack. People simply stopped thinking in those terms; no one knew just when or why, and no one even was much aware that they had stopped. So I think it very possible that while we are saying, "Lo, here!" and "Lo, there!" with our eye on this or that revolution, usurpation, seizure of power, or what not, the superstitions that surround the State are quietly disappearing in the same way.[4]

My opinion of my own government and those who administer it can probably be inferred from what I have written. Mr. Jefferson said that if a centralization of power were ever effected at Washington, the United States would have the most corrupt government on earth. Comparisons are difficult, but I believe it has one that is thoroughly corrupt, flagitious,

4. The most valuable result of the Russian Revolution is in its liberation of the idea of the State as an engine of economic exploitation. In Denmark, according to a recent article in *The English Review*, there is a considerable movement for a complete separation of politics from economics, which, if effected, would of course mean the disappearance of the State.

tyrannical, oppressive. Yet if it were in my power to pull down its whole structure overnight and set up another of my own devising—to abolish the State out of hand, and replace it by an organization of the economic means—I would not do it, for the minds of Americans are far from fitted to any such great change as this, and the effect would be only to lay open the way for the worse enormities of usurpation— possibly, who knows? with myself as the usurper! After the French Revolution, Napoleon!

Great and salutary social transformations, such as in the end do not cost more than they come to, are not effected by political shifts, by movements, by programs and platforms, least of all by violent revolutions, but by sound and disinterested thinking. The believers in action are numerous, their gospel is widely preached, they have many followers. Perhaps among those who will see what I have here written, there are two or three who will agree with me that the believers in action do not need us—indeed, that if we joined them, we should be rather a dead weight for them to carry. We need not deny that their work is educative, or pinch pennies when we count up its cost in the inevitable reactions against it. We need only remark that our place and function in it are not apparent, and then proceed on our own way, first with the more obscure and extremely difficult work of clearing and illuminating our own minds, and second, with what occasional help we may offer to others whose faith, like our own, is set more on the regenerative power of thought than on the uncertain achievements of premature action.

This article appeared in the March 1927 issue of the *American Mercury,* and was reprinted, by Nock, in *On Doing the Right Thing.*

The Path to the River

Normally, one turns into it at about my age; or perhaps I should say, one discovers that one has turned into it, that one is off the main road. The point of departure must have been most inconspicuous; I did not notice it. All I recall noticing is that of a sudden I began to miss many familiar sights and sounds of traffic. The sensation was odd; it was somewhat like the sensation in one's ears when a locust stops chirring. It brought a certain pleasant ease, a feeling of liberation and expansion of spirit, leading up to an untroubled interest in the rich and quiet beauty of my new surroundings.

The path is winding; one can only guess how long it is, for one can not see its end from any point short of its last turn, apparently. Its declivity, so far, is very gentle; one hardly feels it. One has few companions, latterly almost none, and one is content with that. One or two are willing to go the whole way with me, which troubles me a little, and I hope they will not insist. They are young, and taking this journey just for company would break the continuity of their lives, and be but a tedious business, besides. Then, too, since they will some day be taking it on their own, why should they force themselves to take it twice?

My most astonishing realization is that I have lost a great lot of luggage. I can not imagine what has become of it. I thought I was still carrying almost all I started out with, but as I stop to count it up, a great deal of it is gone. Evidently one begins life like a person on his first trip to Europe, by loading up with things that one has no use for, and that get themselves left behind unnoticed, here and there. I discover that my interest in many matters which I thought were important, and would still say, offhand, were important, no longer exists; interest in many occupations, theories, opinions; relationships, public and private; desires, habits, pleasures, even pastimes. I can still play good billiards, for instance, and if anyone asked me, I should reply unthinkingly that I enjoy the game; and then it would occur to me that I have not played for months running into years, and that I no longer care—not really— if I never play again. As an item of luggage, billiards has gone by the board, though I do not know when or how; and many matters of apparently greater importance have gone likewise. Other orders of interest, however, remain intact and, for all I can see, as fresh as ever— I think indeed much fresher, though this may be an illusion. At all events, it is only with these that I feel any longer a genuine concern.

Awareness that this process of unconscious sifting and selection has been going on is presumably final evidence that one is off the main road and well on the path to the river. It is called, rather patronizingly, "the acquiescence of age"; but may not that mean no more than an acquiescence in matters which have in the long run proven themselves hardly worth troubling one's head about? "The fashion of this world passeth away," said Goethe, "and I would fain occupy myself with the things that are abiding." If that be the acquiescence of age, make the most of it.

One in my position is expected, I believe, to have a special interest in questions about what, if anything, takes place on the other side of the river, and whether we are likely to have any hand in it. Do we indeed cross the river or do we melt away forever in its depths? I have never had any curiosity about these matters, nor have I any now. Such thought as I have given them has been unaffected, so far as I am aware (and I can not be responsible for what the Freudians might find going on in my *Unbewusstsein*) by any feeling of personal concern. Perhaps this absence of curiosity and concern may go some way towards giving my thoughts a passing interest for others who are likewise incurious and unconcerned, and I, therefore, write them down.

As a very small boy with a lively imagination and a budding sense of humour, I used to entertain myself at great length with speculations on what the human world would be like if we all lost our bodies. I made it out as on the whole a rather attractive picture, except that eating had to be counted out; this seemed an appalling calamity. It was more than balanced, however, by other considerations which were all to the good, such as the doing away with clothes and houses and, above all, the abolition of work. Work was inseparably related to food, clothes and shelter; and if there were no need for these nobody would have to do any work, which suited me admirably.

There appeared to be no difficulty about imagining a distinct human personality existing apart from physical properties, or pervading them, as magnetism—whatever that is—pervades iron. In fact, the most nearly real world I knew, the only one about which I could approach anything like certainty in my own mind, was the world of consciousness. I got at its phenomena directly and was sure of them. I was not so sure of the phenomena of my physical environment, for I got at these indirectly through sense-perception, and my senses were always letting me down in one way or another; I was always having to true up their findings by experience, mostly disappointing, as in the case of plaster-of-Paris fruit or the apparent soundness of tree-limbs. Again, a sense of the most intimate phenomena of consciousness—those associated with music, for instance—was quite incommunicable by physical means; yet I saw that it was somehow communicated to other persons, to my father and mother and certain cronies, for they made responses so appropriate as to leave no doubt.

So sense-perception impressed me early, if vaguely, as a rather poor and fallible interpreter of my environment, and as having little to do with establishing my most interesting approximations to certainty. As I grew older and understood better what stringent limitations our dependence on sense-perception does really impose on us, I began to wonder how our actual present environment would appear if one could get oneself in immediate contact with it, and be no longer dependent on the very incomplete and special reports of five extremely imperfect and special faculties, or "senses"; one so imperfect, indeed, as to be almost useless, and another not much more valuable.

Thus it came about that when at the age of twenty or so I read the observations of Professor Huxley and others on the subject of consciousness, they seemed simple and clear, and not in the least surprising. "The transition from the physics of the brain to the facts of consciousness," said Romanes, "is unthinkable." Just so did it impress Huxley, as not only inexplicable but actually unthinkable. Consciousness exists, and we know it only as existing in association with that which has the properties of matter and force; yet it is clearly not matter or force or any conceivable modification of either; and an interpretation of it in terms of matter and force is simply beyond the power of thought.

By way of illustrating this as simply as possible, Professor Huxley cites the sense of red colour. I am now writing by the aid of a lamp done in red lacquer; I look at it and see that it is red. Trace the whole process of this perception; suppose, says Huxley, that you could watch all the light-waves, nervous reactions, molecular motion in the brain, possible electrical discharges, "as if they were billiard-balls"; at the end you would be as far from the ensuing fact of consciousness, "the feel of redness," as you were at the outset. The phenomena of consciousness can be to some extent controlled by mechanical means or by some appropriate chemical agent like bhang or alcohol, but this throws no light on the nature of consciousness itself. A colour-blind person's testimony about my lamp might not agree with mine, but the content of his consciousness, whatever it may be, is still as unaccountable in terms of matter and force as mine is.

At high noon one day on a crowded street in Berlin, a man behind me hooked his umbrella into my collar, after the manner of Mr. Squeers; and while he was hand-over-handing me in, I recognized him as an old acquaintance who had also recognized me. Just what was it that we recognized? There was not a particle left of the physical structure that either of us had seen before; we had not met in fifteen years, and our former bodies were all worn out and gone. A resemblance persisted, one may say, and he recognized that. True, no doubt, in the first instance; but he also immediately recognized *me;* and in my turn, instantly getting by the accidents of clothes and physique, I also recognized *him.* One may say, again, that our "personalities" overlived these physical changes, and recognized each other. Very well, but just what is personality, and how does it contrive to do all this over-living, and where do matter and force come in? If personality can overlive three, four or half-a-dozen bodies and get along so handsomely without them, might it not manage, on a pinch, to get along without any?

In other words, since we know consciousness only in association with matter and force, must we regard that association as intrinsic and essential? Can consciousness persist dissociated from them, either independently as bare "personality," or in association with some unknown quantity which has not their properties? If someone says flatly that it can not, we must ask him how he knows that. If he says it can, we must ask the same question. The conditions of inquiry being what they are, if he can give a competent answer either way, all we can say is that he is just the man whom a great many people would like to see.

Such was the conclusion reached by the best science of the last century, and I have not heard that latter-day science has brought forward anything to invalidate or modify it. One may, therefore, I think, be excused from taking interest in any attempts to reach a "scientific proof" that personality survives death, because these attempts must rest on evidence of the senses; and in the premises, this order of evidence, as we have seen, is inadmissible. For example, if a person says to me, "You will never see me again after I die," it is open to me to reply, "Possibly; but since I never yet saw you and do not see you now, why should I expect to see you then? I see a body and some clothes, but the body is not the same one that I saw a week ago or that I shall see a week hence. I never saw *you,* never shall and never can."

Or, on the other hand, suppose he says, "I can prove objectively that I shall be alive after death," I might reply, "Why, bless you, you can't even prove objectively that you are alive now." Nor can he. Or, suppose he puts it thus, "Personality survives death; and to prove it, I will cause bells to be rung, furniture to be moved around, photographs to be taken, and messages to be written, all by invisible agencies. I will even cause a disembodied spirit to invade my own physical organism and control it, and give you assurance by word of my mouth." I might reply, "Yes, that is all very fine, very good, but it may not prove what you say it does. It may prove only that you are an uncommonly smart man. Moreover, if I admit your evidence, I can admit it only *in limine;* that is, admitting that the disembodied spirit is there and is alive, what does that prove about a future state for you, me, Tom, Dick or Harry? Nothing. If the spirit says it does prove something, who knows but the spirit may be wrong? The assumption that it must be right is clearly gratuitous." The *Santissimo Salvatore* spoke with immense philosophical profundity and soundness when He said that "if they hear not Moses and the prophets, neither will they be persuaded though one rose from the dead." If any conviction on this matter is to be reached, its reasonableness must be established by an entirely different method of approach.

This, apparently, is as it should be. Prince Alfonso of Castile is said to have remarked that if he had been present at the creation of the world he would have suggested some valuable improvements. If man were never to progress beyond the first stages of development, we too might suggest some; we might suggest a world in which there should be no pain, sorrow, labour, bereavement, disappointment, hardship. The trouble is that without these any progress in human development is unimaginable; nobody could ever get on. If there were no such thing as pain, if nothing hurt, the race would not last six months; if there were no sorrow or hardship, it could not elaborate any more character than a jellyfish—and so on. When one thinks these matters through to their logical end, taking careful account of everything, one finds it impossible to imagine human development going on as satisfactorily in any other circumstances than those we are in.

Hence it is probably no bad thing that man is held down pretty closely to the consideration of one world at a time. Suppose it were otherwise; suppose that by some miracle he were able to get what we call scientific proof that he would, or that he would not, live after death—cogent, irrefutable proof—it is easy to imagine the utterly enervating preoccupations that would ensue upon him in either case. One can not say whether they would be more debilitating and retarding in the one case or in the other. The flavour of such preoccupations that one gets from the history of mediæval Christianity is enough to intimate the irreparable misfortune that would be brought upon a world possessed by certainty on this point. It is a great advantage to us that by the ordinary standards of analysis we can know no more than we do; that conviction alone is admissible in the premises, and that the reasonableness of conviction, whether affirmative or negative, can be made out only by an order of evidence which is distinctly subjective.

For my own part, I have an extremely strong conviction that human personality overlives death; so strong and apparently so reasonable that I have long ceased to question it. This is not the same thing as saying I believe that my own personality will survive death, for I can not say that; in fact, I doubt it. I have an instinctive feeling that it will, but when I examine the basis available for rationalizing that feeling, I find it too slight to command confidence. These statements are not inconsistent, as I shall presently show.

There are certain orders or categories of human activity which are useful and indispensable, to which, nevertheless, one can not attach the idea of persistence. As I saw in my childhood's fancies, there is an insurmountable incongruity in such an association; natural truth is all

against it. These are what St. Paul calls the ἐπίγεια. The King James
Version gives the translation, "earthly things"; that is to say, lines of
activity which meet purely physical demands, and which can not be
conceived of as going on after these demands have ceased. For example,
one can not possibly imagine oneself manufacturing motor-cars "to all
eternity," as our phrase goes, or selling bonds, or running a bank.
Death would automatically dissociate us from innumerable pursuits
such as these, and we can perceive at once that it must do so.

On the other hand, there are categories of activity with respect to
which an association with persistence is at least imaginable. Natural
truth, if not flatly affirming this association, is at least not flatly against
it. In the light of natural truth there is no absolute, violent, even
ludicrous incongruity in the suggestion, such as instantly appears when
we attempt to contemplate the idea of persistence in the other categories
just mentioned. For example, when the Greek mathematician said that
God "geometrizes continually," his conception strikes us as not precisely
unimaginable or precisely ridiculous. Natural truth goes along with it
far enough at least to intimate that despite philology, geometry is not
quite one of the ἐπίγεια. It has a differentiating quality. As much may
be said of the Aristotelian ποίησις, and of the exercise of certain virtues
and affections. Even the clear and lucid perception of the later Greeks
saw here no actual collision with natural truth. The last words of
Socrates, both to his friends and to his judges, the elegiac lines on
Plato's young and gifted successor, the Master of the Portico, show
conviction open either way; natural truth asserts no jurisdiction. it is
only in the association of persistence with the practice of love[1] that we
first see natural truth legitimized in the parentage of a profound
conviction. Heliodorus and Diogeneia, the devoted lovers, died within
the same hour; and their friend Apollonides declares that death is no
bar to their felicity, but that they are now "as happy lying in the same
tomb as they were when lying in the same bed."

As I have already said, I could not possibly prove, even to myself,
by the accepted standards of scientific analysis, that I am alive at this
moment. *Cogito ergo sum* takes one but a precious little way, as has
often been shown. Yet I know I am alive, I have an unshakable
conviction about it, built up in this way: In the realm of the ἐπίγεια

---

1. Ἀγάπη; στοργή hardly covers it; certainly not ἔρως.

there are certain disciplines, mostly very rigorous, such as the discipline of hard physical work, the discipline of business and its competitions, the various disciplines prescribed by the social order. Engagement with any of these is attended by a keen sense of *life*, and the closer the engagement the more abounding and exalted the sense becomes; and this sense gives rise to strong conviction and supports it. Our vernacular has terms that reflect this experience. A hard set of tennis, for instance, makes on feel "all alive," and so does a fast bout at commercial competition, or leading a forlorn hope in an attack on sales-resistance. Thus too do we speak of the "live man" or the one who is "alive on his job."

Conviction on this point, then, appears to be pretty strictly the fruit of experience. Now, leaving the ἐπίγεια and going over into the categories where natural truth is not so peremptory about its findings, one meets with a precise parallel to all this. Here, too, are certain disciplines; the discipline of pure mathematics (to touch again the matter already spoken of), the discipline of the ποίησις, the discipline peculiar to the successful practice of certain virtues and affections, such as the affection of love.[2] Here, too, the occupation with these disciplines is attended by a strong sense of *life*, but life of a different order, corresponding to the order of experience that excites this sense. Here, too, the more one does with these disciplines, the harder one works at them, the stronger this sense becomes; and when it becomes strong enough it leads to conviction—sometimes, as in my own case, impersonal. I am sure as one can be of anything in this highly uncertain world that *some* will survive death, but my own practice of these disciplines has been too weak-willed and fitful to give me any assurance beyond this; it does not assure me that I shall be among them.

The point is that in both sets of categories alike the sense of life and the conviction proceeding from it are matters of experience alone. Conviction is conditioned by experience; it is practically impossible to entertain a conviction that experience does not to some degree back up. Hence it is not to be wondered at that a conviction of the persistence of personality is relatively uncommon at the present time. Both in the realm of thought and action the general tendency is towards an exclusive preoccupation with the ἐπίγεια; take the ἐπίγεια away, and practically

2. Ἀγάπη again.

the whole of our experience disappears with it; there is nothing left with which we can associate the idea of persistence. It is impossible to make conviction transcend experience; hence the effort to relate persistence to the only kind of life that we have ever experienced results merely in the consciousness of a wholly inadmissible anomaly.

The fifteenth chapter of the First Epistle to the Corinthians is one of the few passages of Scripture that remain at all generally well known; we hear it read at funerals. We may have remarked how impatiently and perfunctorily St. Paul runs off his arguments for persistence, or as he calls it, "immortality," and that in the midst of his arguments he drops in the apparently irrelevant quotation from Menander, that "evil communications corrupt good manners." There is no irrelevance here, however; the quotation conveys the whole point of what he has to say. The civilization of Corinth, like our own, was wholly made up of mundanities; and the gist of the passage is as if he had said, "Here are your arguments, but I might about as well save my breath. You can not take them in, not because they are unsound, but on account of your evil communications; you can not transcend your own experience. The only kind of life you know anything about is not worth being immortal, and you can not help being aware of it."

One may not overpress the point, of course, yet it is worth remarking how persistently the Biblical writers relate the idea of *life* to the practice of special disciplines in the second set of categories that we have been noticing. One such discipline "tendeth to *life*"; in the practice of it "is *life,* and in the pathway thereof there is no death." Another discipline, vividly personified, declares that "whoso findeth me findeth *life.*" Of another it is said, again, that whoso followeth it "findeth *life.*" Of another, that its admonitions "are *life* to those that find them." The great exponent of these disciplines is said to have come that they "might have *life.*" His precepts go forth, "and they that hear *shall live.*" A concordance will show the almost unfailing regularity with which this association occurs; and while, I repeat, too much may not be made of it, one may observe in it, as far as it goes, an interesting correspondence with the suggestions of experience.

Unquestionably, too, as one studies the order of nature, one gets certain intimations of purpose. One must speak of these with great caution, for theologians and poets alike have monstrously exaggerated their evidential value. Nevertheless, they are not, I think, to be flatly disregarded; natural truth invests them with a plausibility that is doubtless slight and vague, but is yet sufficiently definite to keep them in view. Nature appears to be very wasteful and to "make for right-eousness" by very round-about ways; yet on closer inspection her most conspicuous wastes turn out to be made in behalf of some highly interesting economies. The most one may say, perhaps, is that under her régime nothing is going to be saved, finally, that is not worth saving. Whether all that is worth saving will be saved is, of course, another question. Still another question is, how far our present estimate of what is and what is not worth saving will be found in the long run to accord with her inscrutable economy.

For my own part, I could not hold it as any count against the order of nature if my own personality did not survive death. On the other hand, my intimations of purpose in nature, vague as they may be, are distinctly affronted by the suggestion that certain other personalities do not survive death. If Socrates, Marcus Aurelius, Dante, Cervantes, Shakespeare and Rabelais do not survive death, then, as all my intimations lead me to see it, the order of nature is a most inglorious fizzle. My intimations bear the same testimony, too, in behalf of equally eminent practitioners, such as we have all seen and revered, who have passed their days in humbler stations and whose eminence, therefore, remains unknown to the world at large.

I see no reason why the great majority of mankind should survive death, because experience and the intimations of purpose in nature alike present the idea of persistence as an achievement, as a matter of diligent and progressive adaptation to environment; and here, too, the analogy with our physical life seems close and orderly. Von Humboldt says that no one could pass from Siberia into Senegal without losing consciousness; one could not expect to survive a sudden change into an environment wholly alien to one's adaptations. To all appearances, then, in respect of adaptation to any other than a purely secular environment, the vast majority are so dead while they live that one may suppose they stay dead when they die. It is quite conceivable that a person's body might outlive his faculty for adaptation; in other words, that his soul—if for convenience one may so designate that faculty— may die before his body does. Quite conceivably his soul might die without his knowing it. Quite conceivably, too, on the other hand, he might have enough vitality of faculty to stand the actual transition into an alien environment, but not enough to enable the process of adaptation to go on; somewhat like a consumptive who has been too dilatory about measures which, taken in time, would enable him to rebuild himself after moving into a favourable climate.

It is thus, then, that I view the matter; and as I have said, as far as I am aware, I view it without prejudice, and certainly with no sense of personal concern. Experience, the intimations of purpose in nature, and the largest available understanding of nature's economies, all, I think, suggest this view as at least permissible; the view that—

> the energy of life may be
> Kept on after the grave, but not begun;
> And he who flagged not in the earthly strife,
> From strength to strength advancing—only he,
> His soul well-knit, and all his battles won,
> Mounts, *and that hardly,* to eternal life.

My adventures on the main road were uncommonly many and diversified. I sought them with ardent curiosity, turned them inside out, and got all kinds of profit from them, except money and fame. Yet I can think of none that I would wish to repeat, nor do I ever find myself looking back upon any of them with any sentiment except that of thankfulness that almost all of them were good. They were good, I have had them, I am sincerely thankful for them, but now that their time is past, I seldom think of them at all, and never desirously or with regret. Nor am I ever tempted to throw any inquiring glances forward into the future, not even upon the fact of death. One rehearses for it so many thousand times on going to bed at night that one is unlikely to get stage-fright over the full-dress performance. The most beautiful figure in all human history, meditating in his encampment "among the Quadi, at the Granua," told himself with hard common sense that "he who fears death either fears the loss of sensation or a different kind of sensation. But if thou shalt have no sensation, neither wilt thou feel any harm; and if thou shalt acquire another kind of sensation, thou wilt be a different kind of living being, and thou wilt not cease to live."

Among the many keen interests of the present there are one or two little undertakings that for my own satisfaction I should like to complete, or at least to carry farther forward. I hope the path will remain peaceful and easy enough to permit me to work at them while I am still able to work. But I am not aware of any anxiety even about this, for these conditions are not in my control, and if they went against me I could find no reason to complain. My state of mind with reference to them, as far as I know it, is that of one who regards himself as

> . . . a citizen of this great state, the world: what difference does it make to thee whether for five years or three? . . . Where is the hardship, then, if no tyrant or unjust judge sends thee away from the state, but nature who brought thee into it? The same as if a prætor who has employed an actor dismisses him from the stage: "But I have not finished the five acts, but only three of them." Thou sayest well, but in life the three acts are the whole drama; for what shall be a complete drama is determined by him who was once the cause of its composition, and now of its dissolution; but thou art the cause of neither. Depart then satisfied, for he also who releases thee is satisfied.

This beautiful essay—on the "acquiescence of age"—was published anonymously (apparently at Nock's request) in the July 1932 issue of *Harper's Magazine*. Nock was then 63; he would die in thirteen years. He included it as the last essay in his *Free Speech and Plain Language*.

II. THE CASUALTIES OF WAR

I am coming to be much less interested in what war does to people at the time, and much more in what it does to them after it is over.

—Letters From Albert Jay Nock

Peace the Aristocrat

The recommendations of Mr. Garrison and Mr. Daniels and the persistent agitation of Mr. Gardner have at length brought forth fruit in the fairly progressive programme of armament that Congress finally authorized. The general discussion of these measures was singularly trite. On the one hand we had a recrudescence of the doctrine that military efficiency is a sound guaranty of peace—the doctrine of the Big Stick, with which Mr. Roosevelt's years of outpouring have made us more or less familiar. The peace advocates pointed out in rebuttal that in Europe an unparalleled military efficiency has been no guaranty of peace, but, on the contrary, the most highly specialized military establishment in the world has turned out to be nothing but an appalling instrument of organized selfishness and thuggery. Then, with this as a text, they redoubled their excellent discourse: Mr. Jordan, for instance, insisting that war is illogical and brutal; Mr. Babson tabulating its economic waste; and Mr. Carnegie praising the principle of arbitration and an international police.

Mr. Garrison and Mr. Daniels are politicians, and so, *par excellence,* is Mr. Gardner. They have a special point of view—interesting possibly, but quite well understood, and, at all events, not especially pertinent here. The peace advocates also have a special point of view which is not so well understood. It is that of the rationalist philosopher or propagandist, which assumes that men are governed chiefly, or at least much more than actually they are, by reason and logic. The peace advocates are notably disposed to rest their case with proving that war is irrational, illogical, horrible, and costly; and they appear to think it quite enough to do that, in order to make us all forsake war and militarism forthwith, and create a better method of composing our differences.

But, really, men are very little governed by reason and logic; and this accounts for the fact that in an issue between the philosopher and politician, the politician always wins. He may, nay, invariably does, have a worse case: but he quite regularly carries it, because he knows how men act and how they may be induced to act. He must know, for otherwise he could not be a politician; this instinctive knowledge is the primary essential qualification for his squalid trade. As between war and peace, for instance, or between "military preparedness" and disarmament, the peace advocates have all the best of it; there is no answering their arguments, no meeting their representations. From the standpoint of reason and logic, therefore, nothing could be more simply silly than the recommendations of Mr. Garrison and Mr. Daniels, nothing more vicious than the activity of Mr. Gardner. But, I repeat, men are not governed by reason and logic, and hence my purpose in writing is to lodge a humble remonstrance with the peace advocates, begging them to believe that in their sheer dependence upon these they are leaning on a broken reed.

The matter and the time demand plain speech, at any risk of presumption. The peace advocates will therefore forgive me if I say that their efforts against war have always been canceled and nullified because they either do not see, or do not sufficiently consider, how the idea of war presents itself to the common man. The politician sees this plainly; his reaction to it is as instinctive as to the letters of the alphabet; but if long and careful observation of their labors is to be trusted, the peace advocates do not see it or react to it at all. For example, only the other day I attended the organization-meeting of the new Anti-Armament Society, and of the hundred or more present not one, except Commissioner Howe, Benjamin Marsh, and myself, could be presumed to have the faintest idea of war's appeal to the common man. An exception ought possibly to be made for the Reverend Mr. Grant, but of this I am by no means sure.

The fact is that, on account of the auspices and sanctions under which war is presented to him, the common man concerns himself very little with its justification in either reason or morals. "His not to reason why"; he finds no trouble about rolling all this burden of ethical responsibility off on the shoulders of some Kaiser, Parliament, or Congress, or of some Mr. Garrison or Mr. Daniels. A "popular war," such as Germany is at present waging, is evidence of the astonishing reach of this purblind trust and derived morality. It is by another side entirely, by the side of *interest,* that war makes its chief appeal for the common man's suffrage. War and peace are simply two great rival enterprises, standing in competition for the personal interest of the potential recruit; and in the determination of this interest the factors of logic, abstract reason, and abstract morals are extremely insignificant and weak.

As soon as we appreciate—as we may by the very slightest exercise of observation—the fact that war makes no great bid for the approval of the common man's reason or conscience, but bids very high for his *interest,* we immediately perceive the substantial ground of competition between war and peace, and are able to suggest to the peace advocates a most important and wholly positive line of approach to their problem.

If war has always outbid peace for the common man's suffrage, clearly it must have succeeded in making itself more interesting; and on examination, that is precisely what we find it has done. We may dismiss consideration of its appeal to the "primeval man," to the supposititious fund of savagery that is thought to lurk beneath the veneer of civilization in each of us; analysis will show that this appeal amounts to almost nothing. But war addresses some of the best permanent instincts of mankind, addresses them powerfully and shrewdly; and they are the very instincts that have been most continuously baffled and denied by peace.

Foremost, perhaps, among these is the instinct for equality. War has invariably served and promoted this instinct, and peace has invariably disserved and disallowed it. I was in New York at the outbreak of the Spanish War, and curiosity led me to mingle with a number of young men whom I saw in the neighborhood of Union Square, coming forward to enlist. I noticed that, while some of them appeared to be of the class that lives by casual labor, and might not unfairly be regarded as waifs and strays, many came out of shops and stores and small factories, where they might be supposed to get some sort of daily bread. I wondered why they were all so eager to enlist. They did not seem moved by the lust of blood, nor yet, strictly speaking, by the quest of adventure. They were not of the high-spirited type, but on the contrary very miserable. Patriotism did not enlist them, for none of them really knew much about the war or seemed to care greatly. I asked a number of questions and presently got their point of view. They saw war as the great equalizer of opportunity. It was for each of them the one great chance in a disinherited life; it was their emergence into responsibility, their opportunity to be *per se* "as good as anybody." Peace had kept them under the dragging handicap of artificial distinction and artificial privilege; war came, and offered them a start at scratch. When they were once enlisted, the stigma of the dullard, the ne'er-do-well or the unclean starveling was wiped away; they had everybody's chance to prove themselves anybody's equal. They coveted the exhilaration of standing for the first time on their own, shoulder to shoulder with their fellows, doing their share and getting their share of everything that was going.

> It's 'Tommy' this and 'Tommy' that, and 'Chuck 'im out, the brute!'
> But it's 'Saviour of 'is country' when the guns begin to shoot.

This powerful longing for equality and for the joys of equality is undoubtedly one of the strongest impulses that carry men away from peace and into war. The very institutions of war are a moving allegory and symbol of their wish. The regimentation, the marching, the parade, the drill!—here are men with their individuality fully expanded and preserved, yet each with his primary thought continually reaching beyond himself, each consciously responsible for the perfection of alignment toward a common purpose. The little boy paid our nature's instinctive tribute to equality when he asked his mother, "Why is it that when I hear soldiers' music I feel so much happier than I really am?" We all feel that. Martial music forecasts upon our emotions a prophetic picture of human society as we shall one day come to know it; a society whose rhythm and harmony of progress shall reach and animate every one throughout the ranks and make inspiration a common property.

Another immeasurable advantage which war has over peace in competing for the common man's interest, is in its appeal to the sense of purpose. The purpose of war always stands out clear and cogent. There is the enemy massed on the frontier. We know what he means to do; his intention is definite. We are massed to meet him with an intention equally definite. War has its perils and its horrors; but the first glad sense of great definite purpose dawning into stagnant and unillumined lives is sufficient to set them at naught. The conditions of war, terrible as they are, interpret themselves to the common man's satisfaction. They give account of themselves in terms of distinct purpose; and of purpose which with little pressure he inclines to accept, and in accepting it, to accept without complaint the hard conditions of its fulfillment.

But the blight of peace is its aimlessness. Peace, too, has its perils and horrors, and gives no clear sense of what they are for. There is no great unmistakable vision of purpose to suffuse its miseries and mitigate its pains of progress. Its intentions do not stand clear before our minds, shedding their interpretative light upon its immediate conditions. A friend told me lately about an experience he had in Chicago last summer, when the city was sweltering under an unusually long spell of torrid heat. On a Sunday morning he took a train, which he found filled with factory hands going out for a breath of such aid as they could get. He overheard a girl of seventeen telling her escort that in the factory, the day before, five girls had fainted at their work; two, dazed by the heat, had their hands drawn into machines and lost their fingers; and a man, suddenly overcome, fell into some heavy machinery and was killed.

The story is in itself not extraordinary; what my friend chiefly remarked was the girl's unmoved, matter-of-fact way of telling it. She spoke of these frightful happenings as if expecting her listeners to accept them without any waste of emotion, as simply so much in the day's work.

Now when peace imposes conditions like these and induces this mental attitude toward them, good heavens! can one wonder at the chance it stands in competition with war? Does the light of high collective purpose play clearly upon the average life lived on those terms? I urge the peace advocates to ask themselves this question; not in the mind of the reflective philosopher balancing abstract values, but in the mind of the common man confronting a practical choice in interest *for him* between two competing enterprises. When the United States goes to war, we will not be left in doubt about its high and holy purpose; Mr. Garrison and Mr. Daniels will attend to that. Mr. Gardner may be relied on to expound it; Mr. Hobson, Mr. Roosevelt, and Mr. William Randolph Hearst will proclaim it, instant in season and out of season. But the conditions of peace are left without an interpreter. Mr. Carnegie does not interpret them for us; Mr. Butler, Mr. Holt, Mr. Eliot, Mr. David Starr Jordan, Mr. Villard, Mr. George Foster Peabody, representing everything that is influential, distinguished, accomplished, do not interpret them for us. They are left to interpret themselves only in the narrow individualist terms of holding a job, getting a living, or, perchance, keeping a family together. Above this, no august and compelling collective purpose stands out; our society, as the common man sees it, is otherwise aimless; and such as this has never been and never will be the dominating motive in human conduct. It is written, *Man shall not live by bread alone.*

A third instinct, preëminently satisfied by war and notoriously dissatisfied by peace, is the instinct for responsibility. Such as they are, war insists upon its ideals, its standards, even its amenities, with a stringency that admits no hint of favor or exception. Those upon whom war has conferred its peculiar regard must walk worthy of the vocation wherewith they are called. The rewards themselves set the mark of definite expectation, and the expectation must be strictly met. The soldier may not be idle; he may not be lazy, trivial, self-centred, untrustworthy, irresponsible, traitorous, disloyal. If a leader, he must lead; he may not shirk or malinger or dissipate his powers. If he fails, he is superseded; he has but one chance. The code of "an officer and a gentleman" may be conventional and specific—no doubt it is, for all codes are; but it is inexorable. *Noblesse oblige* has always been graven on the sword and spear.

But never on the ploughshare and pruning-hook. Peace makes no such formal demands upon those whom she rewards or distinguishes. Those who receive her best gifts may use them with a scandalously loose discretion, and she remains complacent. Does peace forthwith degrade the captain of industry who exercises a treasonable oppression upon the persons and the social forces he controls? Does peace cashier the rich man's heir or heiress who does not serve society, does not do any work, does not do anything but seek pleasure? Does peace summarily court-martial the man of trained ability who capitalizes his powers and who then withholds them from the common welfare? War would give but very short shrift to such flagrant irreponsibility as this.

By this time I hope I have made it clear that the appeal of war to the common man is something far different from what the peace advocates appear to think it is. Nowhere, speaking broadly, does the common man enlist because he loves war, but because he hates peace. The conditions which peace forces on him make him regard it as something to be broken with at the first attractive opportunity. The skillful politician knows this and counts on it. Not for nothing have the aristocratic modes of government always had the instinct to "keep their people down." The more drab and unrelieved the conditions of

peace, the more gladly will the common man escape them; and while
he may escape them momentarily by the anodyne of drink, gambling,
or commercial amusement, the only escape that carries a substantial
interest for him is by war.

How disappointing, therefore, how purely negative and ineffectual,
are the despondent antiphons of the peace advocates, as they tell us of
the horrors of war and the economic waste of war! This is not what
will do any good. The long-distance recital of horrors makes an
impression upon minds quite accustomed to actual horrors, and the
disinherited are indifferent to pleas against economic waste. Let the
peace advocates hereafter make a clean sweep of this kind of thing, I
entreat them. Let them for once come over to the common man's point
of view, and they will forthwith perceive what a waste of energy it is.
I urge them for once to see war as we see it, if merely for the sake of
giving their efforts a better direction. At the risk of indelicacy, I
personally importune my friends, Mr. Villard and Mr. Peabody, for
once to consider war, not as no doubt it really is, but as it is *for us*.
Peace is very interesting to Mr. Carnegie and Bishop Greer and Mr.
Mead; there is every reason why it should be so. Peace promotes the
philosophical detachment that is so agreeable and becoming to Mr.
Eliot. Probably these gentlemen will find it very hard to understand
how peace can ever fail to interest us, when it interests them so deeply.
But I beg them to make the effort, and I offer the foregoing for their
guidance to our point of view. To us whom peace disinherits, war offers
equality; to us whom peace compels to live aimlessly, war offers a clear
and moving purpose; and to the finer sensibilities that peace disregards
and benumbs, war offers gratification and refreshment. What irony it
is, that even the Kaiser must depend upon the restless urge toward
democracy to fill his ranks!

As soon as one takes this point of view, one sees that the function
of the true peace advocate is not to deplore war but to help make peace
interesting; to create a peace that shall meet war on its own terms and
outbid it; a peace that shall answer these normal and proper demands
of the human spirit at least as well as war now answers them. When
peace interests the rank and file of us as it now interests Mr. Holt and
Mr. Villard, we, too, will be quite proof against the seductions of war.
War will then lose its power of attraction; it will be merely one of the
things that one looks at and passes by. We will then no longer go to

war, because we shall have no time; we shall be entirely preoccupied with the institutions of peace. When Mr. Roosevelt talks about the peril of disarmament, we will not hear. When Mr. Garrison and Mr. Daniels call us to arms, we will not heed—or at most, having Mr. Bernard Shaw's excellent suggestion in mind, we will take up arms only long enough to shoot Mr. Garrison and Mr. Daniels, and then lay them down again and return to our proper business.

One might, perhaps, end with this generalization; but when one presumes to give advice one ought above all things to be practical. So I say further that the first practical step toward permanent peace is to bring about a more diffused material well-being. Permanent peace must have its roots struck deep in this, for peace cannot possibly be interesting or attractive so long as without reason or purpose it keeps so many of us so very poor. The federal investigation of an industry particularly fostered by Mr. Carnegie found a third of its men working seven days a week; half its men working twelve hours a day; and nearly half the force receiving less than two dollars a day. Another federal investigation, covering industries that employ an aggregate of seven million men, found one seventh of them out of employment at one time or another during the year. The New York State Factory Investigating Commission, whose recent hearings were fully reported in that best of newspapers, the New York *Evening Post,* found that out of a total of 104,000 persons, one eighth earn less than five dollars a week; one third, less than seven; two thirds, ten or less; and one sixth, fifteen or more. It found that in New York City, out of 15,000 women industrially employed, 8,000 got less than six dollars and a half a week during the busy season last year.

I touch these matters as lightly as I can. Our old friend Josiah Bounderby could not get it out of his head that the complaints of the Coketown hands were never based on anything but licentious hankerings for venison and turtle soup out of a gold spoon. Possibly some of the peace advocates share this view, and if so their feelings must be respected. I therefore hasten to assure them that I have no thought of muckraking; I condemn nothing, complain of nothing. I merely say that peace cannot possibly compete with war for the suffrage of such as can, by the hardest work, earn no more than two dollars a day; or for the suffrage of seven million men whom peace compels to live so precariously that one seventh of them are mere floaters. I say that it is the sheer delirium of vanity to suppose that a peace which permits so many of us to live under such disabling economic circumstances can be attractive, interesting, or permanent. It is unreasonable to expect it, preposterous to talk about it; and so long as the peace advocates entertain or acquiesce in any such notion, their efforts will appear to us only as the amiable pottering of elderly amateurs.

Within the last five years America has laid hold of this first element in the peace problem. The country is thoroughly interested (though not with peace as the specific object in view) in the wider diffusion of material well-being. Whoever has anything to say about it may command the country's attention. I therefore make the peace advocates a proposition wherein I believe I speak for as many as forty million people. If they will cease expostulating with us about the horrors of war, and plan for us the first constructive move toward a peace that is even reasonably interesting, we will follow to a man. If they will do for the institutions of peace what Lee or Paul Pau has done for the institutions of war, they may count on us for the same grade of loyalty, and just as much of it, as Lee or Paul Pau ever commanded.

We really want peace. We want precisely such a peace as our friends the peace advocates themselves find interesting, and such as with all the superiority of their genius and energy over ours they might lead us into. If they will come forward and be our leaders, if they will head the gigantic army of Americans who instinctively know how attractive, how interesting and beautiful peace ought to be and might be—if they will come forward and plan for us and inspire us in order that we can make it so—we pledge them our confidence, our unfailing support, and our unending patience.

This essay appeared in the May 1915 issue of the *Atlantic Monthly*.

The End and the Means

According to all the Paris dispatches, President Wilson has authorized the statement that the league of nations plan is to be an integral part of the peace treaty. If this be true, we regard it as a deliberate attempt to dragoon the Senate of the United States, and as such, a logical and fitting climax to the whole discreditable course of the Paris conference. It is the familiar trick of the "rider." The people of this country want the peace treaty signed and out of the way, the business interests being especially impatient of delay. At the same time, they are very imperfectly informed about the implications of the league covenant, and reluctant to wade through the diplomatic jargon which half-conceals its sinister purposes. Peace, too, is the immediate consideration; the matters canvassed in the covenant appear remote. If the Senate refuses to ratify a treaty of which the covenant is an integral part, it must carry a fearful burden of obloquy for obstructing peace; and this, apparently, is just what the manœuvres reported from Paris have in view. We may be quite sure, too, that every agency at the disposal of the Administration will do its utmost to manufacture and strengthen public sentiment against the opposition of the Senate; and this, again, is quite as it should be. It is quite appropriate that this measure should prevail, if it does prevail, wholly by force of false pretense, indirection, and dragooning, rather than only in part. This alliance of victorious Governments, masquerading under the pretentious lying title of a league of nations, organized for sheer economic exploitation, has nowhere in its constitution sincerity enough to make fitting one single inch of furtherance by aid of any honorable means whatsoever. It should continue and end under no other than the auspices of its beginning.

We must make it clear at the outset that we do not discuss the general idea of a league of nations. As to that, we spoke fully in our issue of March 8. We believe that a league of nations is inevitable, and that it will come automatically and spontaneously, by means which politicians do not contemplate. The removal of economic barriers and the restrictions now imposed by political governments upon industry and trade, would, we believe, at once effect the same free economic union among world states that now prevails among the United States of America; and we think that a free economic union is the only one that will have stability or permanency. What may be done by way of further political union, or closer political association, among world states, we do not know. While we are skeptical about it, we are aware that many able minds are in favor of trying it, in a belief that some good will come out of the attempt. We wish to refrain from any discouragement of this optimism; hence we must be understood as saying nothing unfavorable at this time about the general aspiration toward a league of nations. We merely wish to expose the character of the particular proposal which President Wilson brought back from France, and which he apparently intends, if he can, to compel the Senate to ratify. We do this the more freely because the very aspiration we mention, the pacific and friendly instinct of mankind, can be so easily perverted to support this proposal by reason of the fact that it bears the name of the thing aspired to. No trick of the politician is more common than this; this it was, for instance, which foisted a bogus reform of the nominating system on the people of New York State by calling it a "direct primary." This it may be, too, which will foist this alliance-contract upon the people of the United States, by calling it the "league of nations."

An equally insidious and undoubtedly more powerful appeal is made by this covenant also to the spirit of easy opportunism. Compromise is the rule of the world. Suppose it is not all one wants; still, it is something, and perhaps one should support it more or less on faith in its being a start in the right direction. But that is precisely what it is not. It has no quality or characteristic which essentially differentiates it from treaties that have hitherto bound the European states into competitive and predatory groups. The war has made the liberal spirit impatient of opportunism and compromise. If all the cost and sacrifice involved in a struggle to "make the world safe for democracy" have purchased nothing better than a rescript of old treaties, if it has not brought about the practical affirmation of a single essential democratic principle, we can not see any place for opportunism in judgment. Faith, under such circumstances, is not faith, but indolent, shirking credulity.

We have never discussed the proposed alliance-contract from the nationalist point of view, for those aspects of it are sure to be quite fully set forth by others. We agree with Mr. J. A. Hobson that "for

America it would be an entangling alliance," and as such subversive of our best traditions—and indeed, as President Wilson himself admitted, subversive of certain elements of our independent sovereignty. These may be valuable or not; we think they are far too valuable to surrender. What interests us especially, however, is the kind of hands into which they are proposed to be surrendered; and here we find the terms of the covenant far from reassuring. Any proposal to surrender them into the hands of a group of gentlemen like those assembled at the Paris conference, for instance, to permit them to serve the purposes and carry out the motives which the Lloyd Georges, Clemenceaus, Orlandos, Balfours, Lansings, and Sazonovs have exhibited with unfailing regularity throughout their course of public life, appears to us absolutely inadmissible. But we are content to leave this view of the covenant to Senator Knox and his associates, knowing that they will say everything for it that can be said. We concern ourselves by preference with that special view of the covenant which may perhaps without prejudice be called the liberal view—and that without any inflated pretensions to being an organ of liberal opinion. We are simply in the very considerable number of those whom President Wilson, by keeping up his perpetual semblance of hitting the right nail on the head without ever really doing it, has bemocked and deluded; and in all we shall find to say about the league covenant, we speak only for ourselves and such of this number as agree with us.

The first half-dozen of the "fourteen points" were calculated to raise liberal hopes and stimulate liberal enthusiasm above measure. Understood for what they meant in the plain natural sense of language—and not for whatever Mr. Wilson's subsequent glosses might make them mean—they could reasonably be accepted, and by many were accepted, as a definite statement of the purposes for which the Allies were fighting—the purposes for which the United States, at least, was certainly fighting. Open diplomacy; freedom of the seas; freedom of trade; disarmament; the principle of self-determination; and the rights of small nations—such was Mr. Wilson's lofty bid for the liberal's toleration of the war. *Caesari appelasti, ad Caesarem ibis.* What we have gotten is a connivance hatched in impenetrable secrecy, a secrecy of which Mr. Wilson was himself among all the machinators present the most jealous; a connivance, further, which enables the carrying out of every execrable secret bargain laid down by the Allied Governments since the war began. So much for the first blandishment in Mr. Wilson's elaborate seduction of liberal opinion. If he has made good his professions with anything more substantial in respect to the other five points of promise, there is nothing in his proposed covenant to indicate the fact. Free seas, free trade, disarmament, self-determination, and the rights of small nations have now the precise status which they had before Mr. Wilson offered them his devotion; and his address of January 8, 1918, has the indelible indorsement of history as a "good-enough-Morgan."

What we have is a calm, arrogant, and ruthless formulation of a plan of world-domination by the five conquering powers, a device for causing the exploitable territories of the earth to stand and deliver without the risk and cost of war. Stripped of its verbiage and a cant that is matched perhaps only in the Act of Algeciras, this is the sheer fact of Articles xvi–xix inclusive. The Governments of the United States, Great Britain, France, Italy, and Japan are the league of nations; they are the executive council; they appoint the dummy directors; they pass finally on the qualifications of candidates; they are, in short, an absolute and irresponsible oligarchy. So far from recognizing freedom of the seas, freedom of trade, disarmament, or self-determination, their collusion precludes these possibilities. International commerce cannot be carried on except at their pleasure, under their jurisdiction, and, it is surely by this time superfluous to add, to their profit. Teleologically considered, we are offered an economic alliance which has as its primary object, in general, the exploitation of a propertyless dependent class the world over, and, as between nations, the exploitation of the vanquished by the victors, and of weaker nations by the stronger. It is an organization of what Mr. Frederic C. Howe calls "financial imperalism" raised to its highest possibility. It contemplates only a political peace, and that a *pax Romana*. Of economic peace it gives no hint; on the contrary, it contemplates the inauguration of unprecedented economic war.

This, then, is the ground of objection to the covenant upon which we choose to stand. We ask that the document be taken upon this ground and examined, with strict attention to the economic implications of every proposal, the possibilities of economic exploitation covered by every arrangement. Especially we urge this upon the propertyless and exploited class in all countries, for it is their chief concern. The past four years fortunately have given them some useful experience of the niceties of diplomatic language, and they now have the opportunity to turn it to most profitable account. They are, too, in a position where they may have something effective to say about the point-blank handing over of their economic destiny to persons or to groups that have hitherto shown themselves conspicuously dishonest in their administration of a similar trust; and they can say it none too soon. The nationalist interest of the document is for us all; its economic interest is peculiarly theirs. Let them consider what the six doctrines for which Mr. Wilson offered a casual and opportunist sponsorship in January, 1918, mean for them; then let them consider the proposals which he now sponsors and insists upon, and see which way their economic interest inclines them.

This short, unsigned editorial appeared in the March 22, 1919, issue of the *Nation*.

An Exhausted Virtue

Public patience with the Peace Conference is no longer patience, but a weak and degenerate pusillanimity. We hope that the Congress will at once cut the foundation out from under the whole intolerable situation by passing a resolution declaring summarily that the state of war is at an end, demanding the immediate withdrawal and demobilization of all our expeditionary forces, renouncing responsibility for further police duty in Europe, and authorizing the resumption of free commerce. It is perfectly competent for Congress to do this. Unless by some unauthorized and improper secret arrangement, of which the Congress may take no cognizance, the United States is independent of the Allied Powers, and has corresponding liberty of action. Our official designation as a "co-belligerent" and an "associated Government" has been carefully preserved, and its implications should now be turned to account. We entered the war as an independent Power for the attainment of certain specific ends. We have Mr. Wilson's word for it—and, what is far more valuable, we have a general popular conviction—that these ends have now been attained. As far as the United States is concerned, everyone knows that the war is at an end and German militarism triumphantly overthrown. Now, therefore, is the time for an official declaration by the Congress, not only for our own moral advantage, but for that of the whole world. If the representatives of this people should thus energetically serve notice of determination to resume an abdicated control and direction of the nation's own business, it would be the most wholesome and powerful stimulant to democratic order, the world over, that could be imagined. There would be a different and far more salutary spirit informing the doings at Versailles after Mr. Wilson had come home in obedience to such an intimation from the Congress. The plain people of Europe—small wonder!—are dissatisfied with the quality of the proposed peace and apparently well aware that any further prescriptions compounded out of the same quack pharmacopoeia will be quite as far from what they need and demand. They are now beginning to express their resentment by such irregular modes as they conceive to be available. How much better, then, how clearing and steadying, if they could have from this country an example of effective expression through the authorized and regular agency set up for such purposes!

The day of makeshift, compromise, and unclear thinking is past. We all see now the inevitable outcome of attempts to reconcile the irreconcilable and to accommodate orders of action between which no accommodation is possible. It was well enough six months ago that the United States should take part in the Peace Conference instead of simply declaring its share in the war at an end and resuming its independent way. Mr. Wilson had been especially active in devising and publishing a whole series of high international ideals. This had its effect upon the popular conscience and will. The country was full of the naïve expectation that this was a war to end war, and that it was so intended by its fautors. This, we can now see, was a fantastic expectation, since war cannot possibly be ended by war, and those who promote war do not do so with any such purpose in view. But our people did not know that, and were easily persuaded otherwise; their best instincts were enlisted. They freely consented, therefore, to the breach of continuity in our foreign policy, in the hope of seeing somewhat at least of the sort of peace that Mr. Wilson and his colleagues had held out to them in prospect.

This hope it was which had already made them endure with incredible patience the most shameful indignities from Mr. Wilson that could be imposed upon any people calling itself free. They endured the abrogation of the constitutional rights they possessed, the eclipse of the Congress, the resolution of their governmental system into an autocracy as sinister and as absolute as any that the Middle Ages ever saw; all for the hope of the Larger Good. This hope reconciled them even to the unrepresentative personnel of the American Commission. But so far from the realization of their hope, they have seen democracy despised and rejected; and the practical outcome of the conference, as Mr. Ramsay Macdonald excellently says, is four gentlemen sitting in Paris, treating Europe as a grocer treats a hogshead of sugar. They have seen an inconceivably impudent recrudescence and brazen stiffening of financial imperialism; the League of Nations covenant a letter-of-marque for unlimited economic exploitation; while the watered-down paraphrase of the peace treaty, which is all that has been officially vouch-safed us, is a deed of chattel slavery for the whole German people for at least thirty years to come. Well, it was a good, a useful lesson. Like most lessons, it might have been learned some easier way; but no matter, it is learned. Now let the Congress decide that our period of tutelage— and theirs—is over, and take the simple step necessary to end it; and let us go on by the light of the expensive wisdom we have gained.

But what would become of Europe? Mr. Taft and the League advocates go up and down the earth promulgating the argument of dreadful consequences, drawing depressing pictures of the desolation that would ensue if the United States drew out of compliance with the will of the Allies. We cannot see it in quite that way. Mr. Taft assumes that the interest of the peoples of Europe is identical with that of the system of financial imperalism represented at Versailles. But that is precisely what it is not; it is squarely opposed to it. We think that this system would suffer greatly if the United States withdrew its supporting hand; but that the *peoples* would suffer much, that they would suffer an iota of what they are suffering now, we greatly doubt. If only they were let alone, we think they would prove quite able to look after themselves. Our withdrawal, with the consequent lightening of pressure upon them from their own exploiters, would, in fact, be a measure of relief amounting almost to emancipation.

But however this may be, the duty that we seem to see resting on the Congress is one imposed by simple honesty and self-respect. Being in the interest of so many people, it is presumably not good politics; at least, not in the tradition of good politics. But traditional politics are now so broken down and discredited that—who knows?—the Congress may be master-politicians enough to discern what is quite obvious to nearly everybody else, that at this juncture a public act of downright, direct, disinterested honesty would turn out to be the most popular thing possible, and therefore the keenest politics of all. Popular instinct now, we believe, is wholly on the side of Richard Cobden's masterly saying, that international peace and good will depend on as little intercourse as possible betwixt *Governments* (the italics are Cobden's own) and as much as possible betwixt *peoples*. The people are tired of the sterile intercourse betwixt Governments at Versailles. A congressional resolution passed at noon today, and ships starting out in free commerce at noon tomorrow, would do more for the peace of the world than twenty centuries of clandestine conniving by the agents of financial imperalism.

––––––––––––––––

This short, unsigned editorial appeared in the June 14, 1919, issue of the *Nation*.

Anglo-American Relations

President Wilson, early in the war, did one of the most just and useful things, probably the most just and useful thing, in his whole career, when he made his famous differentiation between the German Government and the German people. He pointed out that the character, interests and aims of the German Government were wholly different from those of the German people and directly opposed to them; that the Government actively and incessantly worked against the interests of the people, and meanwhile deluded the people with false notions of patriotism in order to get them to accept and fall in with its nefarious purposes. In putting all this so clearly, the President did an inestimable service to the principles of radicalism. Radicalism had been saying just this about the German Government for years and years; it was saying just this when that same Government was in high favour at Washington, when President Roosevelt and the German Emperor were hobnobbing hand and glove.

President Wilson, however, based his admirable statement upon rather different and much less philosophical grounds than those proposed by radicalism. He based it upon the ground that the German Government was autocratic and irresponsible—one of the most curious assertions, one would say, that Mr. Wilson, in view of his own record, would have the hardihood to make. Radicalism criticized and condemned the German Government; radicals the world over beheld it as inimical to the interests of the German people, not because it was autocratic and irresponsible, not, above all, because it was German, but because it was political. By means of its historical investigations into the origin and nature of the State, of political government in general, radicalism perceived that the State, wherever found and whether autocratic, constitutional or republican, invariably operated against the interests of the people; and that its administration was carried on by what, therefore, could be properly regarded (as Mr. Wilson appeared to regard and encouraged us all to regard the German Administration) as a professional-criminal class. Radicalism saw that the primary interest of political government, wherever found and under whatever mode or form, was in maintaining the economic exploitation of one stratum of society by another. Hence radicalism has long been out of the habit, except for purposes of pure geography, of nationalizing political government; quite as sensible persons, long before the war, had given up the habit of nationalizing atrocities committed by armies. Radicalism sees that the German, English and American Governments are German, English, American, only in the same limited and superficial sense that the atrocities in Belgium, India and the Philippines were German, English, American. Louvain, Amritsar and the "water-cure" were *military* atrocities; Hell-roaring Jake Smith was not a product of America but of militarism, which is the same the world over. No special indictment of character can properly be held against the German, English or American peoples on account of these, for it is abundantly demonstrable that wherever an army is and under whatever incidental nationality, there of nature and necessity are atrocities. Thus, to the eye of radicalism, the German, English, American Governments are not essentially German, English, American; they are essentially political. They are not, therefore, properly to be criticized or defended or even considered, according to their geography, but according to their nature and character. No one objects to Asiatic cholera because it is Asiatic, but because it is deadly.

Never to greater profit could this view be tenaciously held and energetically propagated than at the present time. All signs point to an era of misunderstanding and ill feeling between the two peoples who of all on earth have least to quarrel about and most to communicate to a needy world—the English people and ourselves. This misunderstanding is being now most industriously promoted in both countries by those who have lost sight of Mr. Wilson's invaluably just distinction, and are busily identifying the English Government and its aims with the English people and their aims, and the American Government and its aims with the American people and their aims; and there is no telling what misery, distress and error may ensue upon this confusion within the next two years. One section of our press identifies the English Government with the English people as a text for indiscriminate praise, another as a text for indiscriminate blame; and the one is as wrong and contemptible and profoundly dangerous as the other. Talk of the Red Menace!—indeed, the elements that most menace the interests of the American people are, first, the Tory-Federalists and imperialists who day by day release irruptions of adulatory and neurasthenic sycophancy upon England, and, second, those who day by day open upon her the floodgates of their recrimination and invective. They are menacing because both of them alike assume a fixed correspondence in character and purpose between the English Government and the English people; and there is no such correspondence. Meanwhile, like influences in England make the same assumption about our Government and our people; and if such are permitted to have the pre-eminence in both countries, we are likely to see a very pretty quarrel bred by this inveterate and unwarranted confusion.

Probably no one, certainly no radical, would, after the happenings of the last five years, have much of a good word to say for political government, wherever found; any more than President Wilson could find to say for that particular fraction of political government towards which he was endeavouring to arouse all the malignity of which misguided and uninformed human nature is capable. But this is not the point. The point is that in all their consideration of Anglo-American relations, the American people should be clearly aware, and should show themselves clearly aware, that the aims and interests of the English Government are not those of the English people but essentially opposed to them; and that the English people should in their turn, make a similar discrimination. This will be the bond of peace in which a true unity of the spirit can be kept and cultivated to limitless effectiveness. When Mr. Hearst, for example, talks about "England" or "Great Britain," let us clearly understand that he is proceeding upon a monstrous and shocking assumption; and let the English people have the same fixed understanding with regard to Mr. Bottomley's outpourings. When another section of our press spews a turbid spate of sycophancy over some ambassador's sayings or doings, or over some oratory at a Pilgrim's dinner or at a Washington's Birthday celebration in London, let us remember that the interest appealed to is not that of the English people but of political government; and let the English people take a similar saving precaution in the premises.

If Americans wish to get a composite of the English people, to know what their fundamental tradition is and what their fundamental loyalties are, they need not turn to English history or literature, for they will find it more conveniently in their own. Let them resolutely close their eyes to diplomatic exchanges and official pronouncements, and read

Thomas Paine, Thomas Jefferson, Thoreau, Wendell Phillips, Henry George. There is England; there is the fundamental, imperishable tradition of the English people, obstinately held to and continuously pushed forward against every bulwark that political government has raised against it. If the English wish to know the fundamental tradition of the American people, let them look for it in the centuries before the Conquest, in the Peasant's War, in Peterloo, in William Cobbett and in Richard Cobden. Ours is theirs, and theirs is ours; political government is opposed to it here, precisely as it is there. It is the magnificent tradition of economic freedom, the instinct to know that without economic freedom no other freedom is significant or lasting, and that if economic freedom be attained, no other freedom can be witheld.

Economic freedom is that to which political government in both countries, as in all countries, is primarily opposed. Political government in England is having an increasingly hard time with its task, in the face of a high and purposeful economic organization; in the United States it has so far, from purely natural causes, had but little trouble. So much the more, then, should the English people be patient with our imperfect understanding of our tradition; consider the disabilities which political government has put upon us with its inhibiting control of our schools and our press; and assist us in our effort to clear and educate and emancipate ourselves. For our part, it is what Burke calls "the ancient and inbred piety, integrity, good nature and good humour of the English people" that Americans should cleave to, and not the words or works of a Government that is no more essentially English than ours is essentially American. If the distinction that Mr. Wilson drew so precisely be but understood in England and in the United States, then it will be perceived at once that the more diligently political government be slighted and disallowed, and the higher the type of economic organization effected by common effort between the two countries, the sooner will the great common tradition of economic freedom prevail.

This unsigned editorial appeared in the April 14, 1920, issue of the *Freeman*. It was reprinted in *The Freeman Book*.

Pointing a Moral

The situation in the Ruhr, the *coup de main* of Italy and the consequent commotion in the Danube States, make this a most appropriate time to raise an urgent inquiry of those who wish the United States to take a hand in Europe's affairs. What do they want us to do? We have raised that question before, and so have many others, and it has never yet been competently answered. We say competently, because it is no answer merely to reiterate some stock phrase like "The United States ought to join the League of Nations," or to say that our Government ought to cancel the Allied war-debts in return for an equivalent reduction in the German indemnity. Granted, for argument's sake, that the United States should do both these things; let us suppose that they were done to-morrow; let us, indeed, suppose that they had been done two weeks after the promulgation of the Treaty of Versailles. The real question is, what reasonable ground is there for assuming, in the one case, that matters would have gone one whit differently up to the present; or, in the other case, for supposing that they would begin to go differently the day after to-morrow?

Not a single interventionist has ever given an answer to that question, and none ever will. All who have tried to answer it have merely delivered some vague rhetoric about the "moral effect" of such action on the part of the United States; and this is rubbish. The war immensely fortified a universal faith in violence; it set in motion endless adventures in imperialism, endless nationalist ambitions. Every war does this to a degree roughly corresponding to its magnitude. The final settlement at Versailles, therefore, was a mere scramble for loot. We venture to say that there is no human being upon earth who can make anything else of it and look one in the eye while he does so. Now, suppose that the United States Government entered the war from the purest of altruistic motives and that it stuck by the Versailles treaty through thick and thin, League of Nations and all, can any one in his right mind imagine that its "moral effect" would have kept M. Poincaré from looting the Ruhr and setting up his Napoleonic scheme of military hegemony in Europe? Could our moral influence have kept the Poles from grabbing

Upper Silesia or, to come down to date, could it have kept M. Mussolini from laying his hands on Corfu?

To imagine such a thing bespeaks incredible ignorance and incredible credulity. Moreover, the United States Government did not go to war with disinterested motives, and every European Government knows that it did not. M. Poincaré knows it, and so do the Poles and M. Mussolini, just as well as MM. Clemenceau and Orlando and Mr. Lloyd George knew it at the time of the conference at Versailles. To expect disinterested action on the part of our Government now is simply the amiable and hopeful *naïveté* of one who expects to catch a weasel asleep. But assuming that it might be, by some miracle, capable of disinterested action, what form could that action possibly take to be effective?

Fortunately, the cause of intervention has been so thoroughly discredited by circumstances that there is no use in saying much about it now. We doubt whether any politician would dare bring it before the country again. It seems that the time has come to point the moral; and in so doing, we come in sight of the one and only service that America can render—not the American Government, but such Americans as are candid enough and flexible enough to have learned a good many things in the past four years, and to have forgotten a good many as well. This service consists in pointing out that the matters at stake in Europe can not be settled by machinery alone; they must be settled by a wider culture, a firmer will and a better spirit. The League of Nations is machinery, and so is the World Court; machinery, moreover, devised for an entirely different purpose from that to which the interventionists would invoke it. This is plain to every one; as plain as that a reaper is not designed to pull a train. The thing is to abandon a blind and unintelligent faith in machinery, and to give oneself over to the promotion of a culture competent really to envisage a world-order of peace and freedom erected upon the only basis able to sustain it, the basis of social justice. Those who do this are the true interventionists; they proffer Europe the only real help that Americans can give. The interventionists here, and those abroad who ask our aid, never show, we regret to say, that they are concerned by the injustices that afflict Europe; they are concerned only by the inconveniences arising from her condition. Even the British liberals who lately addressed a communication to Americans at large, show hardly more than a perfunctory concern with injustice, but an enormous concern with inconvenience.

The time has come, in our opinion, to disallow all this and to reaffirm the revolutionary doctrine set forth in the Declaration of Independence, that the Creator has endowed human beings with certain inalienable rights; to give more interest to principles and less to machinery; to think less about acting and organizing and instituting, and more about establishing a culture that will afford a proper foundation for national action. The time has come, in short, for inaugurating a really moral movement instead of protracting the succession of ludicrous and filthy hypocrisies which have so long passed for moral movements; for an interest in justice and a belief in human rights wherever there are human beings—in Egypt and Haiti, India and Santo Domingo, quite as much as in Corfu or the Ruhr. It is all very well to go about establishing justice and human rights, in the time of it; but the first step towards establishing them is to believe in them, and that is the step to be taken now.

This unsigned article by Nock appeared in the September 19, 1923, issue of the *Freeman*. It was reprinted in *The Freeman Book*.

III. THE SOCIAL CRITIC

The effective propagandist is the incidental one, and that to be such he must remain always primarily the observant artist and the imperturbable critic of art, the critic, above all, of his own art.
—"Miscellany," the *Freeman*, March 17, 1920

We are concerned with the habit, which seems to us unintelligent and vicious, of regarding potential accessories to civilization as essential elements in civilization. We insist that civilization is not to be measured in terms of longevity, trackage, the abundance of banks and newspapers, the speed and frequency of mails, and the like. Civilization is the progressive humanization of men in society and all these things may or may not sustain a helpful relation to the process.
—"Toodstools," the *Freeman*, December 5, 1923

A Cultural Forecast

We are becoming more or less familiar with the assumption that our immediate cultural prospects are not good. It is the motive of most of the "literature of revaluation," or, as Mr. H. L. Mencken prefers to call it, the *Katzenjammer* literature of the period. As far as the fact is concerned, we may face it frankly. There seems no doubt that it will be a long time before the humane life, as the ages have understood the term, will prevail among us—before our collective life and its institutions will reflect any considerable spiritual activity. Our present collective life, in its ideals and aspirations as well as in its actual practice, is admittedly conducted upon a very low spiritual level. One has only to imagine Plato or Virgil, Dante or Rabelais, contemplating it—souls preeminent in the knowledge and practice of the humane life—and one has no trouble in arriving at the verdict that would be passed upon it by the best reason and spirit of mankind. Moreover, there are no discernible tendencies showing promise of a better state of things, at least within a period short enough to give the question more than an academic interest for our day. Those of our grandchildren, if any, who shall feel within them any vague promptings towards the humane life will be unlikely to find the general current setting that way much more strongly than it does at present.

On the score of fact and truth, therefore, one has nothing against the prophets who keep assiduously telling us all this. Their attitude towards the truth, however, and, by consequence, their attitude towards our present representative society, seem a little uncritical. Most of them appear to expect more of our civilization than it can possibly give them; and their disappointment takes shape in irritation and complaint. This seems historically to have been the chief trouble with the evangelizing spirit, and the chief reason why evangelists themselves usually got no great way in the practice of the humane life, and were, on the whole, rather unpleasant persons to have around. Criticism reckons with the causes of things, and it duly apprehends the length of the course which matters must run under their propulsion, or even under the force of inertia after those causes are no longer operative. Hence, criticism invariably judges social phenomena according to the strength and inveteracy of the causes that give rise to them. In our early days, for example, about a century ago, a representative of Cincinnati's light and learning said to Mrs. Trollope, "Shakespeare, madame, is obscene; and, thank God, *we* are sufficiently advanced to have found it out." Criticism does not stop with remarking that this man's view of both Cincinnati and Shakespeare was very inept, and that he should have done better. Criticism, properly employing the scientific imagination, examines the beginnings and development of Cincinnati's social life, considers its general character and quality, and its only marvel is that any person bred there should have even heard of Shakespeare, or felt it appropriate to have any opinion at all about him, even a silly one. Again, everyone remembers the great fuss that was made last year over the Treasury Department's confiscation of some imported classic, I have forgotten which one; or only the other day, over Mayor Thompson's *opera-buffa* performances in the Chicago libraries. But considering the progress of our cultural life as exhibited consecutively in the great work of Mr. Beard, or as shown by Mr. Bowers, Mr. Sandburg, Mr. Allan Nevins and Mr. Paxton Hibben, in their study of special periods, criticism can only regard it as by some kind of miracle that the humane life exists at all among us, or that our cultural prospects are even as cheerful as they are.

For the humane life does exist among us, and as far as one person's observation goes, it reaches a higher individual development all round among us than in any other society I know of. The reason why our cultural prospects are so poor is not, as is sometimes very superficially said, that there is no culture here. On the contrary, the best culture that I have ever seen, judged by its fruits—culture taking shape in lucidity of mind, intellectual curiosity and hospitality, largeness of temper, objectivity, the finest sense of social life, of manners, of beauty— was in the United States. The aggregate of it is much less, relatively, than elsewhere; but scanty, frail, and unproductive as it is, I have never seen better.

Nor is there any more value in the equally superficial observation that Americans do not much care for culture. What people, left to their own devices and preferences, ever did much care for culture? The general diffusion and prevalence of culture, as far as it has gone, has always been an effect of the high culture of certain classes. In Europe, where people care more for culture than we do, one cannot help observing how largely the love of it is traditional, and how much of the technical apparatus of culture, on which their own culture is patterned, and by which their love of culture is both stimulated and regulated—how much of all this has come to them by way of sheer legacy. Take out the cultural vestiges and traditions of about three royal courts, and anyone travelling through France can easily reckon the mighty shrinkage of French cultural apparatus and the slowing-down of the general tradition's momentum. The approach to culture is laborious and discouraging, and the natural man dislikes work and is easily discouraged. Spiritual activity is too new a thing in the experience of the race; men have not been at it long enough to be at ease in it. It is like the upright position; men can and do assume the upright position, but seldom keep to it longer than necessary—they sit down when they can. The majority have always preferred an inferior good that was more easily acquired and more nearly immediate, unless they were subjected to some strong stimulus which for collateral reasons made the sacrifices demanded by culture seem worth while. Matthew Arnold quotes the learned Martinus Scriblerus's saying (being far from books at the moment, I must quote from memory) that the taste for the bathos is implanted by nature deep in the soul of man, and that it governs him "until, perverted by custom or example, he is brought, or rather compelled, to relish the sublime."

The Church in the Middle Ages could, and did, exercise this power of perversion. It never has had half enough credit for the cultural effect of what it did, even though, for reasons of its own, it did not do all it might have done. The royal courts could exercise the same power, and many of them did, like that of Francis I, for example, and some of the Bavarian kings. Sometimes they coöperated with the Church, thus directing two powerful forces towards the same end. The Church and the court were in a position, not only to organize spiritual activity of various kinds, but also to give it a prestige that made effective headway against the natural taste for the bathos. With these assistances and recommendations, culture got over its initial obstacles, and later could make its own way, relying upon its own power of attraction. The Belgians were always a musical people after their own fashion, and a very good and interesting fashion, but the Elector of Bavaria, Max-Emmanuel, when Governor of the Netherlands, organized music as a function of the civil service, thus giving it a prestige whereby the Belgians were brought "to relish the sublime" in that art, as they still do, and would probably for some time continue to do, even if the royal patronage of music were withdrawn. It is not generally understood, I think, that a very extensive organization of spiritual activity once took place on our continent, in the Mormon polity under Brigham Young; and though it remained in force so short a time, traces of its effect are still plainly to be seen.

Now, it is the lack in America of any influence that by common consent can exercise just this power of perversion, which makes the outlook for culture so unpromising. The person who looks wistfully at culture must go forward practically alone against the full force of wind and tide. Such culture as we have is solitary and uninfluential, existing fortuitously, like stonecrop in the interstices of a much-trodden pavement. One can imagine nothing more disregarded, disparaged, more out of the general run of American affairs. By general consent culture has no place in our institutional life; not in the pulpit, not in the public service or in journalism, notoriously not in our colleges and schools, not in our literature—such of our literature, at least, with rare and very interesting exceptions, as gets itself easily published and considerably read. Here again, however, criticism, while regretting the fact, can see nothing unnatural in it, and nothing susceptible of immediate change. Our whole institutional life is carried on with a view to objects and purposes which are not those of culture; and the complete alienation of culture from its processes is, therefore, quite to be expected. It is simply a fact to be remarked, not a condition to be complained of. In other civilizations the natural taste for the bathos has been, by common consent, severely modified through processes of perversion; but in ours it has been glorified, by common consent, into unapproachable dominance.

To the eye of criticism, some of the consequences of this are interesting. With the natural taste for the bathos everywhere unrestrained and rampant, there is hardly anyone among us who suspects the existence of impersonal critical standards, much less feels it incumbent on him to pay them any respect. A European would see at once, for instance, why a ruler like Frederick the Great, whose position raised him above pettiness and self-interest, with advisers like von Humboldt and Schleiermacher, would be likely to devise a better system of secondary schools than could be worked out by some local school-board appointed by a mayor. An American would not see it so easily; ten to one he would say the local board would do better, as more likely "to give the people what they want"—more likely, that is, to meet the grand average of local taste for the bathos. Thus, there really exists no sense among us of what is first class, second class, third or fourth class, or of what makes it so. Everyone has noticed that our reviewers bestow exactly the same order of praise on a fourth-class work of art—a book, for example—that they do upon a first-class work. I have now before me, for instance, some reviews of a new novel; and two or three of the writers—men of some pretensions, whose word goes a long way with readers, I understand—could not be more earnestly reverential if they were speaking of Cervantes's masterpiece. I have not read the novel, and it may be very great, of course, but really can it be *that* great? With all my best wishes for the author, I fear not. Many fourth-class books indeed deserve high praise; we all have read such books with pleasure, and with no less pleasure because we knew all the time that they were fourth-class books, and knew why they were such, and knew that the pleasure we were getting out of them was of an entirely different order from that which we get out of first-class books. A fourth-class book is not *ipso facto* to be disparaged, for it may be very good indeed; but neither is it to be spoken of in the same terms that one would use of a first-class book, and no writer with any critical sense—no writer, that is, who was depending on something above and beyond a mere personal estimate of the work before him—would dream of doing so.

In this general critical insensitiveness, Americans remind one of those large worms of the species called Eunice, I think, which will begin to eat their own bodies if they discover them lying in range of their mouth. Americans have no Philistine objection to a good thing; on the contrary, they often accept it. But they accept it without exercising any critical faculty upon it; without really knowing that it is good, or knowing what makes it so. Their estimate is purely personal. Until this is understood it seems anomalous, for example, that a work like that of Professor Adams should be a best-seller, as for some time it was. But they will also accept a bad thing with equal interest and with the same critical insensitiveness, especially if it bears some kind of specious recommendation. At the Opéra-Comique, not long ago, I sat beside a very civil and pleasant stranger who turned out to be an American, through all that I could endure of the very worst performance of "Hoffmann" I ever heard in my life. After the first act my neighbour praised it with immense enthusiasm, which embarrassed me into silence. Finally, however, being obliged to say something, I said that, having heard the same opera so lately at Brussels, I supposed I was rather spoiled. "Ah, Brussels!" he said. "Well, now, that's interesting. I overheard somebody saying that same thing out in the street, just as I was coming in. But I didn't pay much attention to it, you know, because I sort of took for granted that the best performances must be here in Paris."

It would be unfair to press this illustration too far, because very few Americans nowadays, especially if they live in New York, have a chance to hear even a tolerable performance of "Hoffmann." But without any unfairness, the reader will have no trouble in getting the implication. A visiting European would have been likely to know that the performance we heard was bad; he would have known why it was bad; and the fact of its being given at the Opéra-Comique in Paris would have had no weight with him whatever. The great majority of Americans (without prejudice to the gentleman who sat beside me) are quite devoid of this critical faculty. What they encounter under some special set of altogether unrelated circumstances they are predisposed to accept and applaud, quite unaware that there is a strict impersonal standard set for such matters, and that, according to this standard, the thing they are accepting may be rated very low indeed. This uncritical attitude appears in every department of spiritual activity, and indulgence in it is unchecked by any organized influence of any kind.

Indeed, every organized influence is actively on the other side; it is on the side of the cultural taste for the bathos. When Francis I or the Elector Max-Emmanuel or Richelieu set out to make some partial and indirect recommendation of the humane life—to show in some measure what a good, desirable, and satisfactory thing it is—he had a fairly clear field. He did not find the natural taste for the bathos immensely fortified by innumerable mechanical accessories, and flattered by all the arts of salesmanship employed in disposing of them. This is the crucial difference, from the standpoint of culture, that criticism observes between the times, say, of the Elector Max and those of Albert I. When the Elector Max established the Monnaie, he had hardly any competition to meet. There was no horde of commercial enterprisers busily encouraging the popular taste for the bathos to believe that it was good taste, just as good as anybody's, that its standards were all right, and that all it had to do was to keep on its natural way in order to come out as well as need be, and to realize as complete satisfaction as the human spirit demands. This is the kind of thing which Albert I, in continuing the Elector Max's tradition, has to meet; and in America where there has never been any authoritative tradition, and no power capable of establishing one, this is the kind of thing which goes on in greater strength and larger extension than anywhere else in the world.

This is the condition that really determines the forecast which criticism is obliged to make for culture in America. The situation, viewed *in limine,* is clearly quite hopeless; and criticism makes this forecast, I repeat, without blame, and, as I shall show presently, without despair or depression. What is the use of recommending the satisfactions of spiritual activity to people who are already quite satisfied amid the inconceivable multiplicity of mechanical accessories and organized promotions of spiritual inactivity? Tell them, as our prophets and reformers do, that the natural taste for the bathos is educable and improvable, and that they ought to do something about it in order to attain the highest degree of happiness possible to humanity, and they reply, "You may be right, but we are not interested. We are doing quite well as we are. Spiritual activity is hard work; nobody else is doing it, and we are getting on comfortably without any work. We have plenty of distractions to take up our time, plenty of good company, everybody is going our way and nobody going yours." What can one answer? Nothing, simply—there is no answer.

There never was a time of so many and so powerful competitive distractions contesting with culture for the employment of one's hours, and directly tending towards the reinforcement and further degradation of the natural taste for the bathos. One has but to think of the enormous army of commercial enterprisers engaged in pandering to this taste and employing every conceivable device of ingenuity to confirm and flatter and reassure it. Publishers, newspaper-proprietors, editors, preachers, purveyors of commercial amusement, college presidents—the list is endless—all aim consciously at the lowest common denominator of public intelligence, taste, and character. One may not say that they do this willingly in all cases, but they do it consciously. But this is not all. Usually for social reasons or, one may say, for purposes of exhibition, the natural taste for bathos still largely pays a kind of acknowledgment to the superiority of culture. This acknowledgment takes the form of a willingness, or even a desire, to assume the appearance of culture and counterfeit its superficial qualities. Commercial enterprise has seized upon this disposition and made as much of it as it can, thereby administering to the natural taste for the bathos the subtlest flattery of all. Thus in literature, education, music, art, in every department of spiritual activity, we have developed an impressive system of passive exercise in culture, a system proposing to produce a sound natural development while the mind of the patient remains completely and comfortably inert upon its native plane of thought and imagination. The apparatus of this substitutionary process is well known to everyone; the "outline" of this or that, the travel bureau, the lecture bureau, the Browning club, the Joseph Conrad club, and so on. Its peak of organization, by the testimony of William James, is reached at Chautauqua. Thus the pursuit of an imitation or Brummagem culture is industriously sophisticated by brisk young college professors with an agreeable gift for miscellaneous volubility, and effeminized by the patronage of women's clubs. I have every wish that this last observation shall not be misunderstood. Whatever may have been the case at the beginning, I feel sure that if the work and influence of women were now subtracted from our society we should after a short time have very little of a civilized environment left. The cartoonist's count against the male of the species, I think, is a true one—I know it is true against myself—that, left to his own devices, he contentedly lapses into squalor. All I suggest is that the natural taste for the bathos knows no distinction of sex. The uncritical attitude towards affairs of the spirit is common to women and men. Among us, spiritual activity, or the counterfeit of it, has always been popularly regarded as lying quite exclusively in woman's province; indeed, our economic system has already brought men pretty well down to the anthropoid level by condemning them to incessant preoccupation with the mere means of existence. Hence our apparatus of culture and our management of it are peculiarly susceptible to the feminine variant of the natural taste for the bathos. Perhaps one sees a fair example of this susceptibility, and the fruits of it, in our development of music, with its relatively great interest in the personality of artists, and its slight interest in the programmes that the artists execute.

It must never be forgotten—one cannot be insisting on it at every paragraph in an essay of this length—that culture has not for its final object the development of intelligence and taste, but the profound transformations of character that can only be effected by the self-imposed discipline of culture. An appearance of culture, effected by no discipline whatever, but only by docility in following one's nose, cannot bring about these transformations. It is not to be doubted, I think, that Americans will soon have a very considerable nodding acquaintance with the best in literature and in the other arts, which is the working apparatus of culture; many influences, mostly commercial, already conspire to promote this. But the transformations of character, which are the only fruit of culture that make it worth serious recommendation, are not to be brought about in that way. It is one thing, for the sake of collateral purposes unrelated to culture, to desire this nodding acquaintance and to undergo the passive exercise necessary to get it; and it is quite another thing to desire the transformations of character attainable only through culture, and to submit to the discipline of culture necessary to effect them.

Probably everyone who is more or less occupied in the works and ways of culture runs across an occasional spirit, usually young and ardent, who desires the fruits of culture and welcomes the discipline that brings them forth. Sanguine persons argue from this phenomenon that matters look brighter, bidding us think of what the grandparents of these young people, and the society that surrounded them, were like. Criticism, however, measures the strength of the opposite pull on these young people of the present day, discriminates carefully between real and apparent culture, as between leaves and fruit; it looks attentively into the matter of motive directed towards either, and it is obliged to regard this sign of promise as misleading. Superficially it is perhaps impressive, but actually it has little significance. I get letters from many such young spirits, and as so many come to an inconspicuous person like myself, I sometimes wonder how many come to persons whose relations with culture are in a sense official. I have two such letters this morning—what is one to say? The worst of it is that my

correspondents mostly tell me they are not poor and that they have no
responsibilities which would prevent their doing measurably what they
like. Apparently they have enough in their favour; it is the imponderabilia
that are against them. There is no trouble about telling them what to
do, but one is all the time oppressed by the consciousness of delivering
a counsel of perfection. How can one say to these correspondents,
"Well, but the farther you progress in culture, the farther out of the
current of affairs you put yourself, the more you are deprived of the
precious sense of coöperation with your fellows; and this is a rather
hard and forlorn prospect for a young person to face"? The author of
the Imitation said with great acuteness that "the fewer there be who
follow the way to heaven, the harder that way is to find"—and, he
might have added, the harder to follow. It is not to be wondered at
that these youthful spirits so often abandon themselves to a sterile
discontent, and to a final weary acceptance of such slender compromise
as the iron force of the civilization about them may yield.

Sanguine persons also get encouragement out of the "revaluation-
process" that they see, or think they see, going on in America, and
hope for great things from it. Criticism again, however, after taking
stock of this process as benevolently as it can, must regard their hopes
as illusory. The pretended signs or symptoms of revaluation mean
actually nothing of the kind. The present popularity of a certain type
of historical and biographical writing, for instance, argues nothing for
culture. It does not imply any unusual energy of aspiration, or indeed
anything necessarily but a vagrant and vulgar curiosity. A very brief
view of the most popular books of this type is enough to show this
clearly; one may see at a glance that their success is a success of scandal.
So much may be said for the type of social study presented in pseudo-
critical essays, and in the fiction produced by what one of my friends
describes as "cheeky reporters with rather nasty minds." Criticism does
not pause to discuss the collateral effects of this body of literature, but
merely observes that it does nothing for culture, and that any expectations based upon its popularity had better be given up. We all know
that this literature is almost invariably approached for the sake of a
kind of delectation which criticism must regard as extremely low. One
approaches it to have one's own vague malevolences, suspicions,
repugnances, formulated and confirmed, and then reflected back upon
one's own consciousness by force of a clever and specious style. How

many readers can one imagine approaching Mr. Sinclair Lewis's novels, for instance, or Mr. Mencken's essays in any other spirit than that of Little Jack Horner? So far, then, from tending towards the transformation of character through culture, our whole body of "revaluation-literature" really withstands and retards it. Hence, too, the "revaluation-process," of which this literature is taken as symptomatic, appears to be greatly misapprehended; and this misapprehension, again, assists in the sacrifice of one generation at least, and, for all that can now be seen to the contrary, of several.

Criticism however, as I said, observes these untoward facts, observes even these lamentable sacrifices, without depression or despair. It is aware that culture and the humane life have one invincible ally on their side—the self-preserving instinct in humanity. This ally takes its time about asserting itself, but assert itself finally and effectively it always does. Ignorance, vulgarity, a barbaric and superficial spirit, may, and from all appearances will, predominate unquestioned for years in America, for ages if you like; no one can set a term on it. But a term there is, nevertheless, and when it is reached, men will come back to the quest of the humane life because they cannot do without it any longer. That is what has always happened, and it will happen again. Probably no one in that day will be able to tell just what has moved them; the general currents of life will simply reverse themselves and set in the opposite direction, and no one will be able to assign any better reason for it than that humanity could not any longer put up with their running the way they were. Perhaps by that time the political entity which we now know as the United States will have disappeared; one sees no reason to attach any peculiar permanence to it over any of the other political entities that have come and gone. Criticism, indeed, attaches very little importance to the bare question of the future of culture in the United States—sub specie æternitatis, what is the United States? Criticism knows well enough what the future of culture will be, and it may tentatively observe that the prospects in one place or another, for a few generations or a few centuries perhaps, seem to show this-or-that probable degree of correspondence with that future; but it interests itself no further. Virgil and Marcus Aurelius had no nationalist conception of culture; anxiety about Roman culture was the last thing

to enter their minds. Socrates and his friends did not inflate themselves
with notions of the humane life as an Athenian property; they turned
over all that kind of bombast to the politicians and publicists of the
period, and threw in some rare humour for good measure, to keep it
company. Their course is the one which criticism suggests as sincerely
practical for Americans of the present time. Contemplating the future
of culture in no set terms of nationality or race or time, they recognized
the self-preserving instinct of mankind as on its side, and did not worry
about it any further. On the contrary, they approached their own age
with the understanding, equanimity, humour, and tolerance that culture
indicates; and instead of expecting their civilization to give them more
than it possibly could give them, instead of continually fretting at their
fellow citizens, blaming, brow-beating or expostulating with them for
their derogations from the humane life, they bent their energies, as far
as circumstances allowed, towards making some kind of progress in
the humane life themselves.

This essay first appeared anonymously in the June 1928 issue of *Harper's
Magazine*. It was the third of three articles on "The Future of America"
contributed by "an eminent biologist," "one of America's leading historians,"
and by Nock, described as "a distinguished critic and man of letters." It
subsequently appeared in Nock's collection *On Doing the Right Thing*.

Note that on page 99 Nock incorrectly lists von Humboldt and Schleiermacher as advisors to Frederick the Great. It should read that they were
advisors to King Frederick William III.

Criticism's Proper Field

Mr. Mumford's remarks, in the first issue of this paper about the good illustrations in our magazines of the 'seventies and 'eighties, reminds me that there was also some pretty good literature in them. I have often wondered why publishing houses did not salvage it out and republish it in cheap form. Houses like Scribner, Harper, the Century, Appleton, must have dozens of dead titles worth resurrection.

Here might be a good way, without prejudice to Mr. Boni's excellent enterprise, to get the public once more accustomed to paper books, as it used to be accustomed to them in the days of the Seaside Library and the Franklin Square Library, half a century ago. These titles could be reprinted for no more than their cost of manufacture, and booksellers might be induced to handle them as a stimulant to the popular taste for books; which it certainly would be. The great vogue of paper books in France was brought about by George Sand's holding her umbrella over the head of Calmann Lévy until he agreed to produce them. Her argument was that they would make the public "book-conscious," and stimulate sales; and so they did.

But Mr. Mumford's article mainly interested me because it showed so positively the evil results of letting criticism be superseded by journalism. Criticism's business is with the past—especially the immediate past; concern with the present is the function of journalism. No critic, historian, biographer, has any business fumbling at what goes on in his own time, for in the first place he can make no judgment of it that is worth anything; and second, more important, because he connives at the neglect of many good values that lie in the years behind him, and hence the educative power of these values is lost upon the present—just as Mr. Mumford shows in respect of the values in our twenty years of a "buried renaissance." Goethe, the greatest of critics, said earnestly, "Don't read your fellow-strivers, fellow-workers."

Let the next batch of critics sift the current books, let them appraise "the modern movements" in music, art, literature; let the present batch stick to their writing. Then we shall really get somewhere, with nothing valuable neglected. Meanwhile let journalism keep its present course,

and not tread on criticism's toes, or steal its colors. I greatly wish that
Mr. Mumford would gather a few like-minded spirits around him who
would limit themselves to producing a sound criticism on this principle;
meanwhile writing occasional articles to maintain, expound and illustrate this principle, and hammer it into the heads of our journalism-
sodden public. Let them lecture about it in colleges and universities,
wherever they can make an opportunity. Let them take as the field of
their activity the period, say, from the beginning of Reconstruction to
the Closing of the Frontier—in figures, roughly, 1865–1900. This would
be, probably, as useful a service as could be rendered our culture at
this time, and Mr. Mumford is just the man to dedicate himself to it,
and to attract others to it.

A note from a correspondent this morning contains two sentences
that should be written in letters of gold and framed in silver, studded
with precious stones. "What is truly living in any period is what is
capable of remaining alive; and this can be established only in relation
to the ages that succeed it. . . . Our freedom of choice depends upon
our ability to make use of the past, and when we lose this, we become
slaves of the immediate, do we not?" Criticism's first job in this country
is the humble ground-floor job of differentiating itself from journalism
by taking its eyes and mind resolutely off the contemporaneous. The
reason for our ludicrous slavery to the immediate is just the loss that
my correspondent speaks of—we really have no freedom of choice—
and the reason for our loss is that we have had no criticism for a
quarter of a century, but only journalism.

This short piece first appeared in Nock's "Miscellany" column in the April 5,
1930, issue of the new Freeman. He included it in The Book of Journeyman.

Artemus Ward

Charles Farrar Browne, known to the world as Artemus Ward, was born ninety years ago in Waterford, Maine. He died at an age when most of us are only beginning to mature—thirty-three. Little more can be told of him by way of formal biography. Mr. Don C. Seitz lately employed himself upon a labour of love by seeking out and publishing all that is known, probably, of the externalities of Ward's life. Mr. Seitz has made the most of what was put before him, and in so doing he has done good service to the history of American letters; yet one closes his fine volume with a keen sense of how little he had to do with, a sense of the slightness and insignificance of his material. All Ward's years were *Wanderjahre;* he had no schooling, he left a poor rural home at sixteen to work in neighbouring printing-offices; he tramped West and South as a compositor and reporter; he wrote a little, lectured a little, gathered up odds and ends of his writings and dumped them in a woeful mess upon the desk of Carleton, the publisher, to be brought out in two or three slender volumes; he went to New York, then to London, saw as much of collective human life in those centres as he had energy to contemplate; he wrote a few pages for the old *Vanity Fair* and for *Punch,* gave a few lectures in Dodworth Hall on Broadway and Egyptian Hall on Piccadilly; and then he died. Little enough of the *pars magna fui* is to be found here for the encouragement of a biographer; Mr. Seitz, I repeat, is to be congratulated on his intrepidity. It is surely a remarkable thing that one whose experience was limited by the span of thirty-three years, whose literary output was correspondingly scanty, and whose predicable hold upon the future was as slight and hazardous as Mr. Seitz shows Ward's to have been, should have managed to live nearly a century; and it is perhaps more remarkable that he should have done it in a civilization like ours, which is not over-careful with literary reputations and indeed does not concern itself deeply with spiritual achievement or spiritual activity of any kind.

Yet that is what Artemus Ward has somehow managed to do, and Mr. Seitz is on hand with a bibliography of eighteen pages, closely printed in small type, to prove it. Some measure of proof, too, is

probably to be found in the fact that a new issue of Ward's complete
works came out in London two years ago, and that an American firm
has taken thought to publish this present volume. How, then, has Ward
contrived to live so long? As a mere fun-maker, it is highly improbable
that he could have done it. Ward is officially listed as the first of the
great American humorists; Mr. Albert Payson Terhune even commem-
orates him as the man "who taught Americans to laugh." This is great
praise; and one gladly acknowledges that the humorists perform an
immense public service and deserve the most handsome public recognition of its value. In the case of Ward, it is all to Mr. Terhune's credit
that he perceives this. Yet as one reads Ward's own writings, one is
reminded that time's processes of sifting and shaking-down are inexorable, and one is led to wonder whether, after all, in the quality of
sheer humorist, Artemus Ward can quite account for his own persistent
longevity. In point of the power sheerly to provoke laughter, the power
sheerly to amuse, distract and entertain, one doubts that Ward can be
said so far to transcend his predecessors, Shillaber and Derby. In point
of wit and homely wisdom, of the insight and shrewdness which give
substance and momentum to fun-making, it would seem that Ward's
contemporary, Henry W. Shaw, perfectly stands comparison with him.
The disparity, at all events, is by no means so obvious as to enable one
to say surely that the law of the survival of the fittest must take its
course in Ward's favour. One is therefore led to suspect either that
Ward's longevity is due to some quality which he possessed apart from
his quality as humorist, some quality which has not yet, perhaps, been
singled out and remarked with sufficient definiteness, or else that it is
due to the blind play of chance.

Several considerations tell against the hypothesis of accident. It might
be enough to say flatly that such accidents do not happen, that the
passing stream of printed matter is too full and swift to permit any
literary flotsam to escape being caught and swept on to oblivion by its
searching current. Two other considerations, however, may be remarked
as significant. First, that Ward very soon passed over—almost immediately passed over, the transition beginning even in the last few months
of his life—passed over from being a popular property to become a
special property of the intelligent and civilized minority; and he has
remained their special property ever since. In his quality of humorist
he could hardly have done this. Even had he really been the man who

taught the Americans to laugh, disinterested gratitude could hardly be carried so far. Artemus Ward himself declined to weep over the memory of Cotton Mather, saying simply that "he's bin ded too lengthy"; and such, more or less, are we all, even the intelligent and civilized among us. Ward was, in his time, a popular property in virtue of his singularly engaging personality, his fine and delicate art as a public speaker and his brilliant dealing with questions and affairs of current interest. But his presence is no longer among us, and the affairs of profoundest public interest in his day are hardly as much as a memory in ours. No power of humour in dealing with those affairs could serve to continue him as a cherished property of the intelligent, any more than it could serve to restore him as a popular property now that those affairs, and the interest that they evoked, have disappeared. His continuance must be accounted for by another quality than those which he shared with his predecessors and contemporaries who have not taken on a like longevity.

The second consideration is that Ward has always been the object of a different and deeper regard in England, where his humour is alien, than in America where it is native. It has long been difficult to get a copy of his complete works in this country, even at second hand; the last edition was published by Dillingham in 1898. In London one buys them over the counter, and I think one has always been able to do so. Since the Dillingham edition, Ward has been kept alive in America chiefly in edited issues like Mr. Clifton Johnson's, of 1912, and this present volume; and also in anthologies and in essays by many hands. These have, however, I think invariably, presented him as a humorist, and without taking account of the quality which has given his work the vitality that it seems to possess. The English writers have done, on the whole, rather better; but even they did not strike straight through to this quality, disengage it from those that made up his strictly professional character, and hold it out in clear view; though there is evidence that they themselves had glimpses of it. They were for the most part content, like Ward's own countrymen, to accept him as a humorist and to assume that he kept his place in literature on the strength of his humour; and they were not aware, apparently, that this assumption left them with a considerable problem on their hands. Mr. Seitz quotes Ward's own view of the quality that gives power and permanence to his work—I too shall quote it presently, as it is admirably explicit—and oddly enough, without perceiving that it leaves him with a considerable problem on *his* hands; a problem which, if he had attended to it, might have caused him to change the direction of about three-fourths of his book.

No, clearly it is not by the power of his humour that Ward has earned his way in the world of letters, but by the power of his criticism. Ward was a first-class critic of society; and he has lived for a century by precisely the same power that gave a more robust longevity to Cervantes and Rabelais. He is no Rabelais or Cervantes, doubtless; no one would pretend that he is; but he is eminently of their glorious company. Certainly Keats was no Shakespeare, but as Matthew Arnold excellently said of him, he is *with* Shakespeare; to his own degree he lives by grace of a classic quality which he shares with Shakespeare; and so also is Ward with Rabelais and Cervantes by grace of his power of criticism.

Let us look into this a little, for the sake of making clear the purpose for which this book is issued. I have already said that Ward has become a special property, and that he can never again be a popular property, at least until the coming of that millennial time when most of our present dreams of human perfectability are realized. I have no wish to discourage my publishers, but in fairness I have had to remind them that this delectable day seems still, for one reason or another, to be quite a long way off, and that meanwhile they should not put any very extravagant expectations upon the sale of this volume, but content themselves as best they may with the consciousness that they are serving a vital interest, really the ultimate interest, of the saving Remnant. Ward is the property of an order of persons—for order is the proper word, rather than class or group, since they are found quite unassociated in any formal way, living singly or nearly so, and more or less as aliens, in all classes of our society—an order which I have characterized by using the term *intelligence*. If I may substitute the German word *Intelligenz*, it will be seen at once that I have no idea of drawing any supercilious discrimination as between, say, the clever and the stupid, or the educated and the uneducated. *Intelligenz* is the power invariably, in Plato's phrase, to see things as they are, to survey them and one's own relations to them with objective disinterestedness, and to apply one's consciousness to them simply and directly, letting it take its own way over them uncharted by prepossession, unchanneled by prejudice, and above all uncontrolled by routine and formula. Those who have this power are everywhere; everywhere they are not so much resisting as quietly eluding and disregarding all social pressure which tends to mechanize their processes of observation and thought. Rabelais's first words are words of jovial address, under a ribald figure, to just this order of persons to which he knew he would forever belong, an order characterized by *Intelligenz;* and it is to just this order that Ward belongs.

The critical function which spirits like Ward perform upon this unorganized and alien order of humanity is twofold; it is not only clearing and illuminating, but it is also strengthening, reassuring, even healing and consoling. They have not only the ability but the *temper* which marks the true critic of the first order; for, as we all know, the failure which deforms and weakens so much of the able second-rate critic's work is a failure in temper. Take, for example, by way of a comparative study in social criticism, Rabelais's description of the behaviour of Diogenes at the outbreak of the Corinthian War, and put beside it any piece of anti-militarist literature that you may choose; put beside it the very best that M. Rolland or Mr. Norman Angell or even Count Tolstoy himself can do. How different the effect upon the spirit! Or again, consider in the following pages the pictures which Ward draws of the village of Baldwinsville under stress of the Civil War. Not one item is missing of all that afflicted the person of *Intelligenz* in every community at some time in the last ten years. Ward puts his finger as firmly as Mr. Bertrand Russell and Mr. H. L. Mencken have put theirs, upon all the meanness, low-mindedness, greed, viciousness, blood-thirstiness and homicidal mania that were rife among us—and upon their exciting causes as well—but the person of *Intelligenz* turns to him, and instead of being further depressed, as Mr. Russell and Mr. Mencken depress him, instead of being further overpowered by a sense that the burdens put upon the spirit of man are greater than it can bear, he is lifted out of his temporary despondency and enervation by a sight of the long stretch of victorious humanity that so immeasureably transcends all these matters of the moment. Such is the calming and persuasive influence of the true critical temper, that one immediately perceives Ward to be regarding all the untowardness of Baldwinsville *sub specie æternitatis,* and one gratefully submits to his guidance towards a like view of one's own circumstances.

The essential humanity of Abraham Lincoln may be largely determined in one's own mind, I think, by the fact that he made just this use of Artemus Ward. Mr. Seitz tells us how, in the darkest days of the Civil War, Lincoln read the draft of his Emancipation Proclamation at a special meeting of his Cabinet, and, to the immense scandal and disgust of his associates, prefaced it by reading several pages from Ward. The incident is worth attention for the further establishment of the distinction drawn among men by the quality of *Intelligenz*. Seward, Chase, Stanton, Blair, had ability, they had education; but they had not the free, disinterested play of consciousness upon their environment, they did not instinctively tend to see things as they are, they thought largely by routine and formula, they were pedantic, *unintelligent*—that is precisely the word that Goethe, the greatest of critics, would have applied to them at once. Upon them then, naturally, Lincoln's performance made the impression of mere impudent levity; and thus one is directly led to see great force in Ward's sly suggestion that Lincoln should fill up his Cabinet with showmen! Alas! how often the civilized spirit is moved to wish that the direction of public affairs might be taken out of the hands of those who in their modesty are fond of calling themselves "practical" men, and given over to the artists, to those who at least have some theoretical conception of a satisfying technique of living, even though actually they may have gone no great way in the mastery of its practice.

In another place Mr. Seitz tells us how the great and good John Bright, the Moses of British political liberalism, attended one of Ward's lectures in London, sat gravely through it, and then observed that "its information was meagre, and presented in a desultory, disconnected manner"! The moment I read that, I laid down the book, saying to myself, *Behold the reason for liberalism's colossal failure!* The primary failure of liberalism is just the failure in *Intelligenz* that we see so amusingly indicated in the case of Mr. Bright; its secondary failure, as we saw in the case of the late Mr. Wilson, for example, is a failure in the high and sound character that depends so largely upon *Intelligenz* for its development. Can one imagine that Ward would be more intelligible to representative British liberals since Bright's day, or that he would make a more serious and salutary impression upon the energumens who in this country are busily galvanizing some of Mr. Wilson's political formulas into a ghastly simulacrum of life, and setting them up as the soul and essence of liberalism—upon ex-Justice Clarke, for example, or ex-Secretary Baker or Mr. George Foster Peabody? One smiles at the thought of it.

Ward said of writers like himself that "they have always done the most toward helping virtue on its pilgrimage, and the truth has found more aid from them than from all the grave polemists and solid writers that have ever spoken or written. . . . They have helped the truth along *without encumbering it with themselves.*" I venture to italicize these remarkable words. How many good causes there are, to be sure, that seem hopelessly condemned and nullified by the personality of those who profess them! One can think of any number of reforms, both social and political, that one might willingly accept if only one need not accept their advocates too. Bigotry, arrogance, intolerance, self-assurance, never ran higher over public affairs than in Ward's day, yet he succeeded in putting upon all public questions the precise critical estimate that one puts upon them now in the perspective of fifty years; its correspondence with the verdict of history is extraordinarily complete. It would be nothing remarkable if one should arrive now at a correct critical estimate of the Negro question, for example, or of the policy of abolition, or of the character and qualities of public men of the day, or of the stock phrases, the catchwords and claptrap that happened for the time being to be the stock-in-trade of demogoguery; but it is highly remarkable that a contemporary should have had a correct critical estimate of them, and that he should have given to it an expression so strong and so consistent, and yet so little *encumbered with himself* as to be wholly acceptable.

Really, there are very few of the characteristic and distinctive qualities of American life that Ward's critical power left untouched. I read somewhere lately—I think in one of Professor Stuart P. Sherman's deliverances, though I am not quite sure—that Americans are just now very much in the mood of self-examination, and that their serious reading of novelists like Mr. Sinclair Lewis or Mr. Sherwood Anderson, and of essayists like Mr. Ludwig Lewisohn or Mr. Mencken, is proof that they are in that mood. I have great doubts of all this; yet if it be true, I can but the more strongly urge them to re-examine the work of a first-rate critic, who fifty years ago drew a picture of our civilization that in all essential aspects is still accurate. Ward represents the ideal of this civilization as falling in with one only of the several instincts that urge men onward in the quest of perfection, the instinct of expansion. The claim of expansion is abundantly satisfied by Ward's America; the civilization about him is cordial to the instinct of expansion, fosters it, and makes little of the obligation to scrupulousness or delicacy in its exercise. Ward takes due pride in relating himself properly to the predominance of this instinct; he says that by strict attention to business he has "amarsed a handsum Pittance," and that when he has enough to permit him to be pious in good style, like his wealthy neighbours, he intends to join the Baldwinsville church. There is an ideal of civilized life for you, a conception of the progressive humanization of man in society! For the claim of instincts other than the instinct of expansion, Ward's America does nothing. It does nothing for the claim of intellect and knowledge (aside from purely instrumental knowledge) nothing for the claim of beauty and poetry, the claim of morals and religion, the claim of social life and manners.

Our modern school of social critics might therefore conceivably get profit out of studying Ward's view of American life, to see how regularly he represents it, as they do, as manifesting an extremely low type of beauty, a factitious type of morals, a grotesque and repulsive type of religion, a profoundly imperfect type of social life and manners. Baldwinsville is overspread with all the hideousness, the appalling tedium and enervation that afflict the sensitive soul of Mr. Sinclair Lewis. The young showman's courtship of Betsy Jane Peasley exhausts its resources of romance and poetry; its *beau ideal* of domesticity is completely fulfilled in their subsequent life together—a life fruitful indeed in certain wholesome satisfactions, but by no means such as a "well-formed mind would be disposed to relish." On the side of intellect and knowledge, Baldwinsville supports the editor of the *Bugle* as contentedly as New York supports Mr. Ochs and Mr. Munsey, and to quite as good purpose; it listens to the school-master's views on public questions as uncritically as New York listens to Mr. Nicholas Murray Butler's, and to quite as good purpose. Baldwinsville's dominant type of morals is as straitly legalistic, formal and superficial as our own; its dominant type of religion is easily recognizable as the hard, dogged, unintelligent fanaticism with which Zenith confronted Mr. Sinclair Lewis. We easily recognize the "dissidence of Dissent and the protestantism of the Protestant religion," which now inspires the Anti-Saloon

League, and which informs and animates the gentle ministrations of
the Ku Klux Klan.

Thus Ward, in his own excellent phrase, powerfully helps along the
truth about civilization in the United States; and all the more powerfully
in that, unlike Mr. Lewis and Mr. Mencken, he does not so encumber
it with himself, so overload it with the dragging weight of his own
propensities, exasperations, repugnances, that his criticism, however
accurate and interesting, is repellant and in the long run ineffectual.
Often, indeed, his most searching criticism is made by indirection, by
the turn of some phrase that at first strikes one as quite insignificant,
or at least as quite irrelevant to any critical purpose; yet when this
phrase once enters the mind it becomes pervasive, and one finds
presently that it has coloured all one's cast of thought—and this is an
effect which only criticism of the very first order can produce. For
instance, consider the first sentence that he writes in a letter to his
wife from the Athens of America:

> Dear Betsy: I write you this from Boston, 'the Modern Atkins' as it is
> denomyunated, altho I skurcely know what those air.

Nothing but that. Yet somehow when that little piece of exquisite
raillery sinks in, it at once begins to put one into just the frame of
mind and temper to meet properly the gentle, self-contained provincialism at which it was directed. Let the reader experiment for himself.
Let him first recall the fearfully hard sledding he had on his way
through, say, Mr. Barrett Wendell's History of American Literature, or
the recent volume of Mrs. Field's reminiscences; let him remember the
groan of distress that now and then escaped him while reading Mr.
Howells's really excellent novel, The Rise of Silas Lapham. Then with
this sentence in mind, let him try reading any one of the three books
again, and see how differently it will impress him.

After the same fashion one may make quite good headway with Mr.
Villard's biography of John Brown if one's spirit is cleared and steadied
by Ward's inimitable critique of "Ossawatomie Brown, or, the Hero of
Harper's Ferry." Amidst the squalor of our popular plays and popular
literature, one preserves a decent equanimity by perusing Ward's reviews
of East Side theatricals and of Forrest's "Othello," and his parodies of

the cheap and lurid romances of his day. Our popular magazines take on a less repellant aspect when one remembers how, after three drinks of New England rum, Ward "knockt a small boy down, pickt his pocket of a New York *Ledger,* and wildly commenced readin Sylvanus Kobb's last Tail." No better criticism of our ludicrous and distressing perversion of the religious instinct can be found than in his account of his visit to the Shakers, the Free Lovers and the Spiritualists. Never was the depth and quality of routine patriotism more accurately measured than by this, from the account of his visit to Richmond after the surrender:

> I met a man today—I am not at liberty to tell his name, but he is an old and inflooential citizen of Richmond, and sez he, "Why! we've bin fightin agin the Old Flag! Lor bless me, how sing'lar!" He then borrer'd five dollars of me and bust into a flood of tears.

Again, how effective is Ward's criticism of the mischievous and chlorotic sentimentalism to which Americans seem invariably to give their first allegiance! During the Civil War the popular regard for motherhood was exploited as viciously as during the last war, or probably in all wars, and Ward's occasional reflections upon this peculiarly contemptible routine-process of militarism are more effective than any indignant fulminations of outraged common sense; as when he suggests, for instance, that "the song writers air doin' the Mother bisness rayther too muchly," or as when in another place he remarks that it seems about time somebody began to be a little sorry for the old man. He touches another fond topic of sentimentalism in his story, which I must quote, of leaving home as a boy to embark in the show business. Where can better criticism than this be found?

> You know, Betsy, that when I first commenced my career as a moral exhibitor with a six-legged cat and a Bass drum, I was only a simple peasant child—skurce 15 summers had flow'd over my yoothful hed. But I had sum mind of my own. My father understood this. 'Go,' he said, 'Go, my son, and hog the public!' (he ment 'knock 'em,' but the old man was allus a little given to slang). He put his withered han' tremblingly onto my hed, and went sadly into the house. I thought I saw tears tricklin down his venerable chin, but it might hav' been tobacker juice. He chaw'd.

But I must end these illustrations, which I have been tempted perhaps unduly to multiply and enlarge upon because their author has never yet, as far as I am aware, been brought to the attention of modern readers in the one capacity wherein he appears to me to maintain an open communication with the future—the capacity of critic. In conclusion I cannot forbear remarking the spring, the abounding vitality and gusto, that pervades Ward's work, and pointing out that here too he is with Rabelais and Cervantes. The true critic is aware, with George Sand, that for life to be fruitful, life must be felt as a *joy;* that it is by the bond of *joy,* not of happiness or pleasure, not of duty or responsibility, that the called and chosen spirits are kept together in this world. There was little enough of joy going in the society that surrounded Ward; the sky over his head was of iron and brass; and there is even perhaps less joy current in American society now. But the true critic has his resources of joy within himself, and the motion of his joy is self-sprung. There may be ever so little hope of the human race, but that is the moralist's affair, not the critic's. The true critic takes no account of optimism or pessimism; they are both quite outside his purview; his affair is one only of joyful appraisal, assessment and representation.

Epitaphs are notably exuberant, but the simple line carved upon Ward's tombstone presents with a most felicitous precision and completeness, I think, the final word upon him. "His name will live as a sweet and unfading recollection." Yes, just that is his fate, and there is none other so desirable. *Mansueti possidebunt terram,* said the Psalmist, the *amiable* shall possess the earth; and so, in the long run, they do. Insight and wisdom, shrewdness and penetration—for a critic these are great gifts, indispensable gifts, and the public has regard for their exercise, it gives gratitude for the benefits that they confer; but they are not enough of themselves to invest a critic's name with the quality of a sweet and unfading recollection. To do this they must communicate themselves through the medium of a temper, a prepossessing and persuasive amiability. Wordsworth showed himself a great critic when he said of his own poems that "they will co-operate with the benign tendencies in human nature and society, and will in their degree be efficacious in making men wiser, better and happier"; and it is just because of their unvarying co-operation with the benign tendencies in human nature and society that Ward's writings have made him in the deepest sense a possession, a cherished and ennobling possession, of those who know him.

_____

This essay was originally written as the introduction to the *Selected Works of Artemus Ward* which Nock edited in 1924. He subsequently included the essay in *On Doing the Right Thing*.

Study in Paradoxes

One of the excellent consequences—or should one say compensations? I think not—of advancing age, is in the rapid dwindling of one's sense of responsibility for Burbanking human society into a new and improved form. This exemption comes entirely from within, nor is it the fruit of disappointment and cynicism. It is released largely by observation and experience of how the things that one believes in actually work out. One believes in them as much as ever, and is all on the side of their being lived out. One also has as much faith as ever in the possibilities of the human race. But unforeseen things happen, and they keep happening so often and so decisively, and with such an air of inevitability about them, that before long one becomes aware that the Burbanking business has more to it than one thought. I sometimes remind myself of a friend living in Brussels sixteen years ago, who rushed into her husband's bedroom one morning at the crack of dawn, saying "Here comes the German army right past the house! Hurry up and put on your dressing-gown." There was no hurry. For two days and three nights that stream of soldiery moved by without cessation. The German army was no circus-procession.

Many matters thus contribute to make our hindsight clearer than our foresight. Viewed by hindsight, some of my most cherished social theories work out in an odd way. For one thing, I am impressed by the ugliness resulting from their operation—freedom and equalitarianism, for instance. I am all for both; yet where liberty and equality most prevail, or are most thought to prevail, the resulting civilization is extremely unlovely. My present habitat in the country is near a seashore resort that thirty years ago rather looked down its nose at Newport's summer society as being an amalgam of the newly-rich. It was somewhat inaccessible; there were transportation-difficulties about getting there, which kept the crowds away. At present, anybody with a motor-car or the price of a middling long bus-ride may go there, and everyone goes. I am glad everyone can. The old life of the place was bottomed on a social theory that I utterly disbelieve in and regard as false and vicious. The new life is bottomed on an equalitarian theory that I believe in and subscribe to with all my heart, yet the old life gave rise to an amenity that was pleasing, beautiful and civilizing, and the new life has nothing of it, but is, on the contrary, tawdry and hideous.

Thus the moment one goes at applying a social principle flatly, certain compensatory reactions seem to be set up. For instance, I am in favor of having everybody able to read. I believe in the principle of it; I am all for equalitarianism in literacy. Yet when my theory is taken up and measurably put into effect, as it is in this country, just see the result—the quantity-production of a contemptible journalism, a contemptible literature, an unconscionable blatant puffing of both, and a corresponding degradation of literary values, literary tastes, literary habits. Of all the repulsive features of an equalitarian society, its literary feature seems to me the ugliest. I say this advisedly, for of late I have been emulating Bruneseau, and have followed the turbid course of some of the best-selling literature of the day, in books and periodicals, by way of knowing what goes on. My cardinal theory of society as shown by the substance of what I read, has set this course straight towards ignorance and vulgarity, while quantity-production salesmanship in literature—an offshoot of my theory—has succeeded in making ignorance and vulgarity arrogant.

Hence it is that one becomes a little circumspect about the imposition of one's theories, vi et armis. I have to recognize, with searchings of heart, that the sense of whatever in human society is enviable, graceful and becoming has been bred by a régime so monstrously unjust and flagitious that it had no right ever to exist on earth. I am not speaking now of inanimate cultural legacies in literature and the other arts, but of the tone of a people's actual social life. I remember being in a European country before the War, and a friend's saying to me, "Well here we are, where according to your social creed and mine everything is absolutely wrong, and yet these are the happiest people on earth." There was no doubt about it, they were. I wonder about the effect on their happiness if my friend and I could by magic have conjured their infamous régime suddenly out of existence and replaced it by a hundred-per-cent democracy. I know the one phenomenon of American life on which there is agreement by all foreign critics and observers, is that nobody seems to be happy. Mr. Edison lately said he was not acquainted with anybody who was happy. Personally, my social theories reach far beyond anything that is contemplated by American institutions, since I am an individualist, anarchist, single-taxer and free-trader. I think also that the general course of things is in those directions. But whenever I feel inclined to hurry up the course of things, I ask myself how much at home I should feel in a society of my own creating, if I had to create it out of the material at present available.

Probably something more than a workable theory is necessary; very likely you have to have a people that knows how to work it. Otherwise you may get a lot of bad by-products. Logically, one would say that as existence becomes mechanically easier, life should become richer and fuller; instead it becomes emptier and poorer, and the more people there are who have access to increased ease of existence, the emptier and poorer it seems to become. The wider the spread of literacy, one would say, the higher should go the level of general intelligence; but it does not work out that way. I have always been a thoroughgoing feminist, strong for the emancipation of women; but while there has been a social gain "in principle" as the diplomats say, through their emancipation, there have been very grave collateral losses which were practically unpredictable. Probably the only way that society can profitably progress is the way it does progress, by the long and erratic ins and outs of trial and error; and blind insistence on any theory, even a sound one, is to little purpose. One may best hang one's theory up in plain sight for any one to examine who is so disposed, and let it go at that. Even if I were in Moscow now, I do not think my wife would get me out in my pajamas at five in the morning to see the Bolshevist theory go by. There is a great deal of it, and it will be a long time on the way; and so I should snooze awhile, shave, dress, get my breakfast, and then repair to the front window and regard it attentively.

This piece originally appeared in the "Miscellany" column of the *new Freeman* in the April 5, 1930, issue. Nock later included it in *The Book of Journeyman*.

Isaiah's Job

One evening last autumn I sat long hours with a European acquaintance while he expounded a politico-economic doctrine which seemed sound as a nut, and in which I could find no defect. At the end he said with great earnestness, "I have a mission to the masses. I feel that I am called to get the ear of the people. I shall devote the rest of my life to spreading my doctrine far and wide among the populace. What do you think?"

An embarrassing question in any case, and doubly so under the circumstances, because my acquaintance is a very learned man, one of the three or four really first-class minds that Europe produced in his generation, and naturally I, as one of the unlearned, was inclined to regard his lightest word with reverence amounting to awe. Still, I reflected, even the greatest mind can not possibly know everything, and I was pretty sure he had not had my opportunities for observing the masses of mankind, and that therefore I probably knew them better than he did. So I mustered courage to say that he had no such mission and would do well to get the idea out of his head at once; he would find that the masses would not care two pins for his doctrine, and still less for himself, since in such circumstances the popular favourite is generally some Barabbas. I even went so far as to say (he is a Jew) that his idea seemed to show that he was not very well up on his own native literature. He smiled at my jest, and asked what I meant by it; and I referred him to the story of the prophet Isaiah.

It occurred to me then that this story is much worth recalling just now when so many wise men and soothsayers appear to be burdened with a message to the masses. Dr. Townsend has a message, Father Coughlin has one, Mr. Upton Sinclair, Mr. Lippmann, Mr. Chase and the planned-economy brethren, Mr. Tugwell and the New Dealers, Mr. Smith and the Liberty Leaguers—the list is endless. I can not remember a time when so many energumens were so variously proclaiming the Word to the multitude and telling them what they must do to be saved. This being so, it occurred to me, as I say, that the story of Isaiah might have something in it to steady and compose the human spirit until this tyranny of windiness be overpast. I shall paraphrase the story in our common speech, since it has to be pieced out from various sources; and inasmuch as respectable scholars have thought fit to put out a whole new version of the Bible in the American vernacular, I shall take shelter behind them, if need be, against the charge of dealing irreverently with the Sacred Scriptures.

The prophet's career began at the end of King Uzziah's reign, say about 740 B.C. This reign was uncommonly long, almost half a century, and apparently prosperous. It was one of those prosperous reigns, however, like the reign of Marcus Aurelius at Rome, or the administration of Eubulus at Athens, or of Mr. Coolidge at Washington, where at the end the prosperity suddenly peters out, and things go by the board with a resounding crash.

In the year of Uzziah's death, the Lord commissioned the prophet to go out and warn the people of the wrath to come. "Tell them what a worthless lot they are," He said. "Tell them what is wrong, and why, and what is going to happen unless they have a change of heart and straighten up. Don't mince matters. Make it clear that they are positively down to their last chance. Give it to them good and strong, and keep on giving it to them. I suppose perhaps I ought to tell you," He added, "that it won't do any good. The official class and their intelligentsia will turn up their noses at you, and the masses will not even listen. They will all keep on in their own ways until they carry everything down to destruction, and you will probably be lucky if you get out with your life."

Isaiah had been very willing to take on the job; in fact, he had asked for it; but this prospect put a new face on the situation. It raised the obvious question why, if all that were so, if the enterprise were to be a failure from the start, was there any sense in starting it? "Ah," the Lord said, "you do not get the point. There is a Remnant there that you know nothing about. They are obscure, unorganized, inarticulate, each one rubbing along as best he can. They need to be encouraged and braced up, because when everything has gone completely to the dogs, they are the ones who will come back and build up a new society, and meanwhile your preaching will reassure them and keep them hanging on. Your job is to take care of the Remnant, so be off now and set about it."

Apparently, then, if the Lord's word is good for anything—I do not offer any opinion about that—the only element in Judæan society that was particularly worth bothering about was the Remnant. Isaiah seems finally to have got it through his head that this was the case; that nothing was to be expected from the masses, but that if anything substantial were ever to be done in Judæa, the Remnant would have to do it. This is a very striking and suggestive idea; but before going on to explore it, we need to be quite clear about our terms. What do we mean by the masses, and what by the Remnant?

As the word *masses* is commonly used, it suggests agglomerations of poor and unprivileged people, labouring people, proletarians, and it means nothing like that; it means simply the majority. The mass-man is one who has neither the force of intellect to apprehend the principles issuing in what we know as the humane life, nor the force of character to adhere to those principles steadily and strictly as laws of conduct; and because such people make up the great, the overwhelming majority of mankind, they are called collectively *the masses*. The line of differentiation between the masses and the Remnant is set invariably by quality, not by circumstance. The Remnant are those who by force of intellect are able to apprehend these principles, and by force of character are able, at least measurably, to cleave to them; the masses are those who are unable to do either.

The picture which Isaiah presents of the Judæan masses is most unfavourable. In his view the mass-man, be he high or be he lowly, rich or poor, prince or pauper, gets off very badly. He appears as not only weak-minded and weak-willed, but as by consequence knavish, arrogant, grasping, dissipated, unprincipled, unscrupulous. The mass-woman also gets off badly, as sharing all the mass-man's untoward qualities, and contributing a few of her own in the way of vanity and laziness, extravagance and foible. The list of luxury-products[1] that she patronized is interesting; it calls to mind the women's page of a Sunday newspaper in 1928, or the display set forth in one of our professedly "smart" periodicals. In another place[2] Isaiah even recalls the affectations that we used to know by the name of the "flapper gait" and the "debutante slouch." It may be fair to discount Isaiah's vivacity a little

1. Isaiah iii. 18–23.
2. Chap. iii. 16.

for prophetic fervour; after all, since his real job was not to convert the masses but to brace and reassure the Remnant, he probably felt that he might lay it on indiscriminately and as thick as he liked—in fact, that he was expected to do so. But even so, the Judæan mass-man must have been a most objectionable individual, and the mass-woman utterly odious.

If the modern spirit, whatever that may be, is disinclined towards taking the Lord's word as its face value (as I hear is the case), we may observe that Isaiah's testimony to the character of the masses has strong collateral support from respectable Gentile authority. Plato lived into the administration of Eubulus, when Athens was at the peak of its great jazz-and-paper era, and he speaks of the Athenian masses with all Isaiah's fervency, even comparing them to a herd of ravenous wild beasts. Curiously, too, he applies Isaiah's own word *remnant* to the worthier portion of Athenian society; "there is but a very small *remnant*," he says, of those who possess a saving force of intellect and force of character—too small, precisely as in Judæa, to be of any avail against the ignorant and vicious preponderance of the masses.

But Isaiah was a preacher and Plato a philosopher; and we tend to regard preachers and philosophers rather as passive observers of the drama of life than as active participants. Hence in a matter of this kind their judgment might be suspected of being a little uncompromising, a little acrid, or as the French say, *saugrenu*. We may therefore bring forward another witness who was preëminently a man of affairs, and whose judgment can not lie under this suspicion. Marcus Aurelius was ruler of the greatest of empires, and in that capacity he not only had the Roman mass-man under observation, but he had him on his hands twenty-four hours a day for eighteen years. What he did not know about him was not worth knowing, and what he thought of him is abundantly attested on almost every page of the little book of jottings which he scribbled offhand from day to day, and which he meant for no eye but his own ever to see.

This view of the masses is the one that we find prevailing at large among the ancient authorities whose writings have come down to us. In the eighteenth century, however, certain European philosophers spread the notion that the mass-man, in his natural state, is not at all the kind of person that earlier authorities made him out to be, but on the contrary, that he is a worthy object of interest. His untowardness is the effect of environment, an effect for which "society" is somehow responsible. If only his environment permitted him to live according to his best lights, he would undoubtedly show himself to be quite a fellow; and the best way to secure a more favourable environment for him would be to let him arrange it for himself. The French Revolution acted powerfully as a springboard for this idea, projecting its influence in all directions throughout Europe.

On this side of the ocean a whole new continent stood ready for a large-scale experiment with this theory. It afforded every conceivable resource whereby the masses might develop a civilization made in their own likeness and after their own image. There was no force of tradition to disturb them in their preponderance, or to check them in a thoroughgoing disparagement of the Remnant. Immense natural wealth, unquestioned predominance, virtual isolation, freedom from external interference and the fear of it, and, finally, a century and a half of time—such are the advantages which the mass-man has had in bringing forth a civilization which should set the earlier preachers and philosophers at naught in their belief that nothing substantial can be expected from the masses, but only from the Remnant.

His success is unimpressive. On the evidence so far presented one must say, I think, that the mass-man's conception of what life has to offer, and his choice of what to ask from life, seem now to be pretty well what they were in the times of Isaiah and Plato; and so too seem the catastrophic social conflicts and convulsions in which his views of life and his demands on life involve him. I do not wish to dwell on this, however, but merely to observe that the monstrously inflated importance of the masses has apparently put all thought of a possible mission to the Remnant out of the modern prophet's head. This is obviously quite as it should be, provided that the earlier preachers and philosophers were actually wrong, and that all final hope of the human race is actually centred in the masses. If, on the other hand, it should turn out that the Lord and Isaiah and Plato and Marcus Aurelius were right in their estimate of the relative social value of the masses and the Remnant, the case is somewhat different. Moreover, since with everything in their favour the masses have so far given such an extremely discouraging account of themselves, it would seem that the question at issue between these two bodies of opinion might most profitably be reopened.

But without following up this suggestion, I wish only, as I said, to remark the fact that as things now stand Isaiah's job seems rather to go begging. Everyone with a message nowadays is like my venerable European friend, eager to take it to the masses. His first, last and only thought is of mass-acceptance and mass-approval. His great care is to put his doctrine in such shape as will capture the masses' attention and interest. This attitude towards the masses is so exclusive, so devout, that one is reminded of the troglodytic monster described by Plato, and the assiduous crowd at the entrance to its cave, trying obsequiously to placate it and win its favour, trying to interpret its inarticulate noises, trying to find out what it wants, and eagerly offering it all sorts of things that they think might strike its fancy.

The main trouble with all this is its reaction upon the mission itself. It necessitates an opportunist sophistication of one's doctrine which profoundly alters its character and reduces it to a mere placebo. If, say, you are a preacher, you wish to attract as large a congregation as you can, which means an appeal to the masses, and this in turn means adapting the terms of your message to the order of intellect and character that the masses exhibit. If you are an educator, say with a college on your hands, you wish to get as many students as possible, and you whittle down your requirements accordingly. If a writer, you aim at getting many readers; if a publisher, many purchasers; if a philosopher, many disciples; if a reformer, many converts; if a musician, many auditors; and so on. But as we see on all sides, in the realization of these several desires the prophetic message is so heavily adulterated with trivialities in every instance that its effect on the masses is merely to harden them in their sins; and meanwhile the Remnant, aware of this adulteration and of the desires that prompt it, turn their backs on the prophet and will have nothing to do with him or his message.

Isaiah, on the other hand, worked under no such disabilities. He preached to the masses only in the sense that he preached publicly. Anyone who liked might listen; anyone who liked might pass by. He knew that the Remnant would listen; and knowing also that nothing was to be expected of the masses under any circumstances, he made no specific appeal to them, did not accommodate his message to their measure in any way, and did not care two straws whether they heeded it or not. As a modern publisher might put it, he was not worrying about circulation or about advertising. Hence, with all such obsessions quite out of the way, he was in a position to do his level best, without fear or favour, and answerable only to his august Boss.

If a prophet were not too particular about making money out of his mission or getting a dubious sort of notoriety out of it, the foregoing considerations would lead one to say that serving the Remnant looks like a good job. An assignment that you can really put your back into, and do your best without thinking about results, is a real job; whereas serving the masses is at best only half a job, considering the inexorable conditions that the masses impose upon their servants. They ask you to give them what they want, they insist upon it, and will take nothing else; and following their whims, their irrational changes of fancy, their hot and cold fits, is a tedious business, to say nothing of the fact that what they want at any time makes very little call on one's resources of prophecy. The Remnant, on the other hand, want only the best you have, whatever that may be. Give them that, and they are satisfied and you have nothing more to worry about. The prophet of the American masses must aim consciously at the lowest common denominator of intellect, taste and character among 120,000,000 people; and this is a distressing task. The prophet of the Remnant, on the contrary, is in the enviable position of Papa Haydn in the household of Prince Esterhazy. All Haydn had to do was to keep forking out the very best music he knew how to produce, knowing it would be understood and appreciated by those for whom he produced it, and caring not a button what anyone else thought of it; and that makes a good job.

In a sense, nevertheless, as I have said, it is not a rewarding job. If you can touch the fancy of the masses, and have the sagacity to keep always one jump ahead of their vagaries and vacillations, you can get good returns in money from serving the masses, and good returns also in a mouth-to-ear type of notoriety:

Digito monstrari et dicier, Hic est!

We all know innumerable politicians, journalists, dramatists, novelists and the like, who have done extremely well by themselves in these ways. Taking care of the Remnant, on the contrary, holds little promise of any such rewards. A prophet of the Remnant will not grow purse-proud on the financial returns from his work, nor is it likely that he will get any great renown out of it. Isaiah's case was exceptional to this second rule, and there are others, but not many.

It may be thought, then, that while taking care of the Remnant is no doubt a good job, it is not an especially interesting job, because it is as a rule so poorly paid. I have my doubts about this. There are other compensations to be got out of a job besides money and notoriety, and some of them seem substantial enough to be attractive. Many jobs which do not pay well are yet profoundly interesting, as, for instance, the job of the research-student in the sciences is said to be; and the job of looking after the Remnant seems to me, as I have surveyed it for many years from my seat in the grandstand, to be as interesting as any that can be found in the world.

What chiefly makes it so, I think, is that in any given society the Remnant are always so largely an unknown quantity. You do not know, and will never know, more than two things about them. You can be sure of those—dead sure, as our phrase is—but you will never be able to make even a respectable guess at anything else. You do not know and will never know who the Remnant are, or where they are, or how many of them there are, or what they are doing or will do. Two things you know, and no more: first, that they exist; second, that they will find you. Except for these two certainties, working for the Remnant means working in impenetrable darkness; and this, I should say, is just the condition calculated most effectively to pique the interest of any prophet who is properly gifted with the imagination, insight and intellectual curiosity necessary to a successful pursuit of his trade.

The fascination and the despair of the historian, as he looks back upon Isaiah's Jewry, upon Plato's Athens, or upon Rome of the Antonines, is the hope of discovering and laying bare the "substratum of right thinking and well-doing" which he knows must have existed somewhere in those societies because no kind of collective life can possibly go on without it. He finds tantalizing intimations of it here and there in many places, as in the Greek Anthology, in the scrapbook of Aulus Gellius, in the poems of Ausonius, and in the brief and touching tribute *Bene merenti* bestowed upon the unknown occupants of Roman tombs. But these are vague and fragmentary; they lead him nowhere in his search for some kind of measure of this substratum, but merely testify to what he already knew *a priori,* that the substratum did somewhere exist. Where it was, how substantial it was, what its power of self-assertion and resistance was—of all this they tell him nothing.

Similarly, when the historian of two thousand years hence, or two hundred years, looks over the available testimony to the quality of our civilization and tries to get any kind of clear, competent evidence concerning the substratum of right thinking and well-doing which he knows must have been here, he will have a devil of a time finding it. When he has assembled all he can get and has made even a minimum allowance for speciousness, vagueness, and confusion of motive, he will sadly acknowledge that his net result is simply nothing. A Remnant were here, building a substratum, like coral insects—so much he knows—but he will find nothing to put him on the track of who and where and how many they were, and what their work was like.

Concerning all this, too, the prophet of the present knows precisely as much and as little as the historian of the future; and that, I repeat, is what makes his job seem to me so profoundly interesting. One of the most suggestive episodes recounted in the Bible is that of a prophet's attempt—the only attempt of the kind on record, I believe—to count up the Remnant. Elijah had fled from persecution into the desert, where the Lord presently overhauled him and asked what he was doing so far away from his job. He said that he was running away, not because he was a coward, but because all the Remnant had been killed off except himself. He had got away only by the skin of his teeth, and, he being now all the Remnant there was, if he were killed the True Faith would go flat. The Lord replied that he need not worry about that, for even without him the True Faith could probably manage to squeeze along somehow, if it had to; "and as for your figures on the Remnant," He said, "I don't mind telling you that there are seven thousand of them back there in Israel whom it seems you have not heard of, but you may take My word for it that there they are."

At that time probably the population of Israel could not have run to much more than a million or so; and a Remnant of seven thousand out of a million is a highly encouraging percentage for any prophet. With seven thousand of the boys on his side, there was no great reason for Elijah to feel lonesome; and incidentally that would be something for the modern prophet of the Remnant to think of when he has a touch of the blues. But the main point is that if Elijah the Prophet could not make a closer guess on the number of the Remnant than he made when he missed it by seven thousand, anyone else who tackled the problem would only waste his time.

The other certainty which the prophet of the Remnant may always have is that the Remnant will find him. He may rely on that with absolute assurance. They will find him without his doing anything about it; in fact, if he tries to do anything about it, he is pretty sure to put them off. He does not need to advertise for them, or resort to any schemes of publicity to get their attention. If he is a preacher or a public speaker, for example, he may be quite indifferent to going on show at receptions, getting his picture printed in the newspapers, or furnishing autobiographical material for publication on the side of "human interest." If a writer, he need not make a point of attending any pink teas, autographing books at wholesale, or entering into any specious free-masonry with reviewers. All this and much more of the same order lies in the regular and necessary routine laid down for the prophet of the masses; it is, and must be, part of the great general technique of getting the mass-man's ear—or as our vigorous and excellent publicist, Mr. H. L. Mencken, puts it, the technique of boob-bumping. The prophet of the Remnant is not bound to this technique. He may be quite sure that the Remnant will make their own way to him without any adventitious aids; and not only so, but if they find him employing such aids, as I said, it is ten to one that they will smell a rat in them and will sheer off.

The certainty that the Remnant will find him, however, leaves the prophet as much in the dark as ever, as helpless as ever in the matter of putting any estimate of any kind upon the Remnant, for, as appears in the case of Elijah, he remains ignorant of who they are that have found him, or where they are, or how many. They do not write in and tell him about it, after the manner of those who admire the vedettes of Hollywood nor yet do they seek him out and attach themselves to his person. They are not that kind. They take his message much as drivers take the directions on a roadside signboard; that is, with very little thought about the signboard, beyond being gratefully glad that it happened to be there, but with very serious thought about the directions.

This impersonal attitude of the Remnant wonderfully enhances the interest of the imaginative prophet's job. Once in a while, just about often enough to keep his intellectual curiosity in good working order, he will quite accidentally come upon some distinct reflection of his own message in an unsuspected quarter; and this enables him to entertain himself in his leisure moments with agreeable speculations about the course his message may have taken in reaching that particular quarter, and about what came of it after it got there. Most interesting of all are those instances, if one could only run them down (but one may always speculate about them), where the recipient himself no longer knows where or when or from whom he got the message; or even where, as sometimes happens, he has forgotten that he got it anywhere, and imagines that it is all a self-sprung idea of his own.

Such instances as these are probably not infrequent, for, without presuming to enroll ourselves among the Remnant, we can all no doubt remember having found ourselves suddenly under the influence of an idea, the source of which we can not possibly identify. "It came to us afterward," as we say; that is, we are aware of it only after it has shot up full-grown in our minds, leaving us quite ignorant of how and when and by what agency it was planted there and left to germinate. It seems highly probable that the prophet's message often takes some such course with the Remnant.

If, for example, you are a writer or a speaker or a preacher, you put forth an idea which lodges in the *Unbewusstsein* of a casual member of the Remnant, and sticks fast there. For some time it is inert; then it begins to fret and fester until presently it invades the man's conscious mind and, as one might say, corrupts it. Meanwhile he has quite forgotten how he came by the idea in the first instance, and even perhaps thinks he has invented it; and in those circumstances the most interesting thing of all is that you never know what the pressure of that idea will make him do.

For these reasons it appears to me that Isaiah's job is not only good but also extremely interesting; and especially so at the present time when nobody is doing it. If I were young and had the notion of embarking in the prophetical line, I would certainly take up this branch of the business; and therefore I have no hesitation about recommending it as a career for anyone in that position. It offers an open field, with no competition; our civilization so completely neglects and disallows the Remnant that anyone going in with an eye single to their service might pretty well count on getting all the trade there is.

Even assuming that there is some social salvage to be screened out of the masses, even assuming that the testimony of history to their social value is a little too sweeping, that it depresses hopelessness a little too far, one must yet perceive, I think, that the masses have prophets enough and to spare. Even admitting in the teeth of history that hope of the human race may not be quite exclusively centred in the Remnant, one must perceive that they have social value enough to entitle them to some measure of prophetic encouragement and consolation, and that our civilization allows them none whatever. Every prophetic voice is addressed to the masses, and to them alone; the voice of the pulpit, the voice of education, the voice of politics, of literature, drama, journalism—all these are directed towards the masses exclusively, and they marshal the masses in the way that they are going.

One might suggest, therefore, that aspiring prophetical talent may well turn to another field. *Sat patriæ Priamoque datum*—whatever obligation of the kind may be due the masses is already monstrously overpaid. So long as the masses are taking up the tabernacle of Moloch and Chiun, their images, and following the star of their god Buncombe, they will have no lack of prophets to point the way that leadeth to the More Abundant Life; and hence a few of those who feel the prophetic afflatus might do better to apply themselves to serving the Remnant. It is a good job, an interesting job, much more interesting than serving the masses; and moreover it is the only job in our whole civilization, as far as I know, that offers a virgin field.

This is one of Nock's most famous essays. It was originally published in the June 1936 issue of the *Atlantic Monthly* and was subsequently reprinted in *Free Speech and Plain Language*.

IV. THE HUMANE LIFE

Of all things that human beings fear (and they are a timorous race) the one that strikes them with abject and utterly demoralizing terror is freedom. They are so afraid of it for other people that almost simultaneously they come to dread it for themselves. . . . They are willing to go to the most fantastic lengths in restriction and repression; but the one thing that they never yet have shown the courage to try is simple freedom, which some day they will have the happy surprise of discovering to be the only thing that really works.

—"Miscellany," the *Freeman*, October 3, 1923

What We All Stand For

---

*The Significance of the Behavior of a Community
Toward Its Citizens Who Burned a Man Alive*

On Sunday evening, August 13, 1911, at the hour when churches dismiss their congregations, a human being named Zack Walker was taken by violence out of the hospital at Coatesville, Pennsylvania, where he lay chained to an iron bedstead, in the custody of the law, suffering from a shot-wound, apparently self-inflicted.

The bedstead was broken in half, and the man, still chained to the lower half, was dragged half a mile along the ground, thrown upon a pile of wood, drenched with oil, and burned alive.

Other human beings to the number of several hundred looked on in approval. When Walker with superhuman strength burst his bonds and tried to escape, they drove him back into the flames with pitchforks and fence-rails, and held him there until his body was burned to ashes. Those who could get fragments of his charred bones took them off as souvenirs.

All this happened because the day before, the 12th, Walker had shot and killed a human being named Rice, a private policeman at the steel-mills. Rice was not shot in the discharge of his duty. He was off duty, and perhaps a quarter of a mile off his premises, his beat. He was on the outskirts of the horrible region called Murderers' Gulch, where the negro mill-hands live. Walker lived, if one calls it living, in a hovel there. Perhaps Walker killed Rice in self-defense. He claimed this, at any rate, in a confession which he made after being captured next day. Whether he told the truth or not will never be known. There were no witnesses.

However, he was burned alive. Why was it done? There was no fear of his cheating the law. Nowhere in the United States could a negro cheat the law for such an offense committed against a white man— unless, possibly, he were a very rich negro, and Zack Walker was miserably poor. The citizens of Coatesville had no fear for the "majesty of the law," whatever that is. It was perfectly safe. No one even thought of it.

Nor were they roused to frenzy by a crime committed against a leading citizen. Rice was far from being a popular idol. He was an obscure person, almost as obscure as Walker himself, not distinguished by anything that would make his life in any sense a public property. In mind and morals he seems to have been about the usual run of man one finds discharging the doubtful function of private policeman for the owners of an industrial plant.

Nor again—and this is worth particular notice—did the crime arise from race-hatred. There is no feverish and sensitive traditional race-feeling in Coatesville which might have brought forth this lynching out of whole cloth, as it does occasionally in some parts of the South. Coatesville is a Northern town. What traditions it has are those of Quakerdom. There is the current accepted commonplace, of course, that the negro is an inferior race—but, dear me, that is everywhere! People have said to me, "Well, but might not this same thing have happened to a Hungarian or Slav laborer, under the same circumstances?" Certainly it might; but it was just a *little more* likely to happen to a negro. Just as when, for instance, a negro boy and a white boy start out under equivalent conditions to look for work in New York, Boston, Detroit, Minneapolis, or Seattle, the negro boy is a *little less* likely to land a job than the white boy. This *little more* and *little less* measure the limit of race-prejudice in Coatesville as elsewhere in the North.

Finally, the lynching of Walker was not hatched out of deliberate and cold-blooded wickedness. It had been premeditated, no doubt, but almost certainly not in the spirit that most of us would suspect. Telephone-messages went out of Coatesville the day before, bearing invitations to the lynching if the man were caught. Telegrams were sent to certain papers in New York and Philadelphia, asking how many words they would run in a lynching-story. But no archdevil with a cool and scheming brain sat up in his office plotting the thing out and apportioning the details around among his minor devilry. No one organized a set scheme of crime for purposes of his own. The crime was without purpose and without fruit. It served no one, appeased no one, consoled no one. It accomplished nothing that process of law was not altogether certain to accomplish better.

If the lynching had been due to any of these causes, this magazine would not publish the story. This magazine is interested in *civilization*— the humanizing of men in society—and we publish this story because through it we are able to present a clear picture of a kind of community life that by many, in spite of repeated warnings, is still thought to have the elements of civilization in it. It neither has them nor can have them. Where life is lived and industry carried forward on the conditions that prevail in Coatesville—and that means nearly all our industrial towns and cities—civilization is wholly impossible. Wealth there may be, and luxury, and all the apparatus of civilization, but civilization itself cannot be had on those terms.

And as our first exhibit we call attention to the fact that the idea of lynching Walker sprang, one may say, out of mere idleness. The people of Coatesville burned Walker in a spirit hardly different from that you see in a crew of gutter-bred youngsters who torture a dog to death— from no deep ground of hatred of the dog or his kind, but more than anything because their ordinary life is lived on a plane where such acts are not seen to be wholly alien, unnatural, and frightful. It was a crime of callousness, of sheer indifference to human distress and pain.

Let us follow the outlines of the story. The whole press of the United States broke forth in a chorus of indignant execration. Governor Tener issued a proclamation. Drinking-places in Coatesville were immediately closed by the authorities, fearing (what irony!) an outbreak of the negroes! The State constabulary was called out, and the quiet streets of Coatesville they patrolled on horseback, with dragoon revolvers at their hand. It was a ludicrous sight; for the negroes made no trouble, gave no intimation of making any, had not the faintest idea of making any. The original mob of whites, too, had melted away in a few moments. As soon as their horrible and savage sport was over, they dispersed at once and went about their business.

Half a dozen arrests were made within a week; all of them very obscure, poor people, some of them boys. Not one of the instigators was apprehended, nor one of the ringleaders.

Under a very vigorous and sweeping charge from Judge Butler the grand jury found some true bills. Mr. Cunningham, the assistant attorney-general, came down from Harrisburg to assist the district-attorney, Mr. Gawthrop. Application was made for a change of venue, to have the trials take place in some other part of the State, before a non-local jury. The Supreme Court of Pennsylvania refused the request. No reason was assigned.

The cases were promptly brought to trial at West Chester, the county seat of Chester County, where Coatesville is. The trial jury brought in a verdict of *not guilty* in each and every case, and the prosecution collapsed. The prisoners received an ovation from such of the Coatesville populace as went to West Chester to attend the trials, and again on their return to Coatesville from the stay-at-homes who came to the station to meet them.

Pinkerton's detectives were put on the case to ferret out the ringleaders, but their work came to nothing. The State police looked into the matter also, but their principal operative, Mr. Cady, died under mysterious circumstances while still at work, and his evidence also mysteriously disappeared. It is supposed to have been sent to Harrisburg, but of this nothing is known.

Thus it was shown that in the year 1911, in Pennsylvania, in the heart of a Quaker settlement, there could be committed as atrocious, idle, and purposeless a crime as ever was committed in the world—a human being burned to death merely to make a hoodlum holiday—and its perpetrators escape scot-free.

When the prosecution failed and the State and local authorities withdrew their agents, the American Association for the Advancement of Colored People quietly entered the field. If the issue of civilization is finally enforced upon Coatesville and the State of Pennsylvania, the credit will belong to this noble society. I am glad of the opportunity to praise them. With inadequate means, lukewarm support, and with most avenues of publicity closed to them, these people have given themselves to the most unpopular cause in the world, yet one which is obviously fundamental to civilization—equality of opportunity for a great, unprivileged, overborne, unhappy section of our people. As long as *any* are victims of inequality, as long as *any* are exploited or dispossessed, there can be no civilization—and this means negro human beings as well as white.

The Association for the Advancement of Colored People employed William J. Burns to put his operatives into Coatesville. This took place in the summer of 1912. In September the chairman of the society, Mr. Oswald Garrison Villard, its attorney, Mr. Wherry, and the writer of this article, accompanied Mr. Burns to Harrisburg and laid the results of the investigation before Governor Tener.

The Governor's attitude was all that could be desired. He was well-informed about the case, fair, candid, and interested. He said plainly that he regarded the Coatesville affair as "one of the failures of the administration." He discussed the most intimate aspects of the case, the reach of Chester County politics, the stress of influential friendships, and all the suspected reasons for the paralysis of statutory justice, in the frankest way. He listened to the advice of Mr. Burns, promised that the case should be reopened at once, and carried through to a summary end, "let the chips fall where they would." He expressed complete agreement with Mr. Burns as to the proper methods to pursue.

Now after these external facts of history, let me give a few inside facts of a plainer and simpler kind—if any could be simpler.

There has never been a time since the lynching of Zack Walker, nor is there now, when a good detective would have any trouble worth talking about in laying hands on the instigators and ringleaders of that crime, or in getting sound evidence against them. The local police force in Coatesville could have had them within fifteen minutes—could have had them, in fact, before the crime was committed. They can get them now. Let alone a detective, a good lively newspaper man could go to Coatesville and get them inside of ten days. Everyone knows this: it is a matter of open and notorious fact. Governor Tener knows it; the State and county authorities know it.

There is no doubt about it. *But what good would it do?*

People are largely addicted to a number of curious delusions about statutory law, one of which is that it works by some kind of natural inherent force residing in itself. Really, it does nothing of the kind. Samuel M. Jones of Golden Rule fame, one of the wisest as well as best of men, said that law means anything the people will back up. It means precisely that. Also, anything the people will not back up is not law, however clearly it is laid down on the statute-books, and cannot be enforced. And here is the reason of the great "failure of justice," as the popular term goes, following the Coatesville lynching. Freely concede that the whole prosecuting force, from the Governor down, was in deadly earnest and did the very best they could—why not? The matter of their sincerity, important when taken by itself, becomes in the larger view almost immaterial. Whatever they did or however they did it, the indisputable fact is that in proposing to enforce the elemental statutory law against murder—murder unprovoked, inexcusable, and peculiarly and indescribably fiendish—they were proposing something that *the people would not and will not back up.*

Why, look at it! The first case tried was on a *confession*—a confession of complicity, under the charge of Judge Butler to the grand jury, whereby he instructed them that every person abetting the act with his presence and assent was legally guilty of murder—and the verdict of the trial jury was *not guilty.* Material witnesses left Coatesville with more money than they had ever seen in a lump sum in the whole course of their lives. No attempt was made to detain them before they left or reach them after they had gone. It is perfectly well known where they went and where they are now.

The case of the police officer Howe failed even to come to trial. He was in charge of the prisoner Walker at the hospital, on guard with a loaded revolver. He made no resistance, fired not a shot—this, too, in face of the fact that only one man at a time could enter the room. Howe was not removed from the force—he was suspended for a few days, but no more. The chief of police, Umstead, *while under indictment for manslaughter,* stood for reappointment, and won. There is no need to say more—one can make a clear enough inference about the direction of public opinion from the items given.

But we are not commenting on this technical "failure of justice," for we are not interested in obtaining convictions or in seeing that the majesty of the law is vindicated—whatever that grandiose term amounts to. So far from believing that if you can only get enough people in jail or on the gallows, everybody will be moral and happy, we seem to see that murder, brutality, violence, and hatred mean about the same thing inside the law as outside, and have about the same effects when administered by law as when administered against the law. Our interest lies in *reasons,* in *causes.* Surely, if any statutory law has a moral sanction, it is the elemental law against murder. Why do the people of Coatesville nullify it? What are the reasons for public opinion remaining at such an appallingly low level?

They are not far to seek. One may see them from the car-windows before one leaves the train at the Coatesville station. Coatesville is typically one of those industrial towns that William Cobbett called *Hell-holes*. It is a perfect miniature model of an American industrial city, so small that you can take it in at a glance, and so accurately drawn to scale that not an essential part is missing or a non-essential feature added. That is why it is such a superb model, the best I have ever seen, for social study. The smaller industrial towns of Massachusetts and Rhode Island I have observed to be much the same. There is great advantage in getting small accurate models of great subjects before one's eyes. Let the most ardent stand-pat protectionist, for instance, sit one forenoon through by the gates of some French town and watch a community trying to tax itself rich by the operation of the *octroi,* or import tax, as the old women bring in their chickens and butter and their handful of eggs. Let Mr. Taft himself do this, and I warrant he will go away a free-trader, because he can *see* the incidence of that tax upon the home consumer as no one can see it when levied at the ports of a great nation. So to see at a glance the whole cross-section of our industrial system, and to see how its works and ways bear upon civilization, one may find one's best model in Coatesville.

Civilization can only be had upon its own terms; and first of these is a diffused, material well-being. Next (if, indeed, it is not rather a part or adjunct of the first) is the thing one observes with such delight in France and Italy—a homogeneous population. Now the distinguishing feature of our *Hell-holes,* our American industrial centers, is the entire absence of these. At Coatesville material well-being is strictly concentrated, and the three several strata of society stand as distinct as layers in a jelly cake. Coatesville has about twelve thousand population. The immense stratum of the exploited is composed of three thousand negroes and thirty-five hundred "foreigners"—in Coatesville the term is applied to human beings who come there from Hungary and the Slavic countries to work for $1.38 per day, and live most wretchedly. All these work in the two great iron and steel-plate mills—the Worth plant and the Lukens plant. Their wages, their conditions of work and

living, preclude either happiness or decency. It is an interesting fact
that while the Lukens mill has been here one hundred and twelve
years, as late as 1900 there were only five "foreigners" in Coatesville.
There are thirty-five hundred now. The "protected American workman"
might note this coincidence if he likes, dating as it does from the palmy
McKinley-Hanna days down through the uplifting administration of
Mr. Roosevelt to the Payne-Aldrich-Taft comedy.

Above the stratum of the exploited is another, a smug, close-mouthed,
unintelligent middle stratum that gets its living out of the town, by
trading and in other ways. This class is characterized by an extreme
apprehensiveness about anything that will "hurt business" or "hurt the
town." Immediately after the lynching this class began to agonize over
the prospect of publicity, just as the same class in Pittsburgh became
hysterical over "the good name of Pittsburgh" when the press began to
air the scandal of councilmanic graft a couple of years ago. Why, it is
almost laughable to see the distrust that members of this class show
toward each other when the lynching is mentioned! It is a tabooed
subject, a thing to be hushed up at all costs. Paraphrasing Sydney
Smith's remark, this class (I hope no one will imagine me ignorant that
there are honorable exceptions) would cheerfully bear any burden of
infamy, however great, rather than any odium of publicity, however
slight.

Above this is the stratum of the exploiting class. It is very small. I
gladly put to its credit the one long mark that it is a resident class. The
mill-owners do not, as in Lawrence, Massachusetts, for example, live
off the scene of their exploitation. The steel-mills are family concerns,
not in the trust, and the owners have made immense fortunes. The
owners are Quakers. I am told that they will not manufacture armor
for battle-ships nor sell their products for any purpose connected
with war. But they pay their laborers less, on the average, than two
dollars a day, and permit or promote for them conditions of living
worse than one can find in the countries from which the "foreigners"
have emigrated.

*"An upper class materialized, a middle class vulgarized, a lower class
brutalized."* There you have precisely the cross-section of Coatesville,
as of Lawrence, Pittsburgh, Pawtucket, Providence, Fall River, all our
myriad *Hell-holes*—nay, you have the cross-section of whole common-

wealths, for from the standpoint of civilization what is Pennsylvania but a magnified Coatesville or Massachusetts but a projection of Fall River? There is no diffused material well-being in either State. There is nothing like a homogeneous people in either State. So if we stop measuring the civilization of a community by its balances of trade, or the number of its newspapers, population, miles of railway, banks, finance companies, manufactured products, and the like, and measure it by the simple tests we have applied to Coatesville, we find that Pennsylvania is not a civilized community, that Massachusetts is not a civilized community.

This conclusion is accurate and sufficient. It modifies our conception of such horrible happenings as the Coatesville *auto da fé*. The lynching of Zack Walker was a frightful tragedy; but let us never forget that it was only a *registration*. It was as much a *registration* of the industrial progress of the United States as the consular reports, or the balance-sheet of an industrial corporation. We do not want to interfere with Governor Tener in his attempt to "uphold the majesty of the law"— we are merely not interested. Plenty of people there will be without us to enthuse over a few convictions—if anybody is ever convicted— and to imagine that society has somehow greatly redeemed and purified itself by a few hangings, a few imprisonments. But we cannot give our interest to so suspiciously short and easy a method with so great a problem. Hanging the murderers of Zack Walker seems to us like smashing the thermometer that has registered an unpleasant temperature. Smash the thermometer by all means, if one gets any comfort out of it; but the weather will be just as hot. Hang the lynchers of Zack Walker by all means, if one has any appetite for mere vengeance; but we wish to point out that nothing has been done for civilization as long as we leave untouched an industrial system that keeps on producing *an upper class materialized, a middle class vulgarized, a lower class brutalized.*

The lynching was a frightful crime, but it is over, it is past remedy. The warning remains—a warning to examine carefully the ground of our industrial life, the life which has made our immense fortunes and our immense poverty and misery, made our millionaires, made our obstinate inequalities, made our *Hell-holes;* and instead of giving us civilization, a homogeneous people, progressing toward a harmonious and general perfection, issues only in *an upper class materialized, a middle class vulgarized, a lower class brutalized.*

This essay appeared in the February 1913 issue of the *American Magazine* during the time Nock was a staff member.

Prohibition and Civilization

Prohibition, as a policy, has had a great deal of public attention, but the kind of civilization connoted by prohibition has had very little. This is unfortunate, because the general civilization of a community is the thing that really recommends it. The important thing to know about Kansas, for instance, is not the statistics of prohibition—as most writers on the subject seem to think—but whether one would really want to live there, whether the peculiar type of civilization that expresses itself through prohibition is really attractive and interesting.

The Reverend Floyd Keeler, for example, writing in the July *Atlantic,* devotes a whole article to proving that, in Kansas, prohibition does prohibit, within limits. This is not without interest, of course; still, it would seem much more interesting and truly practical to tell us what life is like under a general social theory of negation and repression: for such is what life in Kansas comes to. That, after all, is the determining test. Burke says—and I earnestly commend his words to the advocates of our grand new policy of Americanization, whatever that means: "There ought to be in every country a standard of manners that a well-formed mind would be disposed to relish. *For us to love our country, our country ought to be lovely.*" No one can fail to remark, in the present war, the immensely superior spirit of the French in defense of a truly lovely civilization. The final test, indeed, of any civilization—the test by which ultimately it stands or falls—is its power of attracting and permanently interesting the human spirit.

Concerning Kansas, therefore, the question is not whether prohibition prohibits, but whether, under prohibition, the general civilization is such as "a well-formed mind would be disposed to relish." Kansas, as I showed in my former paper, is essentially Puritan: and the secret of Puritanism's downfall was in its failure to meet this test. An English critic of Puritanism gives a vivid example of the precise line of criticism by bidding us imagine Shakespeare and Virgil coming over on the *Mayflower,* and think what intolerably bad company they would have found the Pilgrim Fathers! William James was probably as distinguished a lover of the humane life as America ever produced; and we all

remember with amusement his naïve cry of relief at leaving the vapid
and orderly perfections of Chautauqua, that vast playground of middle-
class Puritanism. Well, similarly, one has but to imagine some disinterested lover of human perfection like William James making a candid
examination of the civilization of Kansas, and one knows at once what
the verdict would be. It is beside the point to say that Kansans would
not agree to this verdict; that Governor Capper, who "really knows
Kansas," would repudiate it; that Mr. William Allen White would treat
it lightly and Mr. Walt Mason make a jingle about it. There is a standard
set for such matters by the best reason and judgment of mankind; and
in any disinterested estimate of a civilization, a verdict of William James
would be apt to come nearer the mark of general human experience
than one of Governor Capper or Mr. Mason, or even, probably—though
I do not like to think so—than one of the accomplished Mr. White.

By far the greater part of the power and permanence of a civilization
resides in its charm. It is surely noticeable, for instance, that wherever
French civilization once strikes root, it remains forever. The border
provinces, the Province of Quebec and our own State of Louisiana, are
as obstinately and unchangeably French as ever they were. The reason
is that French civilization satisfied the human instinct for what is
amiable, graceful and becoming, and men cleave to it. It appeals to
them as something lovely and desirable, rather than as something
merely rational and well-ordered, which is the chief appeal of the
German type. Under the State Socialism of Germany one is continually
confronted with the social relations and consequences of practically
every move one makes. The principle of prohibition is extended to
cover an endless range of conduct (though, significantly, drink is
exempt). The home scheme of social life is ordered with excellent and
obvious rationality, but it is devoid of charm, it has no savor, and all
its reasonableness cannot make up for the deficiency, cannot make the
normal spirit really enjoy it. One feels the same restlessness and
perverseness under it that William James declared he felt under the
régime at Chautauqua. One doubts whether such smooth-running social
order is worth having at the price. I remember some years ago, after a
long time spent in observing the ghastly perfections of German municipal
machinery, I came home ready to rejoice in the most corrupt, ring-
ridden and disreputable city government that I could find in America,

if only I might draw a free breath once more and forget the infinity of things that are *verboten*.

Such is the universal perversity of human nature, and it is something to be reckoned with. In my mind, it has always been the one insuperable objection to Socialism. The Socialists are at a loss to see why we do not all fall in at once with their orderly and rational scheme, just as Mr. Keeler, speaking in the *Atlantic* for the people of Kansas, wonders why we do not all fall in with prohibition. The answer is the same in both cases. Men look at the essentially Socialistic civilization and the essentially Puritan civilization, give them due credit, acknowledge their virtues, and then pass them by. Nay, further: we look at the type of people produced by these civilizations, we consider them attentively, and then make up our minds quite firmly that no amount of social benefit would be worth having if we had to become like them in order to get it.

The civilization of Socialism, however, is rational. It has that sound merit, just as civilization of one Latin type has the merit of beauty and amiability. But Puritan civilization has neither. It has all the flat hideousness of Socialism, without the rationality which Socialism has managed to redeem by its contact with great world-currents of thought. Puritanism is essentially a hole-and-corner affair, with its arid provincialism untempered by contact of any kind. Its ideals are grotesque and whimsical; its methods are unintelligent—the methods of dragooning. Mr. Keeler must forgive my plain speaking; it comes of a sincere desire to resolve his doubts about the sanity or integrity of the brute mass of us who look unmoved on the progress of prohibition in Kansas. We cannot accept prohibition without accepting the civilization that goes with it, for prohibition cannot stand on any other soil. To get even the attenuated benefit of prohibition in Kansas, our community-life must become more or less like that of Kansas, and we ourselves more or less like Kansans; and this is wholly impossible and unthinkable.

Indeed, it is from precisely this condition that the general spirit of America is struggling to emerge. The original implantation of Puritanism, with all its crudeness and rawness and lack of imagination, for a long time dominated our life and narrowed our ideals. But its influence is rapidly passing away. As evidence of this, it is most encouraging to note the disappearance of the old unintelligent forms of partisanship and sectarianism, and the steady fixture of the right of final private

judgment upon public affairs. Our institutions have become more
rational, flexible and responsive, and our methods more enlightened.
Even in our prison and police methods we have already swung a long
way from the Puritan theory of punishment towards the more civilized
theory of reclamation.

Along with these changes there has come the perception that society
should leave to each person an ever-increasing maximum portion of
his own life to regulate for himself. This is not only true with reference
to organized or statutory interference, but with reference to the arbitrary
and unreasoning pressure of public opinion. The Puritan theory of "thy
brother's keeper" has been largely disallowed. We scarcely realize the
extent of these wholesome changes in our social life until our attention
is called to them by some recrudescence of the Puritan spirit. Not long
ago, for instance, the Superintendent of Police in Chicago swore in half
a dozen policewomen to suppress what Mr. Howells once called "public
billing and cooing" in the parks. Some members of the Virginia legislature
put in a bill to ban the short skirt and low-cut waist. The time was, not
more than twenty-five or thirty years ago, when whimsies and antics
like these on the part of public officials went almost unquestioned—
when our theory of public office was practically that of a New England
village beadle in Colonial times. Now, however, they appear to us as
morbid and silly extravagance, carrying their own sufficient condemna-
tion in their sheer absurdity. And yet it is well worth while to note such
happenings, because they indicate the temper of Puritanism so clearly,
and show the length of nonsensical hypocrisy to which it is ready to go.

The advocates of prohibition ought to get a clear grasp of the fundamental objection to their theory, and meet it with something more
substantial than feeble talk about the influence of "the liquor interests."
Our objection is to Puritanism, with its false social theory taking shape
in a civilization that, however well-ordered and economically prosperous, is hideous and suffocating. One can at least speak for oneself: I
am an absolute teetotaler, and it would make no difference to me if
there were never another drop of liquor in the world; and yet to live
under any régime of prohibition that I have so far had opportunity to
observe would seem to me an appalling calamity. The ideals and instruments of Puritanism are simply unworthy of a free people, and, being
unworthy, are soon found intolerable. Its hatreds, fanaticisms, inacces-
sibility to ideas; its inflamed and cancerous interest in the personal con-

duct of others; its hysterical disregard of personal rights; its pure faith in force, and above all, its tyrannical imposition of its own *Kultur:* these characterize and animate a civilization that the general experience of mankind at once condemns as impossible, and as hateful as it is impossible.

The drink problem is, as I said in my former paper in the Review, by no means a problem of the first order, and it is perfectly open to a solution that is rational and consistent with a type of civilization appropriate to this country. It can be solved by a process analogous to the "Safety First" movement directed against the far more important problem of industrial accidents, or like the movement for a "safe and sane" Fourth of July. These reforms were effected in perfectly cool temper, without any rampant orgy of law-making, and without involving any reflection on either our national dignity or intelligence. Contrast them, for instance, with our ill-considered and ineffectual handling of the problem of the white slave traffic, resulting in the stupidities of the Mann Act—the most efficient agent of blackmail, probably, that any Government ever devised. There is no reason why the United States might not become a sufficiently temperate nation without the sacrifices required by prohibition.

Why might not some State, for instance, make a simple experiment in differential taxation; and with that, why might not some community take up the problem of retail distribution—the saloon problem—with seriousness and commonsense, providing such a type of resort as exists everywhere on the Continent and is being introduced in England? Such a policy as this is constructive, not negative, and, when laid down, is done with once for all. A graded tax bearing very heavily on high alcoholic content, and a method of retail distribution modelled after the Public-House Trust: if any State should make this constructive experiment, it would be interesting to compare the results with those that are to be observed in Kansas or in any other State that has embarked on a course of prohibition.

This essay was the second of two articles ostensibly on prohibition that Nock wrote for the *North American Review.* It is a fine, early example of Nock's constant interest in what is necessary for real civilization. It appeared in the September 1916 issue.

Our Pastors and Masters

The first year of national prohibition has gone by, and the practical consequences of the Eighteenth Amendment and the Volstead Act are about what the judicious foresaw they would be. Such benefits as have accrued to the country are those which the most determined opponents of sumptuary legislation would have cheerfully conceded before the fact. The question now is only whether they are worth having at the price. No one pretends, probably, that in those sections of the country where public opinion is unfavourable, the law is well obeyed or well enforced; and this is not good for law in general. If law in a democracy is "whatever the people will back up"—which we think is one of the best definitions of law that we ever met—then obviously no very healthy respect for law can be bred by the cynicism which creates statutes known to be unenforceable. But we have recently spoken in some detail of this aspect of sumptuary legislation, and mention it now only to wonder at the curious inconsistency which rallies so many of the self-styled friends of law and order to the support of sumptuary law. If they were true friends or wise friends, one would think that they might be more jealous of the general respect for law, and dislike to see it frittered away in mere cynical and hypocritical levity.

Our own great objection to prohibition, however, has never been nearly as much to prohibition itself as to the civilization that goes with it. Prohibition's chief interest, we think, is only as the index to what manner of spirit we, as a nation, are of. A civilization which is ever striving after a more and more highly organized interest in personal conduct, is not a happy civilization to live in, even for one whose personal conduct is wholly blameless. We think that some of our liberal friends who advocated prohibition, or at least did not resent it, may perhaps have overlooked this. The teetotaller finds, quite as much as the drinker, that the hardness and dullness of our civilization, never over-gracious or over-amiable, its tedium and ennui, have of late greatly increased; and he can easily perceive that this is not because of prohibition itself, but because of the sudden and immense predominance of the spirit which has among many others, one outward and visible expression in prohibition. Prohibition in itself makes but little one way or another; but as a registration of that spirit, it is discouraging and benumbing.

It is natural that we as a people should be apt to mind one another's business and enjoy regulating one another's conduct. Our history furnishes several good reasons for this, and we have in recent issues gone somewhat into the more obscure and powerful of them. To speak of them compendiously *en passant,* however, perhaps we can not do better than resort to our old device of dramatization, and say that the commercial life of our nation was shaped by Gradgrind, our religious life by Chadband, our social and public life on its lighter side by Quinion, and on its more serious side by Pecksniff. These four worthies have fixed our ideals in all those departments of life; and they have exercised an iron control over our education, over our secondary schools, colleges and universities, and over the institutional voices of our society, such as the press, the theatre and the pulpit. Now, these four old friends of ours have a constitutional horror of human freedom. The natural human aspiration for freedom is to them something irregular and vicious; and even worse and more perverted is the notion that human beings should find happiness in freedom. Therefore when anyone has come forward to erect this aspiration into a philosophy of conduct and to preach that philosophy, and justify it by the happiness which ensues upon its practice, they regard him as a dangerous enemy of the race. Under these circumstances it is, as we say, natural that as a people we should be exceedingly suspicious and distrustful of freedom and instinctively move to repress it when we can. It is also natural for every one to make a great virtue of his own training and tenets; and we can all find an easy and profitable opportunity to do that by keeping a good sharp eye on our neighbours and seeing to it that they walk as closely as possible to the line which Gradgrind, Chadband, Quinion and Pecksniff have marked out as the proper one for all humanity to walk by. During the war this opportunity was enormously enlarged; one could put in almost all one's time in the assiduous practice of this virtue; and it is due, we think, to this unwonted exercise—of which national prohibition was but a single practical outcome—that the tone and temper of American life has so remarkably changed in respect of its general amenity and interest.

For the one trouble with any civilization dominated wholly by our

four old friends, is that it is not *interesting;* it does not permanently
satisfy the human spirit. The human race has an indefeasible love for
what is graceful, amiable and becoming, and is somehow aware that
those qualities can flourish only under freedom. Hence its restlessness,
irritability, its rather conventional and outright hypocrisy under the
dragooning of our four old friends. We are all more or less like young
Tom Gradgrand and his sister Louisa; in spite of all the counter-
attractions of Coketown's life, in spite of the best schooling that
McChoakumchild can give, in spite of the moving and ever-present
example of Josiah Bounderby, our perverse hearts will wander off in
scandalous dalliance with Sleary and the performing dog. Our civilization
offers Gradgrind's old cure for these vagrant instincts after freedom:
namely, more and stricter legislation; more objects to be proscribed;
more ways of life to be closed or straitened; more unhappiness and
unloveliness to be deliberately cultivated; and the end of all this, and
the end of the innumerable Toms and Louisas too, alas!—will be what
they must be.

Unless, indeed, we all resolutely turn our backs upon our four sturdy
old monitors, realizing that the forces of nature are on our side and
not on theirs, that the instincts for freedom, for beauty, for a graceful
and amiable social life, are true primary instincts and that our business
is to follow them. Whisky, tobacco, cards, dancing, one or another
mode of Sunday observance—these do not in themselves much matter.
It does not in itself greatly matter that a Boston sculptor was the other
day haled before the judgment-seat and fined ten dollars for working
at his art on Sunday. It does not in itself greatly matter that a business
man of New York was lately yanked out of his office and brought to
book for being at his desk on Sunday. What matters is the permanent
failure in interest, the hardness and hideousness, of a civilization that
makes place for this inflamed concern with personal conduct, that
resents and disallows any just conception of the individual, and tends
constantly to a featureless uniformitarianism. What matters is that, for
life to be truly fruitful, life must be felt as a joy; and that where freedom
is not, there can be no joy; and that where Gradgrind, Chadband,
Quinion and Pecksniff prevail, there can be no freedom. What matters,
in a word, is the heightened and continued ascendancy of Gradgrind,
Chadband, Quinion and Pecksniff in our civilization; and until that

ascendancy be, from first to last, utterly broken down, nothing else matters much, or can matter.

This short unsigned piece appeared in the January 26, 1921, issue of the *Freeman*.

The Decline of Conversation

The more one thinks of it, the more one finds in Goethe's remark that the test of civilization is conversation. The common method of rating the civilization of peoples by what they have got and what they have done is really a poor one; for some peoples who have got much and done a great deal strike one at once as less civilized than others who have got little and done little. Prussia, for example, was relatively a poor State a century ago, while fifteen years ago it was rich and active; yet one would hardly say that the later Prussia was as civilized a country as the Prussia of Frederick's time. Somewhat the same might be said of Tudor England and modern England. The civilization of a country consists in the quality of life that is lived there, and this quality shows plainest in the things that people choose to talk about when they talk together, and in the way they choose to talk about them.

It can be taken for granted, I suppose, that man has certain fundamental instincts which must find some kind of collective expression in the society in which he lives. The first and fundamental one is the instinct of expansion, the instinct for continuous improvement in material well-being and economic security. Then there is the instinct of intellect and knowledge, and instinct of religion and morals, of beauty and poetry, of social life and manners. Man has always been more or less consciously working towards a state of society which should give collective expression to these instincts. If society does not give expression to them, he is dissatisfied and finds life irksome, because every unused or unanswered instinct becomes a source of uneasiness and keeps on nagging and festering within him until he does something about it. Moreover, human society, to be permanently satisfactory, must not only express all these instincts, but must express them all in due balance, proportion, and harmony. If too much stress be laid on any one, the harmony is interrupted, uneasiness and dissatisfaction arise, and, if the interruption persists, disintegration sets in. The fall of nations, the decay and disappearance of whole civilizations, can be finally interpreted in terms of the satisfaction of these instincts. Looking at the life of existing nations, one can put one's finger on those instincts which are being collectively overdone at the expense of the others. In one nation the instinct of expansion and the instinct of intellect and knowledge are relatively over-developed; in another, the instinct of beauty; in another, the instinct of manners; and so on. The term *symphonic,* which is so often sentimentally applied to the ideal life of society, is really descriptive; for the tendency of mankind from the beginning has been towards a functional blending and harmony among these instincts, precisely like that among the choirs of an orchestra. It would seem, then, that the quality of life in any society means the degree of development attained by this tendency. The more of these instincts that are satisfied, and the more delicate the harmony of their interplay, the higher and richer is the quality of life in that society; and it is the lower and poorer according as it satisfies fewer of these instincts and permits disharmony in their interplay.

American life has long been fair game for the observer. Journalistic enterprise now beats up the quarry for the foreigner and brings it in range for him from the moment the ship docks, or even before; and of late the native critic has been lending a brisk hand at the sport. So much, in fact, has been written about the way we live, how we occupy ourselves, how we fill up our leisure, the things we do and leave undone, the things we are likely to do and likely to leave undone, that I for one would never ask for another word on such matters from anybody. As a good American, I try to keep up with what is written about us, but it has become rather a dull business and I probably miss some of it now and then, so I cannot say that no observer has ever made a serious study of our conversation. In all I have read, however, very little has been made of the significance of the things we choose to talk about and our ways of talking about them. Yet I am sure that Goethe's method would give a better measure of our civilization than any other, and that it would pay an observer to look into it. For my own part, ever since I stumbled on Goethe's observation—now more than twenty years ago—I have followed that method in many lands. I have studied conversation more closely than any other social phenomenon, picking up from it all the impressions and inferences I could, and I have always found that I got as good results as did those whose critical apparatus was more elaborate. At least, when I read what these critics say about such people as I know, especially my own, they seem to tell me little with which I was not already acquainted.

Speaking as Bishop Pontoppidan did about the owls in Iceland, the most significant thing that I have noticed about conversation in America is that there is so little of it, and as time goes on there seems less and less of it in my hearing. I miss even so much of the free play of ideas as I used to encounter years ago. It would seem that my countrymen no longer have the ideas and imagination they formerly had, or that they care less for them, or that for some reason they are diffident about them and do not like to bring them out. At all events the exercise of ideas and imagination has become unfashionable. When I first remarked this phenomenon I thought it might be an illusion of advancing age, since I have come to years when the past takes on an unnaturally attractive colour. But as time went on the fact became unmistakable and I began to take notice accordingly.

As I did so a long-buried anecdote arose to the top of my mind and has remained there ever since. I am reminded of it daily. Years ago Brand Whitlock told me the story of an acquaintance of his—something in the retail clothing way—junior partner in a firm whose name I no longer remember, so for convenience we will make acknowledgments to Mr. Montague Glass and call it Maisener and Finkman. Mr. Finkman turned up at the store one Monday morning, full of delight at the wonderful time he had had at his partner's house the evening before— excellent company, interesting conversation, a supreme occasion in every respect. After dinner, he said—and such a dinner!—"we go in the parlor and all the evening until midnight we sit and talk it business."

Day after day strengthens the compulsion to accept Mr. Finkman as a type. This might be thought a delicate matter to press, but after all, Mr. Finkman is no creation of one's fancy, but on the contrary he is a solid and respectable reality, a social phenomenon of the first importance, and he accordingly deserves attention both by the positive side of his preferences and addictions and by the negative side of his distastes. I am farthest in the world from believing that anything should be "done about" Mr. Finkman, or that he should be studied with an ulterior view either to his disparagement or his uplift. I am unequivocally for his right to an unlimited exercise of his likes and dislikes, and his right to get as many people to share them as he can. All I suggest is that the influence of his tastes and distastes upon American civilization should be understood. The moment one looks at the chart of this civilization one sees the line set by Mr. Finkman, and this line is so distinct that one cannot but take it as one's principal lead. If one wishes to get a measure of American civilization, one not only must sooner or later take the measure of Mr. Finkman's predilections, but will save time and trouble by taking it at the outset.

As evidence of the reach of Mr. Finkman's influence on the positive side, I notice that those of my American acquaintance whose interests are not purely commercial show it as much as others. Musicians, writers, painters, and the like seem to be at their best and to entertain themselves best when they "talk it business." In bringing up the other instincts into balance with the instinct of expansion, such persons as these have an advantage, and one would expect to see that advantage reflected in their conversation much more clearly and steadily than it is. Where two or three of them were gathered together, one would look for a considerable play of ideas and imagination, and one would think that the instinct of expansion—since one perforce must give so much attention to it at other times—might gladly be let off on furlough. But I observe that this is seldom the case. For the most part, like Mr. Finkman, these people begin to be surest of themselves, most at ease and interested, at the moment when the instinct of expansion takes charge of conversation and gives it a directly practical turn.

One wonders why this should be so. Why should Mr. Finkman himself, after six days' steady service of the instinct of expansion, be at his best and happiest when he yet "talks it business" on the seventh? It is because he has managed to drive the whole current of his being through the relatively narrow channel set by the instinct of expansion. When he "talks it business," therefore, he gets the exhilarating sense of drive and speed. A millstream might thus think itself of more consequence than a river; probably the Iser feels more importance and exhilaration in its narrow leaping course than the Mississippi in filling all the streams of its delta. By this excessive simplification of existence Mr. Finkman has established the American formula of success. He makes money, but money is his incidental reward; his real reward is in the continuous exhilaration that he gets out of the processes of making it. My friends whose interests are not exclusively commercial feel the authority of the formula and share in the reward of its obedience. My friend A, for example, writes a good novel. His instincts of intellect, beauty, morals, religion, and manners, let us say, all have a hand in it and are satisfied. He makes enough out of it to pay him for writing it, and so his instinct of expansion is satisfied. But he is satisfied, not exhilarated. When, on the other hand, his publisher sells a hundred thousand copies of another novel, he is at once in the American formula of success. The novel may not have much exercised his sense of intellect, beauty, morals, religion, and manners—it may be, in other words, an indifferent novel—but he is nevertheless quite in Mr. Finkman's formula of success and he is correspondingly exhilarated. He has crowded the whole stream of his being into the channel cut by the instinct of expansion, and his sensations correspond to his achievement.

Thus by his positive action in establishing the American formula of success, Mr. Finkman has cut what the Scots call a "monstrous cantle" out of conversation. Conversation depends upon a copiousness of general ideas and an imagination able to marshal them. When one "talks it business," one's ideas may be powerful, but they are special; one's imagination may be vigorous, but its range is small. Hence proceeds the habit of particularizing—usually, too, by way of finding the main conversational staple in personalities. This habit carries over, naturally, into whatever excursions Mr. Finkman's mind is occasionally led to make outside the domain of the instinct of expansion; for his disuse of imagination and general ideas outside this sphere disinclines him to them and makes him unhandy with them. Thus it is that conversation in America, besides its extreme attenuation, presents another phenomenon. On its more serious side it is made up almost entirely of particularization and, on its higher side, of personalities.

These characteristics mark the conversation of children and, therefore, may be held to indicate an extremely immature civilization. The other day a jovial acquaintance who goes out to dinner a good deal told me a story that brings out this point. It seems he had just been hearing bitter complaints from a seasoned hostess who for years has fed various assorted contingents of New York's society at her board. She said that conversation at her dinner-table had about reached the disappearing-point. She had as much trouble about getting her guests into conversation as one has with youngsters at a children's party, and all the conversation she could prod out of them nowadays, aside from personalities, came out in the monotonous minute-gun style of particular declaration and perfunctory assent.

"She's right about that," my friend went on. "Here's a *précis* of the kind of thing I hear evening after evening. We go in to dinner talking

personalities, no matter what subject is up. The theatre—we talk about
the leading lady's gowns and mannerisms, and her little ways with her
first husband. Books—we hash over all the author's rotten press-agentry,
from the make of his pajamas to the way he does his hair. Music—we
tell one another what a dear love of a conductor Kaskowhisky is, and
how superior in all respects to von Bugghaus, whose back isn't half so
limber. Damned quacks actually, you know, both of them! Good Lord!
man, can you wonder that this country killed Mahler and put Karl
Muck in jail?

"Well, we sit down at the table. Personalities taper off with the end
of the soup. Silence. Then some puffy old bullfrog of a banker retrieves
his nose out of his soup-cup, stiffens up, coughs behind his napkin,
and looks up and down the line. 'Isn't it remarkable how responsibility
brings out a man's resources of greatness? Now who would have thought
two years ago that Calvin Coolidge would ever develop into a great
leader of men?'

"*Guests, in unison, acciaccato*—'Uh-huh.'

"Next course. Personalities pick up a little and presently taper off
again. Somebody else stiffens up and pulls himself together. 'Isn't it
splendid to see the great example that America is setting in the right
use of wealth? Just think, for instance, of all the good that Mr.
Rockefeller has done with his money.'

"*Guests, fastoso*—'Uh-huh.' "

My lively friend may have exaggerated a little—I hope so—but his
report is worth an observer's careful notice for purposes of comparison
with what one hears oneself. His next remark is worth attention as
bringing out still another specific characteristic of immaturity.

"But what goes against my grain," he continued, "is that if you pick
up some of this infernal guff and try to pull it away from the particular
and personal, and to make real conversation of it, they sit on you as if
you were an enemy of society. Start the banker on a discussion of the
idea of leadership—what it means, what the qualifications for leadership
are, and how far any President can go to fill the bill—how far any of
them has ever gone to fill it—and all he'll do is to grunt, and say, 'I
guess you must be some sort of a Red, ain't you?' A bit of repartee like
that gets him a curtain call from the rest every time. It's a fine
imaginative lot that I train with, believe me! I have sat at dinner-tables
in Europe with every shade of opinion, I should say, and in one way

or another they all came out. That's what the dinner was got up for. How can you have any conversation if all you are expected to do is to agree?"

It is a mark of maturity to differentiate easily and naturally between personal or social opposition and intellectual opposition. Everyone has noticed how readily children transfer their dislike of an opinion to the person who holds it, and how quick they are to take umbrage at a person who speaks in an unfamiliar mode or even with an unfamiliar accent. When the infant-minded Pantagruel met with the Limosin who spoke to him in a Latinized macaronic jargon, he listened awhile and then said, "What devilish language is this?—by the Lord, I think thou art some kind of heretic." Mr. Finkman's excessive simplification of life has made anything like the free play of ideas utterly incomprehensible to him. He never deals with ideas, except such limited and practical ones as may help get him something, and he cannot imagine anyone ever choosing, even on occasion, to do differently. When he "talks it business," the value of ideas, ideals, opinions, sentiments, is purely quantitative; putting any other value on them is a waste of time. Under all circumstances, then, he tends to assume that other people measure the value of their ideas and opinions as he does his, and that they employ them accordingly; and hence, like my friend's banker, when some one tries to lead up into a general intellectual sparring for mere points, he thinks he is a dangerous fellow with an ax to grind.

This puts the greatest imaginable restraint upon conversation, a restraint which betrays itself to the eye of the observer in some rather odd and remarkable ways. I have been much interested, for example, to see that the conversion of conversation into mere declaratory particularization has lately been taken up in a commercial way. One reads advertisements of enterprising people who engage to make you shine in conversation. They propose to do this by loading you up with a prodigious number of facts of all kinds, which you can fire off at will from the machine-gun of your memory. On this theory of conversation, a statistician with Macaulay's memory is the ideal practitioner of social amenities; and so indeed, with Mr. Finkman's sensibilities in view, he would be.

Another odd manifestation of this restraint is the almost violent eagerness with which we turn to substitutes for conversation in our social activities. Mr. Finkman must not be left alone in the dark with his apprehensions a moment longer than necessary. After such a dinner as my debonair friend described, it is at once necessary to "do something"—the theatre, opera, cabaret, dancing, motoring, or what not—and to keep on doing something as long as the evening lasts. It is astonishing to see the amount of energy devoted to keeping out of conversation; "doing something" has come to be a term of special application. Almost every informal invitation reads, "to dinner, and then we'll do something." It is even more astonishing to see that this fashion is followed by persons whose intelligence and taste are sufficient, one would think, to put them above it. Quite often one finds oneself going through this routine with persons quite capable of conversation, who would really rather converse, but who go through it apparently because it is the thing to go through. When this happens, one marvels at the reach and the authority of Mr. Finkman's predilections—yet there they are.

My friend was right in saying that conversation is managed differently in Europe. I was reminded of this not long ago, when the German airship made its great flight to this country. Everyone remembers the vast amount of public interest in this event, and how the pilot of the airship, Doctor Eckener, was fêted and fussed over from one end of the country to the other. Three or four days after the landing, a friend of mine, a German banker, asked me to luncheon at his house. There were four of us—Doctor Eckener, his assistant, our host, and myself. We talked for something over two hours, largely about music, a good deal about the geography and history of the region around Fried-richshafen, and for half an hour, perhaps, about European public affairs. From first to last, not one word was said about the flight of the airship or about the business of aviation or the banking business. The conversation was wholly objective and impersonal; each one spoke his mind, and none of us felt any pressure towards agreement. I remember that I myself put out some pretty heretical opinions about the structure of music-drama. No one agreed with me, but no one dreamed of transferring to myself the brunt of his objections to my opinion.

This kind of thing gives the impression of maturity, and, as far as my experience goes, it is as common in Europe as it is uncommon here. There has been much comment lately upon the attraction that

Europe exerts upon certain American types. I am led to wonder if it be not perchance the attraction of maturity. Children may be delightful, may be interesting, may be ever so full of promise, and one may be as fond of them as possible—and yet when one has them for warp and filling, one must get a bit bored with them now and then, in spite of oneself. I have had little to do with children, so I speak under correction; but I should imagine that one would become bored with their intense simplification of life, their tendency to drive the whole current of life noisily through one channel, their vehement reduction of all values to that of quantity, their inability to take any but a personal view of anything. But just these are the qualities of American civilization as indicated by the test of conversation. They inhere in Mr. Finkman and are disseminated by his influence to the practical exclusion of any other. I can imagine, then, that one might in time come to be tired of them and to wish oneself in surroundings where man is accepted as a creature of "a large discourse, looking before and after," where life is admittedly more complex and its current distributed in more channels—in other words, where maturity prevails.

One is impressed, I think, by the way this difference is repeatedly brought out in ordinary conversation in Europe and America—in the choice of things to talk about and in the way people talk about them. I am impressed by it even in conversation with children, though as I said, due allowance ought to be made for the fact that my experience with children is not large. Yet even so, I do not think it is special or exceptional. I have a friend, for instance, whom I go to see whenever I am in Brussels, and it is the joy of my life to play at sweethearts with his three daughters who range from seven to sixteen. My favourite is the middle one, a weedy and nonchalant charmer of twelve. She does not impress me as greatly gifted; I know several American girls who seem naturally abler. But in conversation with her I detect a power of disinterested reflection, an active sense of beauty, and an active sense of manners, beyond any that I ever detected in American children; and these contribute to a total effect of maturity that is agreeable and striking.

An observer passing through America with his mind deliberately closed to any impressions except those he received from conversation could make as interesting a conjectural reconstruction of our civilization as the palæontologists with an armful of bones make of a dinosaur. He would postulate a civilization which expresses the instinct of expansion to a degree far beyond anything ever seen in the world, but which does not express the instinct of intellect and knowledge, except as regards instrumental knowledge, and is characterized by an extremely defective sense of beauty, a defective sense of religion and morals, a defective sense of social life and manners. Its institutions reflect faithfully this condition of excess and defect. A very brief conversation with Mr. Finkman would enable one to predicate almost precisely what kind of schooling he considered an adequate preparation for life, what kind of literature he thought good enough for one to read, plays for one to see, architecture to surround oneself with, music to listen to, painting and sculpture to contemplate. It would be plain that Mr. Finkman had succeeded in living an exhilarating life from day to day without the aid of any power but concentration—without reflection, without ideas, without ideals, and without any but the most special emotions—that he thought extremely well of himself for his success, and was disposed to be jealous of the peculiar type of institutional life which had enabled it or conduced to it. The observer, therefore, would postulate a civilization marked by an extraordinary and inquisitional intolerance of the individual and a corresponding insistence upon conformity to pattern. For in general, it is reflection, ideas, ideals, and emotions that set off the individual, and with these Mr. Finkman has had nothing to do; he has got on without them to what he considers success, and hence he sees no need of them, distrusts them, and thinks there must be a screw loose with the individual who shows signs of them.

There is a pretty general consensus among observers that this picture corresponds in most respects with the actual civilization of the United States, and many of them deplore the correspondence. I do not deplore it. It seems to me important that Mr. Finkman should have room according to his strength, that he should be unchecked and unhampered in directing the development of American civilization to suit himself. I believe it will be a most salutary experiment for the richest and most powerful nation in the world to give a long, fair, resolute try-out to the policy of living by the instinct of expansion alone. If the United States cannot make a success of it, no nation ever can, and none, probably, will ever attempt it again. So when critics denounce our civilization as barbarous, I reply that, if so, a few generations of barbarism are a cheap price for the result. Besides, Mr. Finkman may prove himself right; he may prove that man can live a full and satisfying inner life without intellect, without beauty, without religion and morals, and with but the most rudimentary social life and manners, provided only he has unlimited exercise of the instinct of expansion, and can drive ahead in the expression of it with the whole force of his being. If Mr. Finkman proves this, he will have the laugh on many like myself who at present have the whole course of human history behind our belief that no such thing can be done. But this is a small matter. The important thing is that we should then have a new world peopled by a new order of beings not at all like ourselves, but by no means devoid of interest on that account. So, whether the result be in success or failure, the great American experiment—for just this is the great American experiment—seems to me wholly worth while.

This essay appeared in the May 1926 issue of *Harper's Magazine* and was subsequently reprinted in *On Doing the Right Thing.*

One's Own Smoke

A light plague of mosquitoes in the part of New York where I have been living lately, has enabled me to understand the psychology of the imperialist and the Prohibitionist. After being attacked and pestered for two or three nights, I bought a patent net, a first-class device with a framework of flexible steel that folds up out of the way in the daytime, and is stretched out at night to form a canopy. While enjoying the protection of this excellent apparatus, I felt an almost bloodthirsty sense of triumph as I watched mosquitoes roosting on the outside of the net and wishing they could get at me, and then I reflected that after all they were only obeying their nature's fundamental demand in taking their food wherever they could get it; and once or twice I dropped to sleep in a state of sentimental wonderment about the ethics of doing them out of a square meal. But I gave all that up when I read a newspaper-report of some scientificker's discovery that the mosquito's blood-lust is a morbid appetite and that indulgence in it probably shortens its life. I perceived then that I was really doing the mosquito for its own good, like the British in India, and that if it starved it would perish morally and correctly. There is a good deal of comfort in this state of mind. I go to sleep now soothed and sustained by the consciousness that I am a true moralizer and benefactor, as much so as any imperialist who ever took up the white man's burden.

While one would not willingly encourage hardness of heart, one must allow something, I think, for a possible light touch of morbidness in one's sentiment toward human sorrows, both individual and social. It is easy to get a bit too much worked up over distresses lying in one's purview—distresses, I mean, which with the best will in the world one can not possibly alleviate, and with which perhaps one can not even sympathize intelligently, since one has never experienced the like oneself. For instance, I have never had a headache, never been seasick, but I have seen a great many people laid out with one or the other; and I dare say headache or seasickness is really not so bad as I imagine it must be. Indeed, I am pretty sure it is not, for I have seen the afflicted people recover quite suddenly, and in almost no time at all become as chipper as squirrels; and if the distresses of headache or seasickness are at all up to what my fancy paints them, these victims could never do that. Hence my sympathetic concern with sufferers, when I see them about me, no doubt is tinged with morbidness. Therefore, since there is nothing that I can do to help them, I do not hover around them any to speak of. If I could help them, I would; when I can, I do; but having cleared myself on this point, I move on and forget about them as quickly as I can.

This policy, which seems to be instinctive with the world of mankind, is the only rational one to be adopted with most of the spiritual woes and difficulties with which one comes in contact. The person who indiscriminately tries to take them upon himself very seldom makes a success with them; he usually makes a mess of things all round. The three friends of Job remain the classical example of both the right way and the wrong way with such matters. When Job's troubles fell upon him, his friends came and sat with him seven days and seven nights, "and none spoke a word unto him, for they saw that his grief was very great." That was superb. They were promptly on hand, ready day or night in case anything was needed, meanwhile keeping their mouths shut like the fine old Oriental gentlemen they were. But when seven days were over, Job began to tell his troubles; he "opened his mouth and cursed his day," and this was too much for his friends. They tried to take his troubles on themselves, argued them over, tried to sympathize with him, console him and get him into a better frame of mind; and they made an awful mess of it. They did him no good, and utterly ruined their own equanimity. How much better all around, one would say, if when Job opened his mouth and began to curse his day, they had quietly and decorously tiptoed off about their business, and let him cuss.

There is an old saying which I think has a lot of good sound Christian doctrine in it, that there are two classes of things one should not worry about; the things one can help, and the things one can't help. If you can help a thing, don't worry about it; help it. If you can't help it, don't worry about it, for you do no good, and only wear yourself down below par. The spiritual distresses of individuals are in the nature of things quite incommunicable to any good purpose. We are not structurally equipped to burn anyone's smoke but our own. I say again that this is no deprecation of sympathy, but only an observation of the very limited range of sympathy's effective operation. One can be all in favor of the weak brother, and still refrain from an exercise of sympathy that obfuscates his sense of responsibility and really tends to keep him weak. I often think of a letter that Golden Rule Jones wrote to somebody who had appealed to his sympathies and asked for help, saying that whiskey had been the cause of his downfall. Jones replied, "I don't believe that whiskey was the cause of your downfall. I believe it was the whiskey that you drank." Giving one's life for others is the best thing that one can do, but there is more than one way of doing it. Maintaining a rational attitude, free from morbidness, toward other peoples' troubles that are in their nature irremediable by any outside agency and also, strictly speaking, incommunicable—this enables one to do best for oneself and thereby to do best for others; and the man who for the sake of others preserves his own integrity of spirit and personality inviolate, I hold to be the noblest Roman of them all.

One may say the same of one's attitude toward what is called the woes of society, the sorrows of the world. There is a huge deal of nonsense talked about those, to begin with. There is no such thing as the woes of society, and the world has no sorrows. Only individuals have woes and sorrows. When you hear a person speak of being overcome by the sorrows of the world, you may wager he has not got this fact quite straight. Many people, moreover, borrow the world's troubles in the conviction that they are great altruists, when in fact they are only bilious and would be benefitted by some liver-medicine and hard work in the open air. Richard Whately, the logician and Archbishop of Dublin, a great man with all a great man's hatred of nonsense, had a clergyman in his diocese who was always telling him what a tough place the world was, and how hard it was to bear up under the wretchedness of human society. One day Whately was vigorously spading up a bed in his large garden, when out of the tail of his eye he saw this clergyman approaching. He gave no sign, however, until the parson got within twenty feet, when he suddenly raised the spade and ran at him. The parson thought the archbishop had suddenly gone crazy, and took to his heels with Whately after him hot-foot. Whately chased him around and around the garden until he judged his victim was about played out; then he stopped, threw down the spade, and said, "Now, sir, what have you to say?" The parson had nothing to say. The unaccustomed exercise had got his circulation going briskly and normally, and made the woes of society take on a very different look. Put a few people like Whately on the track of most of our neurasthenics and sentimentalists, and the psychoanalysts would find themselves permanently out of a job.

_____

This essay originally appeared in the *new Freemen* of October 1, 1930, and was subsequently reprinted in *The Book of Journeymen*.

American Education

Complaint within the teaching profession about the quality of education in America has lately taken an interesting turn. For forty years, to my knowledge—I do not know how much longer—professional criticism has confined itself pretty strictly to matters that went on under the general system, and has not questioned the system itself. It has run to questions of pedagogic method and curricular content; to the *what* and the *how*. One notices with satisfaction, however, that within the past year some of our educators have gone beyond these matters and touched the system's structural principles. The presidents of Brown, Haverford and St. Stephen's have spoken out plainly. Professor Giddings, of Columbia, has been very explicit, and even the president of Columbia has made some observations that might be construed as disparaging. These gentlemen have spoken informally, mostly by implication, and not pretending to present anything like a complete thesis on the subject; nevertheless their implications are clear.

One wishes they had gone further; one hopes they may yet do so. My own reason for writing is that perhaps a layman's view of the situation may call out additional professional comment on it. One need make no apology for the intervention, for the subject is quite within the layman's competence. Matters of content and method (the *what* and the *how*) are primarily a professional concern, and the layman speaks of them under correction. But the system itself is not a technical affair, and its points of strength and weakness lie as properly under lay review as under professional review. In any kind of fairness, indeed, if professional opinion takes responsibility for correctness in technical matters it has enough on its shoulders, and lay opinion may well take the lead on matters which are not technical.

On its moral and social side, our educational system is indeed a noble experiment—none more so. In all the history of noble experiments I know of none to match it. There is every evidence of its being purely an expression—no, one may put it even stronger than that, an organization—of a truly noble, selfless and affectionate desire. The representative American, whatever his faults, has been notably characterized by the wish that his children might do better by themselves than he could do by himself. He wished them to have all the advantages that he had been obliged to get on without, all the "opportunities," not only for material well-being but also for self-advancement in the realm of the spirit. I quite believe that in its essence and intention our system may be fairly called no less than an organization of this desire; and as such it can not be too much admired or too highly praised.

But unfortunately Nature recks little of the nobleness prompting any human enterprise. Perhaps it is rather a hard thing to say, but the truth is that Nature seems much more solicitous about her reputation for order than she is about keeping up her character for morals. Apparently no pressure of noble and unselfish moral earnestness will cozen the sharp old lady into countenancing a breach of order. Hence any enterprise, however nobly and disinterestedly conceived, will fail if it be not also organized intelligently. We are having a fine illustration of this great truth in the fate of the other noble experiment which Mr. Hoover commended on moral grounds in one of his campaign speeches; and an equally conspicuous illustration of it is furnished by the current output of our educational institutions.

Our educational pot has always been sufficiently astir; there can be no doubt of that. It would seem that there is no possible permutation or combination in pedagogic theory and practice that we have not tried. The roster of our undergraduate and secondary courses reads like the advertisement of a bargain-counter. One of our pioneer women's colleges offers, among other curious odds-and-ends, some sort of "course" in baby-tending! Our floundering ventures in university-training have long been fair game for our cartoonists. Only this morning I saw a capital cartoon in a New York paper, prompted by a news-item on some new variant of a cafeteria or serve-self educational scheme vamped up in one of our top-heavy state universities. But now, after all this feverish and hopeful fiddling with the mechanics of education, the current product seems to be, if anything, a little poorer than any that has gone before it.

This statement may rest as it lies. I see no point in a digression to define education or to describe the marks that set off an educated person. If I were writing on oyster-culture, I should consider it a waste of space to define an oyster, because everyone likely to read my paper would know well enough what an oyster is; at least, he would know very well what it is not. Similarly, everyone likely to read this essay may be presumed to know an educated person from an uneducated person. But if this seems a cavalier way of dealing with one's readers, one may establish a perfect understanding by a reference to Mr. James Truslow Adams's paper in the November 1929 issue of the *Atlantic Monthly*. It is enough to say that one who, by whatever means, has compassed just the discipline intimated by Mr. Adams—a discipline directed as steadily towards *being* and *becoming* as towards *doing* and *getting*—and who in all his works and ways reflects that discipline, is an educated person. One who has not compassed it, and whose works and ways do not reflect it, may not properly be called an educated person, no matter what his training, learning, aptitudes and accomplishments may be.

Mr. Adams's paper makes it clear that the educated American is not often to be met with; and there is a pretty complete consensus that he is at present much scarcer than he was, say, twenty-five years ago. An Italian nobleman of high culture, who has seen a great deal of our college and university life, lately told me that he had made a curious observation while here, and asked me whether I thought it was a fair one, and if so, how I should account for it. He said he had now and then met Americans who were extremely well educated, but they were all in the neighbourhood of sixty years old; he had not seen a single person below that age who impressed him as having been even respectably educated, although interest in the matter had led him to look everywhere. It is unsafe to generalize from a single opinion, but it may be worth remembering that this reference is the judgment of one foreign observer of experience and distinction.

This state of things is obviously not due to any deficiency in our mechanical equipment. What impresses one most, I think, at sight of the Continental school, is the very moderate character of its plant and general apparatus of learning, as compared with ours. I have elsewhere remarked that no live-wire, up-to-date, go-getting American college president would look twice at the University of Poitiers or the old university at Brussels. Even Bonn, the aristocrat of German universities, is a very modest and plain affair in its physical aspects. The secondary schools of France and Belgium have in our eyes an appearance of simplicity almost primitive. Yet see what comes out of them. Compare the order of disciplined intelligence that somehow manages to squeeze itself out of Poitiers and Brussels with that which floats through one of our universities. With every imaginable accessory and externality in his favour, the American simply makes no comparison. Put a cost-accounting system on education in France and America, with reference to the quality of the product—if such a thing were possible—and the result would be, I think, a most disquieting surprise.

Nor have the French and Belgians any natural advantage over us in respect of raw material. I firmly believe that the run-of-mine American is just as intelligent as the run-of-mine Frenchman, and the picked American as the picked Frenchman. The trouble is not there, nor can I see that it lies anywhere in the technique of pedagogy; I must needs be shown wherein our pedagogy is not entitled to a clean bill. Yet the fact is that with relatively poor equipment, with no better raw material and no better pedagogy than ours, French institutions turn out extremely well-educated men, and ours do not.

The whole trouble is that the American system from beginning to end is gauged to the run-of-mine American rather than to the picked American. The run-of-mine Frenchman does not get any nearer the university than the adjacent woodpile. He does not get into the French equivalent of our undergraduate college. If he gets through the French equivalent of our secondary school, he does so by what our ancestors called the uncovenanted mercies of Providence, and every step of his progress is larded with bitter sweat. The chief reason why my Italian friend found no educated Americans under sixty years of age is that forty years ago the run-of-mine American did not, as a rule, get much nearer the founts of the higher learning than the run-of-mine Frenchman does to-day, and for the same reason—he could not, speaking strictly, "make the grade." The newspapers some time ago quoted the president of Columbia as saying that during the past half-century the changes in school and college instruction, as to both form and content, have been so complete that it is probably safe to say that to-day no student in Columbia College, and perhaps no professor on its faculty, could pass satisfactorily the examination-tests that were set for admission to Columbia College fifty years ago.

The root-idea, or ideal, of our system is the very fine one that educational opportunity should be open to all. The practical approach to this ideal, however, was not planned intelligently, but, on the contrary, very stupidly; it was planned on the official assumption that everybody is educable, and this assumption still remains official. Instead of firmly establishing the natural limit to opportunity—the ability to make any kind of use of it—and then making opportunity as free as possible within that limit, our system says, Let them all come, and we will scratch up some sort of brummagem opportunity for each of them. What they do not learn at school, the college will teach them; the university will go through some motions for them on what the college failed to get into their heads. This is no jaunty exaggeration. I have a friend who has spent years in a mid-Western state university, trying to teach elementary English composition to adult illiterates. I have visited his classes, seen what they were about, seen his pupils, examined their work, and speak whereof I know. A short time ago, in another enormous university—a university, mind; not a grade school, but a university dealing with adult persons—two instructors published samples of the kind of thing produced for them by their students. Here are a few:

> Being a tough hunk of meat, I passed up the steak.
> Lincoln's mind grew as his country kneaded it.
> The camel carries a water tank with him; he is also a rough rider and has four gates.
> As soon as music starts, silence rains, but as soon as it stops it gets worse than ever.
> College students as a general rule like such readings that will take the least mental inertia.
> Modern dress is extreme and ought to be checked.
> Although the Irish are usually content with small jobs, they have won a niche in the backbone of the country.

At the hands of some upper-classmen and second-year men, Shakespeare fared as follows:

> Edmund, in *King Lear,* "committed a base act and allowed his illegitimate father to see a forged letter." Cordelia's death "was the straw that broke the camel's back and killed the king." Lear's fool "was prostrated on the neck of the king." "Hotspur," averred a sophomore, "was a wild, irresolute man. He loved honor above all. He would go out and kill twenty

Scotchmen before breakfast." Kate was "a woman who had something to do with hot spurs."

Also Milton:

"Diabetes was Milton's Italian friend," one student explained. Another said, "Satan had all the emotions of a woman, and was a sort of trustee in heaven, so to speak." The theme of *Comus* was given as "purity protestriate." Mammon, in *Paradise Lost,* suggests that the best way "to endure hell is to raise hell and build a pavilion."

Would it be unfair to ask the reader how long he thinks that order of intelligence would be permitted to display itself at the University of Brussels or the University of Poitiers?

The history of our system shows a significant interplay between the sentiment for an indiscriminate and prodigal distribution of "opportunity" and certain popular ideas or pseudo-ideas that flourished beside it. One of these was the popular conception of democracy. It is an interesting fact that this originally got its currency through the use of the word by politicians as a talking-point. Practically all publicists now quite arbitrarily use the word "democratic" as a synonym for "republican"—as when, for instance, they speak of the United States and France as "great democracies." The proper antithesis of democracy is not autocracy, monarchy, or oligarchy, but absolutism; and, as we all know, absolutism is much deeper entrenched in these republican countries than in monarchical Denmark, say. The term, too, became debased on its more special uses. In the America which Dickens visited, a democratic society meant one in which "one man was just as good as another, or a little better"; this phrase itself is of sound American coinage current with the merchant. Democratic manners to-day, as a rule, mean merely coarse manners; for instance, the ostentatiously "democratic" luncheon-etiquette of our booster clubs means that all hands shall, under some sort of penalty, call each fellow member by his given name, regardless of the previous acquaintance or the lack of it.

Thus the educational free-for-all sentiment got a very powerful endorsement. It was democratic. Poverty-stricken Tom, from the slashes, should go through school, college and university hand in hand with Dick the scion of Wall Street, and toplofty Harry of the Back Bay. Democracy so willed it, in spite of Nature's insuperable differentiations whereby Tom had first-rate school-ability. Harry had excellent ability in other directions but no school-ability, and Dick was a *Dummkopf* with no ability of any kind. Privately these differentiations might be recognized, indeed must be, but it was of the essence of democracy that there should be no official or institutional recognition of them. The unspeakable silliness of our truant laws, which make compulsory attendance a matter purely of school-age instead of school-ability, appropriately expresses this limitation.

The very human but rather ignoble tendency to self-assertion which led us to put the label of democracy on what was merely indiscriminate or vulgar led us also to put the label of greatness on what was merely big. With a whole civilization groveling in the unintelligent worship of bigness, a great school must be a big school. The thing to notice is how admirably this fell in with pseudo-democratic doctrine and also with the noble but ill-starred sentiment pervading our system. To make a big school, students must be got; to get them, standards of eligibility must be brought down to a common denominator of intelligence, aptitude and interest. Then, when they are got, something has to be found for them to do that they can do, or at least upon which they are able to mark time—such as "courses in English," the number of which exhibited annually by our institutions will amaze the reader, if he has curiosity enough about it to look it up—and this means a profound sophistication of requirements. It can be seen at once how solidly sentiment and pseudo-democratic doctrine stood behind these developments and encouraged them.

By another interesting coincidence—these coincidences in the history of our system are really remarkable—these developments also met, as if made to order, the great and sudden expansion of the nation's industrial life, the glorification of profit-making, and the implied disparagement of all intellectual, æsthetic, and even moral processes which did not tend directly or indirectly to profit-making. It was promptly perceived that the ineducable person might become a successful banker, industrialist, broker, bond-salesman or what not; plenty such there were who could manage no more than to read the stock-quotations and write their own signatures—Daniel Drew, for instance, and Cornelius Vanderbilt. Thus vocationalism came at once to the burdened system's aid. Circumstances were created whereby the ineducable person might bear directly on the business of banking, brokerage, industry, and so on, with the prestige of a college or university career thrown in. The elective bargain-counter was extended all over the academic floor-space; its limit was only at the line where imaginative ingenuity broke down and ceased to work; and certain fragile windflowers, such as "courses in English," were distributed over it here and there, partly by way of garnishment, partly as camouflage. Thus everything was made satisfactory all around. The ineducable person was taken care of with an academic career to all appearances as respectable as anybody's; sentiment was assuaged; democratic doctrine was satisfied; the general regard for size was satisfied, and so was the general preoccupation with profit.

In discussing the effect of all this, I wish to make it as clear as possible that I am not laying the slightest blame upon our educators. They had to take the system as they found it; its faults were none of their making. They had to meet measurably the egregious demands of a noble but undiscriminating sentiment, a preposterous misconception of the democratic principle, a childish reverence for bigness, and an exclusive preoccupation with profit-making. It is a large order; if in practice they were able to meet these demands by ever so little obliquely, one might reasonably ask no more. With this clearly understood, we may observe that one immediate effect is a calamitous overlapping of effort, whereby the lines marking off the school from the college and the college from the university have been obliterated. As in the case I cited, the university is doing work that by the handsomest possible concession one would say should be done in the eighth grade. The secondary school and the undergraduate college, again, are overlapping on the university in their furtherance of vocationalism. Hence, whatever may be done for senti-ment or democracy or the promotion of profit-making, none of them are doing anything for education. An institution, like an individual, has only twenty-four hours a day, and only a limited amount of attention at its disposal; and so much of time and attention as it devotes to one pursuit must be taken from another.

This overlapping, indeed, gives rise to a great deal of justifiable avoidance on the part of educators, or what I understand is better known as "passing the buck." In looking over an undergraduate college last year, I remarked to the president that, on the one hand, he seemed to be doing a good deal of rather elementary school-work, and at the same time trespassing pretty heavily on the university, especially in his science courses; so that on the whole his college made me think of the small boy's objection to some asparagus that his mother offered him— it tasted raw at one end and rotten at the other. He said this was so; he had to give way to vocationalism somewhat—much more than he wished; he was doing his best against it. As for the other matter, it was the fault of the schools; they left ragged holes in the boys' preparation. "Don't you think we should do something for the poor fellows who come to us with these deficiencies?"

"Certainly," I replied. "Fire them."

"Ah, but then we should have no students, and should be obliged to shut up shop."

"Well, but at that," I suggested, "would it really be such a killing misfortune?"

"Possibly so, I think," he answered, after a moment's reflection. "My ideas are the same as yours precisely, but needs must when the devil drives. We are doing only half a job, I know—perhaps not that—but we are doing it better than any other college, and perhaps that justifies us in keeping on."

There may be something in this—I personally doubt it—but that is another matter. The point is that we can see clearly just what it is to which this lamentable situation runs back. The secondary school must take in all the shaky material sent up from the grade-school, for of such is the kingdom of democracy. In its turn the grade-school must take in all the enormous masses of human ineptitude that are dumped on it by the truant laws; and thus from one end of our system to the other do we see the ramification of the four social principles that our civilization has foisted on it as fundamental.

A second immediate effect is the loss, in practice, of any functional distinction between formative knowledge and instrumental knowledge. Formerly a student gave up, in round numbers, the first twenty years of his life to formative knowledge; his pursuits during this time were directed exclusively toward the *being* and *becoming*. That was the stated business of the school and college, and they kept him so busy with it that he hardly knew there was such a thing as instrumental knowledge in the world. He got his introduction to that later, at the university or technical school, where first he began to concern himself with the *doing* and *getting*. I have not space to discuss this aspect of our system at length—done properly, it would take many pages—but I think the reader will have no trouble about perceiving it in all its relations with what has been said already.

A third effect is the grotesque and monstrous shift of responsibility from the student to the teacher. Formerly the teacher had none of it; now he has practically all of it. The student who formerly presented himself was capable of learning; that was what he was there for; it was "up to" him to do it, and he did it. The teacher directed him, perhaps helped him a little—precious little, in my experience—but took no responsibility whatever for the student's progress. The run-of-mine student now arrives, incapable of anything, usually indifferent and incurious toward everything. Well, what is to be done? He may be relied on to do nothing particularly striking for himself—Nature has attended to that—therefore what is done must be done either for him or with him; and thus the burden of responsibility immediately passes to the teacher, and there it remains.

For some reason that I have never been able to discover, Mr. Jefferson seems to be regarded as a great democrat; on public occasions he is regularly invoked as such by gentlemen who have some sort of political axe to grind, so possibly that view of him arose in this way. The fact is that he was not even a doctrinaire republican, as his relation to the French Revolution clearly shows. When Mr. Jefferson was revising the Virginia Statutes in 1797, he drew up a comprehensive plan for public education. Each ward should have a primary school for the three R's, open to all. Each year the best pupil in each school should be sent to the grade-school, of which there were to be twenty, conveniently situated in various parts of the state. They should be kept there one year or two years, according to results shown, and then all dismissed but one, who should be continued six years. "By this means," said the good old man, "twenty of the best geniuses will be raked from the rubbish annually"—a most unfortunate expression for a democrat to use! At the end of six years, the best ten out of the twenty were to be sent to college, and the rest turned adrift.

As an expression of sound public policy, this plan has never been improved upon. Professor Chinard, who has lately put us all under great obligations by his superb study—by far the best ever made—of Mr. Jefferson's public life, thinks it quite possible that those who formed the French system had this plan before them. Whether so or not, the French system is wholly in accord with Mr. Jefferson's hard good sense in accepting the fact that the vast majority of his countrymen were ineducable, and with his equally hard realism in permitting this fact to determine the fundamentals of his plan. The Faculty of Literature at the University of Poitiers is domiciled in the Hôtel Fumée, an exquisitely beautiful family mansion, built about 1510 by a rich lawyer. From an outside view, which is all I ever had of either property, I should say the Hôtel Fumée carries about as much floor-space as Mr. James Speyer's residence on Fifth Avenue. I venture to say that if Columbia University cleared out all its ineducable students, root and branch, its Faculty of Literature could do a land-office business in a house the size of Mr. James Speyer's, with maybe a room or two to rent.

From what Professor Giddings and the presidents of Brown, Haverford and St. Stephen's have said, I infer that this is the season of repentance. Whether or not it will lead to a season of good works is another matter; I think it highly improbable. Nevertheless it seems useful at the present time that the situation should be diagnosed, and its "indications," as the doctors say, taken into account. Artemus Ward once said the trouble with Napoleon was that he tried to do too much and did it. Just this is the trouble with American education. In my judgment, the indications are simply that the whole school-population of the country, above the primary grade, should be cut down by ninety per cent. If anyone thinks that this proportion is too high, let him take it out on Mr. Jefferson, who is much bigger than I am; my figures are fairly liberal as compared with his. With him on my side I make bold to believe that nine-tenths of our student population, in university, college, grade schools and secondary schools, have no more justification for being where they are than they would have for an intrusion upon the French Academy or the Royal Society; and that unless and until this mass is cut adrift, the prospects for American education will show no improvement worth considering.

Professional criticism has already suggested that the college and university—and I believe there has been some similar hint about the secondary school—should slough off the otiose bulk of those brought to them by the mere *vis inertiæ*, and those who present themselves because it is the thing to do, or as a liberation from home or a furlough for parents; likewise those who are going in for contacts, athletics, husbands, the atmosphere and flavour of college life, or for what I understand the authorities now delicately call "extra-curricular activities," whereof the coonskin coat and pocket-flask are said to be the symbols. At present this would no doubt account for sixty per cent of Mr. Jefferson's "rubbish," probably seventy, but that is not enough. The intention of Mr. Jefferson's plan was to off-load all ineducable persons, no matter what their disposition, and to have this relief applied continuously at every point in the system above the primary school.

This reform seems unlikely to be carried out, and I do not urge it or even recommend it. Conversance with human history begets a deal of respect for Nature's well-established policy of progress by trial and error, and a profound circumspection about trying to anticipate it. The experienced person regards root-and-branch reforms, even good ones, with justifiable doubt. One may be by no means sure—far from it— that it would be a good thing "by and large" and in the long run for the United States to produce any educated people, or that in its present summary sacrifice of its educable individuals it is not taking precisely the right way with them. I am not disposed to dogmatize either way, and hence I do not recommend this reform, or, indeed, any reform. I am merely recording observations of certain social phenomena, placing them in their right relations and drawing the conclusions that seem warranted in the premises. As to the final desirability of the state of things contemplated by these conclusions, I have nothing to say.

Still, education seems as yet to be a subject of experiment with us, and I observe with interest that, according to some educators, the next experiment will be with the revival of the small college. There is obviously no more saving grace in smallness than in bigness; everything depends upon what the small college is like. The forecast, however, sets one's fancy going. Perhaps—one must have one's doubts about it, but perhaps—without too much infringement on Nature's policy, or deflection of our great moral and social mission to the world at large, one small laboratory experiment might be tried, such as has never yet been tried by us. I mean an experiment in educating educable persons only. It would be interesting and possibly useful to set up two small institutions, a school and an undergraduate college, both so well endowed as not to care a straw whether a student came near them or not, and both committed wholly to the pursuit of formative knowledge; the school's attendance limited, say, to sixty, and the college's to two hundred. The school should take pupils at the age of eight, and carry them on until they could meet the college's requirements. Neither institution should take any account whatever of bogus democratic doctrine, the idolatry of mass, vocationalism or the pretended rights of ineducable persons. If such persons presented themselves they should be turned away, and if anyone got in and afterward was found for any reason or to any degree ineducable, he should be forthwith bounced out.

These institutions should be largely a reversion to type, their distinction being that of representing the pure type, without a trace of hybridization. Requirements for entrance to the college should be the ability to read and write Latin and Greek prose with such ease and correctness as to show that language-difficulties were forever left behind; knowledge of arithmetic and of algebra up to quadratics; nothing more. The four years' course in college should cover the whole range of Greek and Latin literature from Homer's time to that of Erasmus, mathematics as far as the differential calculus, a compendium of formal logic, and one of the history of the English language (not literature), and nothing more; and this should lead to the degree of Bachelor of Arts, the only degree that the college should confer.

My notion is that the instructors in these institutions could pretty well follow their own devices for five years, having no students to teach, but that in ten years things would look up a little, and that in fifty years a review of the experiment would be interesting. One could then make the observations and comparisons necessary to determine what it was worth. I can not say flatly that I recommend this experiment;

I merely say that it would be interesting, might be useful enough to be worth its cost, and incidentally some poor few, at least, of our educable fry would lay up out of it a treasure more to be desired than gold—yea, than much fine gold. Yet it is nothing that I would urge, for quite possibly the Larger Good requires that things should go on as they are now going.

Probably, however, I should give (though in all diffidence) some decorous hint about the sort of thing I should look for from it, if it were carried out under strictly aseptic experimental conditions. The literature of Greece and Rome represents the longest continuous record available to us—a matter of some twenty-five hundred years or more, if mediæval and Renaissance literature were included, as it should be—as well as the fullest and most diversified record, of what the human mind has ever been busy about. Therefore the one great benefit of the "grand old fortifying classical curriculum," as far as it went, was that on one's way through it one saw by centuries instead of weeks, by whole periods instead of years, the operation of the human mind upon every aspect of collective human life, every department of spiritual, industrial, commercial and social activity; one touched the theory and practice of every science and every art. Hence a person came out from this discipline with not only a trained mind but an experienced mind. He was like one who had had a profound and weighty experience. He was habituated to the long-time point of view, and instinctively brought it to bear on current affairs and happenings. In short, he was mature.

"Sobald er reflektirt," said Goethe of Lord Byron, "ist er ein Kind." Byron was one of the great natural forces in literature—all praise to him for that–but of maturity, the best assurance of a right interpretation and right use of personal experience of the world and its affairs, he had none. So, too, the composite American is one of the greatest natural forces that have ever appeared in human society. Perhaps it is as such, and such only, that Nature proposes to use him, and she may intend to fade him out and supersede him when this function in her inscrutable economy is fulfilled—she has never been any too scrupulous about turning such tricks—and, if so, it would be hazardous to tamper with the fundamentals of a training that fits him for her purpose. Our system seems to have been constructed in anticipation of just this purpose on the part of Nature; it confirms him in a perpetual adolescence, permits his inner adjustment to the world and its affairs to proceed by a series of juvenile, casual and disorderly improvisations—*sobald er reflektirt ist er ein Kind.*

This essay originally appeared in the May 1931 issue of the *Atlantic Monthly* and was subsequently reprinted in *Free Speech and Plain Language.*

Snoring as a Fine Art

And the Claims of General
M. I. Kutusov as an Artist

What colossal irony!" I said to myself as I closed Caulaincourt's memoirs of the Russian campaign of 1812. "It seems that Napoleon was utterly ruined and Napoleonic France was utterly destroyed, all by a man who actually did nothing about it but snore through staff meetings, write sprightly letters to Madame de Staël, read French novels, and hold his army back as tight as he could from aggressive military operations of any kind. What a distressing thought to carry to St. Helena!"

The rationale of the Russian campaign seems to have been a standing puzzle to historians on both sides. Some seventy years ago Count Tolstoy published a book called *War and Peace,* in which he undertook to show that both the Russian and the French historians were equally all wrong, and that the real rationale of the campaign was something quite different. Later historians, with the usual fine professional contempt for secular learning, paid little attention to Count Tolstoy's views, and, as far as I know, have never thought them worth discussing.

But now comes Caulaincourt's journal, which backs up Count Tolstoy's conclusions with astonishing particularity, and makes it pretty clear that the old Count was right. I was so struck by this that I got out my dog-eared copy of *War and Peace* and penciled cross-references between it and Caulaincourt's journal, with results which convinced me that in all essential respects the old man had a large edge on the historians. If any reader has curiosity enough to put the two books side by side and read from one to the other, as I did, I believe he will come away with the same opinion.

This Caulaincourt was Napoleon's right-hand man in the campaign. They saw it through together, and when at last Napoleon deserted the pitiful remnant of his soldiery and ran away to Paris, Caulaincourt went with him and loyally stuck by him to the last; he was about the only one who did. Throughout the campaign, Caulaincourt kept a full journal of each day's doings; it is one of the most fascinating books I ever read. This journal did not see daylight for a century; it was supposed to be lost. It was discovered, I believe by accident, five or six years ago; it was then published, and has lately been translated into English.

The one thing which perhaps has been most bothersome to historians, especially Russian historians, is that if the Russian commander had done everything that they all assume a good general should have done, he could have made a most spectacular military success. He did none of those things, however, though everyone expected them. The Tsar expected them; so did the court and all Russian officialdom, and the entire Russian staff; and so, above all, did the French. Nothing in Caulaincourt's whole story is more interesting than his naïve disclosure of French bewilderment at Kutusov's[1] actions.

Early in the campaign, when Kutusov took up an impregnable position at Maley-Yaroslavetz and then most unaccountably and unreasonably abandoned it overnight, Caulaincourt reports Napoleon's saying, "That devil Kutusov will never make a fight of it." Nor did he. On the great retreat from Moscow, he could have captured Napoleon, Murat, Davoût, Ney, anyone he liked, a dozen times over. He could have cut off the retreat, devastated the French army, slaughtered thousands, taken prisoners wholesale and raised the devil generally, all to the praise and glory of holy Russia. At the campaign's end, Napoleon walked straight into a nutcracker at the Berezina; he had Wittgenstein's army closing in on his right, Kutusov's own army on his left, and waiting for him in front, on both ends of the Berezina bridge, was Tchitchagov; but Kutusov did not close the nutcracker. Instead, he ordered Wittgenstein to slow up a little, slowed up his own march, and sent word to Tchitchagov to keep his eyes open and take it easy.

Nobody understood these tactics. After Maley-Yaroslavetz, Napoleon said to Caulaincourt, "I beat the Russians every time, but that does not get me anywhere." From then on, Caulaincourt reveals the amazement of the French at almost every step. Why abandon one good position

---

1. Field Marshal Prince Mihail Ilarionovitch Kutusov-Smolensky (1745–1813); served under Suvorov, gaining a great military reputation; twice governor of Vilna; commanded the Russian forces against Napoleon at Austerlitz; commanded against the Turks, 1810–1811; commander in chief against Napoleon, 1812.

after another? Why not follow up the advantage at Tarutino, Krasnoe, Vyazma? Why not cut off the retreat at this, that, or the other point? Why above all, since Tchitchagov had kept the French under close observation at the Berezina for thirty-six hours, did he not send out a stand of cannon and blow them to Jericho while they were crossing the river on their improvised bridges?

The Petersburg court and the official set were equally mystified, and also disgusted; no more so than the Tsar, who never liked Kutusov, and had repeatedly blistered him for his inaction. Kutusov's own staff had given him up as hopeless. They would meet, discuss aggressive strategy, urge attacks, plan battles, suggest forays, and all that sort of thing, while the old man's nose sent forth loud trumpeting sounds which betokened a complete lack of interest; and when at last they had it all out of their systems, he would wake up and mutter something to the effect that the supplies had not come up yet, or the soldiers' boots were worn out, or the troops did not know how to execute such complicated manœuvres; and that would be that.

So some historians put it that Kutusov was no better than an "old dowager," as Napoleon called him, an incompetent and crafty courtier, not worth his salt as a soldier. The trouble with that theory is that he had a gilt-edged record all the way down from Suvorov's time to his conclusive windup of the Turkish war in 1811, only a few months before Napoleon crossed the frontier. Others put it that he was a weak and dissolute old man, too far gone in his dotage to know what he was about; but that will hardly wash either, for, hang it all, he got results. When his lackadaisical campaign was over, Napoleon was finally and completely done in; done in for good and all—Waterloo was only a *coup de grâce*. Napoleonic France was also permanently done in; and when the *Grande Armée* straggled across the border there was not enough of it left to be worth counting.

What more could one ask? Even the Tsar had to bottle up his chagrin in face of the fact that, even if his old general's management had not been exactly what one would call stylish, it had nevertheless somehow turned the trick in the cheapest and most effective way.

Two things revealed by the composite Tolstoy-Caulaincourt narrative struck me with peculiar force. The first is that from the moment

Moscow was captured and occupied Kutusov seems to have known exactly what Napoleon was going to do. Moreover, it is clear that he was the only one who did know. Caulaincourt shows beyond peradventure that through the whole month spent in Moscow Napoleon himself had not the faintest idea of what his own next move would be; nor, naturally, had anyone on the French side, and of course no one but Kutusov on the Russian side had any idea of it, especially in view of circumstances which I shall presently mention.

Something like this had happened once before. Kutusov commanded the Russian forces at Austerlitz; and there too he knew exactly what Napoleon was going to do. He warned the Russian and Austrian emperors that if they took the offensive, as they and the Austrian strategists were keen for doing, the battle would be a total loss because Napoleon was not going to do anything like what they were expecting, but something quite different. If his advice had been taken, it is anybody's guess what might have been the outcome. He was overruled, however, and the thing turned out precisely as he had said it would. He presided at the staff meeting held the evening before the attack, and throughout the two hours consumed by the Austrian general Weyrother in reading the disposition of the troops he was sound asleep and snoring manfully. In the battle next day he acted with great energy and ability, but he knew that no matter how the troops were disposed the battle would be lost by reason of contingencies which he, and no one else, foresaw.

After the occupation of Moscow, however, the case was different. Kutusov could not tell the Tsar or anyone else what he knew, because it was something so fantastically improbable that he would instantly have been deprived of his command, if not certified to an asylum as a hopeless lunatic. Napoleon was a good officer; he was supposed to be the best general in Europe. He had already conquered a large slice of Russia and had taken Moscow. After that, there were several courses equally open to him, any one of which a good officer might creditably choose. The course which he actually did choose, however, and which Kutusov apparently knew he would choose, was one that no kind of officer, even a shavetail lieutenant just out of West Point, would ever dream of taking.

Napoleon could have wintered in Moscow, where, as the French historians admit, he had six months' supplies available, despite the fire.

He could have rested and refitted his army there for a week or so, and then pushed on to threaten Petersburg (which Alexander I thought he would do) and negotiated an advantageous peace. He could have moved over to Nizhni-Novgorod, or, if he wished to shorten up his communications, he could have fallen back on Smolensk or Vilna for the winter. The road into the rich southern provinces was open to him; so was practically any road anywhere, in fact, for Kutusov was encamped in front of Kaluga, offering him no obstruction, but merely lying low and waiting for the outcome which he had foreseen as inevitable, and on which he was confidently risking the whole fate of Russia. Again, if Napoleon had decided to retreat, he might have retreated through a region well furnished with supplies, by the road along which Kutusov subsequently pursued him; or, as one might better say, chaperoned him.

With all these choices before him, what Napoleon actually did was to remain idle in Moscow for a month; then march out, ill-prepared at the very worst time of year, in a half-hearted search for the Russian army; and then, after the indecisive collisions at Maley-Yaroslavetz and Tarutino, which Kutusov did his best to avoid, he broke into a headlong stampede for the frontier by the worst route he could have chosen—the road by Mozhaisk towards Smolensk, which led through utterly devastated regions. Who could possibly have predicted anything like that from the greatest military genius of Europe? Yet, as I say, apparently Kutusov knew Napoleon would do just that, and knew it so well that with Tsar and court and his own staff all against him he staked the future, not only of Russia but of Europe, on his knowledge.

Kutusov seems to have been one of those peculiarly and mysteriously gifted persons of whom one can say only, as we so often do say in our common speech, that they "had something." Such people appear in history all the way from Balaam the son of Beor down to contemporary examples which I shall presently cite; there are more of them, perhaps, than one would think. They "have something," but nobody knows what it is or how they got it; and investigation of it is always distinctly unrewarding. In the late J. A. Mitchell's story called *Amos Judd*—one of those sweet and unpretentious little narratives of the last century which I suppose no one nowadays could be hired to read—Deacon White says, "There's something between Amos and the Almighty that the rest of us ain't into"; and that is about as far as scientific inquiry into these matters has ever carried us, or probably ever will.

Yet the something is there. We can all cite instances of it in our most commonplace experience, without troubling to look up impressive historical examples. A friend who was wading through the Barchester series last winter remarked to me that it had an inordinate number of dull pages, "but the odd thing is that one doesn't skip them." Another friend not long ago asked me what makes Edward FitzGerald a great letter-writer. The answer is, of course, that nothing does; he simply isn't. Yet if you start reading his letters, trivial and actually uninteresting as they are, you keep on reading and rereading; and I do not believe Oxford's whole Faculty of Literature, in council assembled, could account for your doing it in terms which would boil down to anything more scientifically respectable than "because you do." What makes Madame Mertens, contralto at the Brussels opera, a great artist? Again, nothing; she isn't; not voice, not method, beauty, grace of movement, sex attraction, dramatic power, nor any combination of them. Like Trollope and FitzGerald, she simply has something; some fascinating endowment which keeps your recollection of her fresh and clear long after the memory of this-or-that really great artist has faded.

The peculiar something which Kutusov had, the "something between Amos and the Almighty" which made him so confidently aware that the unlikeliest thing in the world was the thing which was going to happen, seems to be entirely dissociated from intellect and personal will. Count Tolstoy says that young Prince Bolkonsky went away from an interview with Kutusov feeling greatly reassured about the old general's conduct of the campaign, because "he will put nothing of himself into it. He will contrive nothing, will undertake nothing. . . . He knows that there is something stronger and more important than his will; that is, the inevitable march of events; and he can see them and grasp their significance; and seeing their significance, he can abstain from meddling, from following his own will and aiming at something else."

The whole passage in *War and Peace* which describes this interview is worth a great deal of close meditation; it is the fifteenth and sixteenth chapters of Part X.

I shall return to this aspect of the matter in a moment. Before doing so I wish to remark that the gift (I call it a gift only for convenience, to save words) which we are discussing is not only dissociated from intellect, but also from conventional morals. Certain Old Testament characters who unquestionably had it, and on occasion let it put itself to good use, were nevertheless what by our conventional ethical standards we would call pretty tough citizens; our old friend Balaam, for instance, and Elisha. It has been said, and I believe it is accepted in some quarters—of course there is no knowing—that Joan of Arc was not in all respects a model of sound peasant character; but granting it be so, she still most conspicuously "had the goods."

Kutusov himself, like Lieutenant-General Bangs in Kipling's amusing ballad, had the reputation of being "a most immoral man." At sixty-three, very big, very fat, with one eye blinded and his face scarred by a bullet in one of Suvorov's wars, he seems somehow to have kept his attractiveness to the ladies, for his friendships with them—some of high degree, some not so high—were many and close. Even during his fourteen months' stay in Bucharest while he was starving out the Turks, he passed his enforced idleness in dalliance with a handsome and spirited Wallachian gal; rumors whereof got back to Petersburg, to the great scandal and discomposure of Alexander's court, for which he seems to have cared not a button. "The Spirit breathes where it will," said the *Santissimo Salvatore;* and oftentimes the breath of its most intimate inspiration blows upon persons whom we, in our modesty, would at once put down as morally disqualified.

The other striking impression which I got from the Caulaincourt-Tolstoy narrative was of Kutusov's attitude of complete quiescence towards the something which he had. Not only is that something, as I said, dissociated from intellect, but also if the intellect be applied to it in any attempt at rationalization, however cautious and tentative, it refuses to turn its game for you and leaves you in the lurch.

The case of the poet Wordsworth, for example, strongly suggests that this is so. Wordsworth unquestionably had something; and when he was content to leave that something in full charge of his poetical operations—when he resolutely bottled up the conscious and intellectual Wordsworth, and corked it down—he was a truly great poet. When he summoned up the conscious Wordsworth, however, and put it in charge, as unfortunately he too often did, the conscious Wordsworth was such a dreadful old foo-foo that the poetry churned out under its direction was simply appalling.

Kutusov seems to have done everything he could to keep his consciousness from playing upon the sequence of events which he alone knew was going to take place. In the chapters I have referred to (and I repeat, they are a great study) Count Tolstoy says, "All Denisov had said was practical and sensible; what the general was saying was even more practical and sensible; but apparently Kutusov despised both knowledge and intellect, and was aware of something else which would settle things—something different, quite apart from intellect and knowledge." In view of this, he took every means to keep himself as nearly as possible in a state of complete selflessness. He attended to routine, watching everything, putting everything in its place, holding everything up to the mark; but beyond that he kept his mind as far off the actual course of the campaign as he could. He read French novels, corresponded with his lady-friends, meditated on all sorts of non-military matters; and, most effective and rewarding of all conceivable relaxations, he snored. Like nearly all old persons, he dropped off to sleep easily, almost at will; and being big and fat, he snored; and when a person is snoring he is about as inaccessible and unsuggestible and selfless as a living human being can become.

I once had an acquaintance whom I shall call Smith, for that is not his name; he is still alive and flourishing, I believe, and would presumably boggle at this kind of publicity. It was he who really completed my understanding of Kutusov's elaborately purposeful quiescence; not consciously, however, because, as I found out later, he had never even heard of Kutusov. Smith's career was unusual. He had great intelligence, ability, energy, determination, and in his earlier years he had thrown the whole sum of these into various enterprises, all of which went wrong. He wanted money, quite disinterestedly too, for he had some highly commendable semi-public purposes in view; but money ran like a scared dog whenever it saw him coming. Rather late in middle life (this is his own account of it) he discovered that he "had something," or that something had him; something, as Tolstoy says, quite apart from intellect and knowledge, which—provided he kept his conscious self in complete abeyance towards it—would really settle things. After that, everything he touched went right. I do not know how his affairs came out in the long run, this being some time ago, but at the period I speak of he appeared to be raking in money with both hands.

Smith told me most extraordinary stories of his prescience concerning the course of certain business operations; and since, like Kutusov, he had the goods to show for it, there seems no reasonable doubt that the stories were true. One which I remember particularly, since it brought Kutusov to my mind at once, was that he had just come from an important conference where the one thing most unlikely to happen had happened, precisely as he knew it would. "I was so sure of it," he said, "that when I went in I merely took my seat, said nothing, kept my mind as much as possible off the discussion, and waited for things to turn out as I expected; and so they did. If I had told anybody they would turn out that way, I should have been laughed at, but they did."

What most interested me about Smith was this attitude of studied quiescence. He had somehow, quite independently and off his own bat, formed the idea that the effort to do any examining or analyzing or rationalizing would be ruinous. I never saw a man who had such a nervous horror and hatred of "psychical research," or any kind of experimentation with spiritism, clairvoyance, telepathy, and the like. Rather to my surprise, since I did not suspect him of knowing our American classics, he cited Mr. Jefferson's remark about the virtue of resting one's head contentedly on the pillow of ignorance which the Creator has made so soft for us because He knew we should have so much use for it. Smith's philosophical position, as I understood it, was that of an intensively ignorant and incurious pragmatism. There the thing is, and it works; that is all one knows, and for all practical purposes it is all one needs to know. The attempt to discover anything about what it is, or how or why it works, is unfruitful, and apparently will always be so; and it seems also to be invariably damaging. Besides, Smith asked pointedly, if you should conceivably get anywhere with this sort of research, or even supposing you got as far as you can possibly imagine yourself getting, what good would it do?

Association with Smith kept continually bringing to my mind the profound saying of Joubert, that "it is not hard to know God, provided you do not trouble yourself to define Him." Smith carried his diffidence even to the point of having a great dread of verbal symbols; he never used them. They might be all right, he said, if it were clearly understood that they had no definite significance, but it was hard to keep up that clear understanding even with oneself, because, as Goethe says, man never knows how anthropomorphic he is; therefore one had best steer clear of them. The old prophet spoke of "the word which the Lord hath put in my mouth"; Socrates and Marcus Aurelius spoke of "the intimations of the dæmon." Such symbols might be all well enough, Smith said, as long as one were sure they were not being made to mean something; but it is hard to be always sure of that, and anyway they are unnecessary, so why not give them a wide berth? Organized Christianity, for example, had put a good many such symbols into currency and had attached definite meanings to them, or tried to, and see what a terrific lot of damage it has done!

With one exception, I am sure that Smith is the only man who ever discussed this subject with me. The other one was a retired gambler; it is really quite embarrassing that both my prize exhibits should be such as the righteous would at once frown upon as men of sin, for Smith also was no great shakes at either conventional piety or conventional morals. The ex-gambler told me he perfectly understood what I was driving at. Quite often in his career of skinning the unwary, he said—not always, but fairly often—he had sat into a game with a clear presentiment of how it would turn out. If he knew he would lose, he lost in spite of all the skill and brainwork he could put into the effort to beat his presentiment; but he had discovered that if he were due to win he could do so only if he resolutely kept all brainwork off the game and played it out mechanically, simply "going along." If he did that, he said, he never failed to win.

And now I ask myself why I have burdened the printing press with this rather rambling and inconsequent recital. I hardly know. What I have written is not at all the kind of essay for which editors believe our "reading public," whatever that is, to be always thirsting. As the good and great John Bright said of Artemus Ward's lecture, "its information is meagre, and presented in a desultory, disconnected manner." As I rake over the débris of my thoughts, the only semblance of a purpose I can discover is to suggest that possibly, under certain circumstances, snoring should be regarded as a fine art and respected accordingly. If this be admitted, I might suggest further that our civilization does not so regard it, as it should, and gives the practice no encouragement, but rather the contrary.

Consequently one might with reason think that there is too little snoring done—snoring with a purpose to guide it, snoring deliberately directed towards a salutary end which is otherwise unattainable—and that our society would doubtless be better off if the value of the practice were more fully recognized. In our public affairs, for instance, I have of late been much struck by the number of persons who professedly had something. The starry-eyed energumens of the New Deal were perhaps the most conspicuous examples; each and all, they were quite sure they had something. They had a clear premonition of the More Abundant Life into which we were all immediately to enter by the way of a Planned Economy. It now seems, however, that the New Deal is rapidly sinking in the same Slough of Despond which closed over poor Mr. Hoover's head, and that the More Abundant Life is, if anything, a little more remote than ever before.

I do not disparage their premonition or question it; I simply suggest that the More Abundant Life might now be appreciably nearer if they had put enough confidence in their premonition to do a great deal less thinking, planning, legislating, organizing, and a great deal—oh yes, a very great deal—more snoring.

"Counselors and counselors!" said Kutusov to Prince Bolkonsky. "If we had listened to all of them, we should be in Turkey now. We should not have made peace, and the war would never have been over. . . . Kamensky would have come to grief there if he hadn't died. He went storming fortresses with thirty thousand men. It's easy enough to take fortresses, but it's hard to finish off a campaign successfully. Storms and attacks are not what's wanted, but *time* and *patience*. Kamensky sent his soldiers to attack Rustchuk, but I trusted to them alone—time and patience—and I took more fortresses than Kamensky, and I made the Turks eat horseflesh."

He shook his head. "And the French shall, too. Take my word for it," cried Kutusov, growing warmer, and slapping himself on the chest. "I'll make them eat horseflesh!"

What in any case it all boils down to, I suppose, is the rather trite fact that merely "to have something" is by no means enough. If one is sure one has something, the next thing is to know what to do about it; and in most circumstances—in more, at any rate, than is commonly supposed—snoring is a sovereign procedure. It is presumable that many persons who have something, and know they have it, lose out on it by a futile effort to coördinate "the intimations of the dæmon" with suggestions of desire, curiosities of intellect, impulses of will. Thus they come to disbelieve in the something which they actually have, and to regard it as mere fantasy; and from this most unfortunate disability a resolute devotion to snoring would have saved them.

But I did not intend to moralize, knowing myself to be uncommonly puny at that sort of thing; so, in fear of being led further, I shall end my prosaic disquisition here.

This essay originally appeared in the *Atlantic Monthly* of November 1938. It became the title essay in *Snoring as a Fine Art and Twelve Other Essays.*

Pantagruelism

When you kindly asked me here, I was a little afraid to come, because I felt that an audience like this would more or less expect me to get at Rabelais by his professional side, and I am not able to do that. I know nothing about the practice of medicine today, let alone how it was practiced four hundred years ago. I have always been pretty healthy, or I might know more, but I am contented. Probably you have noticed how contented ignorant people are. I am not sure that Aristotle is right in that fine sentence of his about all mankind naturally desiring knowledge. Most of them would rather get along without knowing anything, if they could, because knowing things is hard work. I often wish I knew less than I do about a great many things, like politics, for instance, or history. When you know a great deal about something, you have hard work to keep your knowledge from going sour—that is, unless you are a Pantagruelist, and if you are a professor of politics, like me, nothing but Pantagruelism will ever save you. Your learning goes so sour that before you know it the Board of Health comes sniffing around, asking the neighbours whether they have been noticing anything lately. Maybe something of that sort is true of medicine too, but as I said, I do not know about that. Pantagruelism is a natural sort of preservative, like refrigeration; it keeps the temperature right. Some people put too much bad antiseptic stuff into their learning—too much embalming-fluid. What do you suppose would happen if Congress enacted a spiritual food-and-drugs law. In my line of business practically all our textbooks of politics would be confiscated, and as for an election, I do not see how we could ever have one, unless we got up some way of bootlegging all our campaign-material.

There seems to be no doubt that Rabelais's professional standing was high. According to all testimony, he must have been one of the most eminent and successful practitioners in Europe. For two years he was at the head of the great hospital at Lyon, perhaps the foremost in France, and I think also the oldest in continuous service. It is about a thousand years old. It was moved once, from one quarter of town to another, and it has been dusted up and renovated every now and then, but it still stands where Rabelais found it. Some fragments of structure which belong to his day are said to exist, but I could not identify them. The whole affair looked pretty old to me, but I imagine it is probably all right. I should not care to be a patient there, but I should not care to be a patient anywhere. I suppose if you are ill enough, you do not much mind where you are, but I was never ill enough for that.

Rabelais did some good things at that hospital. In two years he ran the death-rate down three percent. It is not easy to see how he did that. One might suppose that the death-rate would be pretty constant, no matter what diseases the patients had. Rabelais had an average of about two hundred patients, sleeping two in a bed, sometimes three, in air that was warmed only by an open fire, and with no ventilation worth speaking of. It must have been a little stuffy in there sometimes. Rabelais examined all his patients once a day, prescribed medicines and operations, and superintended a staff of thirty-two people. He managed everything. His salary was about forty dollars a year, which was high. His successor got only thirty. What do you think of that? I believe he had his board thrown in. The hospital was rich, but the trustees capitalized its prestige. They thought a physician ought to work for nothing, for the honour of it. Probably you never heard of any trustees like that, so I thought I would mention it.

The thing he did that interests me most was to beat that hospital out of five dollars. He did it in his second year there, nobody knows how, nobody can imagine how. I think that is more extraordinary than reducing the death-rate. Any man who could beat a French hospital corporation out of five dollars need not worry about the death-rate. He could raise the dead. The French auditor of the hospital was frightfully depressed about that five dollars. He left a marginal note on the account, saying that it seemed to be all wrong, but there it was, and for some reason apparently nothing could be done about it. The note has a mournful tone; you can see just how sad and distressed he was. The incident makes one think of Panurge and the money-changers, in the sixteenth chapter of the Second Book, where Rabelais says that whenever Panurge "changed a teston, cardecu or any other piece of money, the changer had been more subtle than a fox if Panurge had not at every time made five or six sols vanish away visibly, openly and manifestly, without making any hurt or lesion, whereof the changer should have felt nothing but the wind."

Rabelais held a more important position, even, than this one at Lyon. For twenty years he was personal physician to two of the ablest and most prominent men in the kingdom, Cardinal Jean du Bellay and his brother Guillaume. Great men they were. Both of them were always ailing, always worn down by heavy labours and responsibilities in the public service. They were in pretty constant need of the best medical skill, and could command it; and Rabelais was their chosen physician and confidential friend. Probably this speaks as well for his professional quality as any other evidence we have.

Then, too, there is his record at the University of Montpellier, which you historians of medicine know better than I do, and know how remarkable it was, so I need not go into it. The University of Montpellier always made a great specialty of medicine. It was like the Johns Hopkins in that. Except for a few years when Toulouse was ahead of it, I believe the Faculty of Medicine there was said to be the best in France. It is interesting to go in and look at the pictures of the sixteenth-century professors. Rabelais is there, and Rondellet, who some think was the original of the physician Rondibilis, in the Third Book. I am none too sure of that, but it does not matter. That sort of question never matters. Rondibilis is the same, no matter who his original was, or whether he had any. What of it? Think of scholars like F. A. Wolf and Lachmann tying themselves up for years over the question whether Homer was one man or eighteen. What difference does it make? You don't read Homer for any such notions as that. You read him to keep going, to keep your head above water, and you read Rabelais for the same reason.

Scurron, Rabelais's preceptor at Montpellier, has his picture there, and so has Saporta, whom Rabelais mentions as a fellow-actor in the comedy of "The Man Who Married a Dumb Wife." They had college dramatics in those days, too. Anatole France rewrote this comedy from the synopsis of it that Rabelais gives, and Mr. Granville Barker put it on the stage for us. I wish we could see it oftener, instead of so many plays that are only slices out of our own life, and usually out of the dullest and meanest part of our own life, at that. Some think that Rabelais wrote the original comedy, but this is only a guess; there is no evidence either way.

It gives one a fine sensation to look at those pictures at Montpellier, even though you can't say much for them as works of art. They are pretty poor in that way. They look wild and scary. I was going to say they look like modernist portraits. You might think the University had given some talented sign-painter a blanket commission to produce the lot, but as a rule you can make out that they are supposed to represent human beings. If Rabelais looked like his picture, then phrenology and physiognomy are not worth a red cent as sciences. But one gets a great sense of nearness to the period out of looking at those pictures in those surroundings. Montpellier is a modern city now, but the School of Medicine still has a good deal of its old quality, and the recollections of one's visit are exceedingly happy.

Rabelais makes some running comments on physicians and their ways that interest a layman. Some physicians are fussy. They want to regulate everybody and lay down the law about what is good for everybody, and especially about what is not good for anybody. Did you ever hear of that before? They begrudge you any interesting food and anything interesting to drink. Then pretty soon another batch of little rule-of-thumb doctors comes along and tells us the first batch was all wrong, and that we ought to do something different. They were just like that in Rabelais's day, too. A friend of mine has been calling my attention to some dietary rules laid down in that period—why, according to those rules, you would say it was not safe to eat anything. This sort of thing even got under Gargantua's skin, you remember. He told Friar John that it was all wrong to drink before breakfast; the physicians said so. "Oh, rot your physicians!" said Friar John. "A hundred devils leap into my body if there be not more old drunkards than old physicians." Friar John went by what philosophers used to call "the common sense of mankind." He believed that the same thing will not work for everybody, and that seems to have been Rabelais's idea too. Rabelais mentions two or three diets in the course of his story, and they seem very reasonable and sensible. He thought that Nature had some resources of her own, and he was willing to let her have something to say about such matters. The little whimsical doctors of his time would not let Nature have any chance at all, if they could help it. They laid out the course that they thought she ought to follow, and then expected her to follow it. Sometimes she did not do that, and then the patient was out of luck.

Of course, you may lay down some general rules. Rabelais knew that. For instance, he says it was sound practice for Gargantua to eat a light lunch and a big dinner, and that the Arabian physicians, who advised a big meal in the middle of the day, were all wrong. There is sense in that. It is a good general rule. But then, you have to remember that one man's light lunch is another man's square meal. Also, something depends on what you have for breakfast, and when you get it, and what you have been doing during the morning. If you have ever been around a French restaurant at lunchtime, you have probably noticed Frenchmen getting away with a pretty hefty square, and it is a great sight to see the way they dig into it. It reminds you of the old days when you were a boy on the farm, feeding a P. K. Dederick hay-press. As Panurge said, it is as good as a balsam for sore eyes to see them gulch and raven it. Well, if you had a French breakfast that morning, it is a fair bet that you would be doing the same thing. A French breakfast disappears while you are looking at it. Then again, Gargantua was a huge giant, and his light lunch would founder an ordinary stomach. It would be worse than an old-style American Sunday dinner. When he was a baby, it took the milk of 17,913 cows to feed him. No ordinary baby could do anything with that much milk. So, you see, you have to allow for exceptions to your general rule, after all, probably quite a lot of them.

By the way, did you ever hear that our term Blue Monday came out of those Sunday dinners? The mayor of one of our mid-Western cities told me that. He said he never had such a frightful time with reformers and the moral element in his town as he did on Monday morning. They ate their heads off every Sunday noon, and when they came to on Monday morning, they were full of bile and fermentation and all sorts of meanness, and that made them want to persecute their neighbours, so they would run around first thing to the mayor's office to get him to close up something that people liked, or stop something that they wanted to do. Every Monday morning he knew he was in for it. It was Blue Monday for him every week.

I have often wondered how much of this sort of thing is behind our great reform movements. One of them, you know, was started by a bilious French lawyer. He was a fearful fellow. Most people have no idea of the harm he did. He was a contemporary of Rabelais, and they were probably acquainted. He was down on Rabelais, and did as much as anybody to give him a bad name. That was because Rabelais would not join in on his reform. That is always the way with these bilious reformers. You have to reform things their way, or they say you are a scoundrel and do not believe in any reform at all. That is the way the Socialists and Communists feel nowadays, when we do not swallow their ideas whole, and yet maybe we want things reformed as much as they do. Rabelais wanted to see the Church reformed. He did his best for it. He was hand in glove with Erasmus on that. But he was a Pantagruelist, so he knew that Calvin's way and Luther's way would not really reform anything, but would only make a botch of it. Well, we see now that it all turned out just as he knew it would. Swapping the authority of a bishop for the authority of a book was not even a theoretical reform, and all it did practically was to set up a lot of little Peterkins all over Christendom, each one sure he was the only one who knew what the book meant, and down on all the others, fighting and squabbling with them and saying all sorts of hateful things about them. Rabelais knew that was sure to happen, and knew that kind of reform was just no reform at all. So he would not go in with Calvin, and Calvin, being a good bilious reformer, abused him like a pickpocket. You have to look out for bilious reformers. Maybe you have some of them down here. Calvin was an enormously able man, but his liver was out of commission. It is a strange thought, isn't it, that if somebody had fed Calvin eight or nine grains of calomel at night every week or so, and about a quarter of a pound of Rochelle salts in the morning, the whole tone of Protestant theology might have been different. It almost makes mechanists of us. But maybe you are all mechanists here. I hear that modern physicians are mostly mechanists, so perhaps you are too.

Rabelais had much the same sort of notion about reform in medicine. His position on that has puzzled a great many people. That is because they look at him in a little, sectarian, rule-of-thumb way. He was for going back to Galen and Hippocrates, cleaning off the glosses on their texts, and finding out what they really said. Well, then, some say that shows he was a hide-bound old Tory in medicine. On the other hand, he made dissections and lectured from them, which was a great innovation. He went in for experiments. He laughed at some ideas of Democritus and Theophrastus, and in the seventh chapter of the Third Book you find him poking fun at Galen himself. Well, then, others say, he was a great radical, and he has even been put forward as the father of experimentation in medicine. All that is nonsense. To the Pantagruelist, labels like radical and Tory mean just nothing at all. You go back to the classics of a subject for the practical purpose of saving yourself a lot of work. You get an accumulation of observation, method, technique, that subsequent experience has confirmed, and you can take it at second-hand and don't have to work it all out afresh for yourself. Maybe you can improve on it, here and there, and that is all right, but if you don't know the classics of your subject, you often find that you have been wasting a lot of time over something that somebody went all through, clear back in the Middle Ages. What is there radical or Tory about that? It is just good sense.

I think Americans are peculiarly impatient about the classics of any subject. In my own line, I know, I next to never meet anybody who seems to have read anything that was written before about 1890. That is one reason why we get done in so often by other people, especially in business and finance. You take a good thing wherever you find it— that was Rabelais's idea. If somebody worked it out satisfactorily for you forty years ago, or four hundred, or four thousand—you know, we have a record of quite a few little matters that were worked out very capably as long ago as that—why, you are just that much ahead. You have that much more chance to work out something else, some improvement maybe, or something new. Knowing the classics matures and seasons the mind as nothing else will, but aside from that, in a practical way, it is a great labour-saver. When I was at Ems a couple of years ago, one of their experimenters had just discovered that the Ems salts helped out a little in cases of pyorrhea. That was known four hundred years ago. It is mentioned in a report on the springs, written in the sixteenth century. Then it was forgotten, and discovered again only the other day.

But I must stop this sort of thing, and speak about Pantagruelism. I hear you have a good many Pantagruelists here in Baltimore, and that does not surprise me, because there used to be such a marvellous lot of germ-carriers in this university. If you caught Pantagruelism from Gildersleeve or Minton Warren or William Osler, there was no help for you. You had it for life. There was a big quarantine against Baltimore on account of those people. That was the most expensive quarantine ever established in the world. It cost the American people all their culture, all their intelligence, all their essential integrities, their insight, their dignity, their self-respect, their command of the future, to keep Pantagruelism from spreading. We did it, though. The country is practically free of Pantagruelism now. There is less of it here than in any other country I know. Hardly anyone ever heard of it. Probably you know how the great exponent of Pantagruelism is regarded. Why, only the other day when I was talking to a few people informally about Rabelais, a man came up to me afterward and said he was sorry his wife was not there. He had left her at home because he thought she might have to hear some improper language. That was his idea of Rabelais, and he was a professor in one of our colleges, too. Just think of a miserable little coot like that. When you look the situation over and see the general part that this country is playing in the world's affairs, and see what sort of thing she has to play it with, you begin to think that quarantine cost too much.

Pantagruelism is not a cult or a creed or a frame of mind, but a quality of spirit. In one place Rabelais says it is "a certain jollity of mind, pickled in the scorn of fortune," and this is one of its aspects: an easy, objective, genial, but unyielding superiority to everything external, to every conceivable circumstance of one's life. It is a quality like that of the ether, which the physicists of my day used to say was imponderable, impalpable, harder than steel, yet so pervasive that it permeates everything, underlies everything. This is the quality that Rabelais communicates in every line. Read the Prologue to the Second Book, for instance—better read it aloud to yourself—well, there you have it, you can't miss it, and if it does not communicate itself to your own spirit, you may as well give up the idea that you were cut out for a Pantagruelist.

And at what a time in the world's life was that Prologue written. It was a period more nearly like ours than any other in history. The difficulties and temptations that the human spirit faced were like ours. It was a period of unexampled expansion, like ours; of revolution in industry and commerce; of the inflation of avarice into a mania; of ruinous political centralization; of dominant bourgeois ideals—not the ideals of the working bourgeois, but those of the new bourgeois of bankers, speculators, shavers, lawyers, jobholders; and it was a period of great general complacency towards corruption. This is one thing that makes Rabelais particularly a man of our own time. The quality of spirit that he exhibits was brought out under circumstances almost exactly like ours, and contact with it helps us to meet our own circumstances in the way that he met his.

Pantagruelism means keeping the integrity of one's own personality absolutely intact. Rabelais says that Pantagruel "never vexed nor disquieted himself with the least pretence of dislike to anything, because he knew that he must have most grossly abandoned the divine mansion of reason if he had permitted his mind to be never so little grieved, afflicted or altered on any occasion whatsoever. For all the goods that the heaven covereth and that the earth containeth, in all their dimensions of height, depth, breadth and length, are not of so much worth as that we should for them disturb or disorder our affections, trouble or perplex our senses or spirits."

You see, the Pantagruelist never admits that there is anything in the world that is bigger than he is. Not business, not profession, not position. The case of the American business man is much discussed now, as you know. What has the typical American business man come to? He thought his business was bigger than he was, and he went into slavery to it and let it own him, and he was proud to do that, he thought that meant progress, thought it meant civilization, and he thought because his business was so great that he must be a great man; and he kept letting us know he thought so. He was like the misguided girl who had lived with so many gentlemen that she thought she was a lady. Well, then, a pinch comes, and now we are all saying the business man is only a stuffed shirt, that there is nothing inside his shirt but wind and fungus. We see that the big men of business have had to have a tariff wall around them, or get rebates from the railways on their freight, or get some other kind of special privilege, and that they were not great men at all, for almost anybody with the same privilege could have done as well.

Then think of the people in politics, the jobholders and jobhunters. There are a lot of them around just now, telling us what ought to be done and what they are going to do if they are elected. The trouble with them is that they think the job is bigger than they are, and so they destroy the integrity of their personality in order to get it or to hold it. Why, by the time a man has connived and lied and shuffled his miserable way up to the point where he can be an acceptable candidate, there isn't enough of him left to be a good jobholder, even if he wants to. The Athenians blamed Socrates, you know, because he wouldn't have anything to do with politics; he would not vote or go into any campaigns or indorse any candidates—he let it all alone. He was a great Pantagruelist, one of the greatest, so he told the Athenians that what they were blaming him for was the very reason why he and his followers were the best politicians in Athens. That closed *them* out. He was such a good Pantagruelist that finally the boys had to get together and poison him. We are having an election coming on in a few days now, and the good Pantagruelists are having a little fun out of asking their friends just what it is that they think they are going to vote for.

Pantagruelism is utterly unselfconscious; it works like a kind of secondary instinct. Have you ever noticed how Rabelais's wonderful art comes out in the relations between Pantagruel and Panurge? Pantagruel liked Panurge, was interested in him, amused by him, tolerant of all his ingenious deviltry, but never once compromised his own character. On the other hand, he was never priggish, never patronizing or moralistic with Panurge, not even in their discussion on borrowing and lending. His superiority was always unselfconscious, effortless. I think the delicate consistency that Rabelais shows on this point is perhaps his greatest literary achievement; and the climax of it is that Panurge, who was never loyal to anything or anybody, was always loyal to Pantagruel.

But Pantagruelism is not easy. In the Prologue to the Third Book we come on another characteristic which is the crowning glory of Pantagruelism. Rabelais has been talking about the blunders of an honest-minded Egyptian ruler, and some other matters of the kind, how well-intended things are sometimes misapprehended, and so on, and then he says that by virtue of Pantagruelism we are always ready to "bear with anything that floweth from a good, free and loyal heart." Maybe that is easier for you than it is for me. I don't mind saying frankly and very sadly that my Pantagruelism breaks down oftener on that than on anything. On this point Pantagruelism is like Christianity. I have often thought I might have made a pretty consistent Christian if it had not been for just that one thing that the blessed Apostle said about suffering fools gladly. How easily the great Pantagruelists seem to do that, but it only seems easy, it really is very hard to do. How easily, how exquisitely Rabelais did it. I wish I might have him in New York so he could hear some of my friends talk about the great transformations that are going to take place when Mr. Roosevelt is elected or Mr. Hoover is reelected. I always walk out on them, but Rabelais would not. He would play with them a while, and probably get some results, for they are really first-rate people, but all that sort of thing seems beyond me.

The quarantine I spoke of a moment ago appears to be pretty well lifted. We are not quarantining against much of anything, these days. Now, in conclusion, may I ask if it ever occurred to you to think what a thundering joke on the country it would be if this university should quietly, without saying anything about it, go back to its old contraband business of disseminating Pantagruelism? For that was its business. You got good chemistry with Remsen, and mathematics with Sylvester, and semitics with Paul Haupt, and a degree at the end of it, and all that sort of thing, but mark my words, before time gets through with you it will show that the real distinction of this university was that it exposed you to Pantagruelism day and night. Let us dream about it for a moment. Suppose we say you sold your campus and your plant— they may be an asset to you, but they look to me like a liability; suppose you threw out all your undergraduate students—and this time I am very sure they are a liability; suppose you went back to the little brick houses where Huxley found you, and suppose you got together a dozen or so good sound Pantagruelists from somewhere and shut them up there with your graduate students, your bachelors and masters. What a colossal joke it would be. The country has virtually ruined itself in the effort to stamp out Pantagruelism. All its institutional voices have been raised in behalf of ignoble, mean, squalid ideals, and telling us that those mean progress, those mean civilization, those mean hundred-percent Americanism. Now that the country has got itself in such distraction from following this doctrine that none of the accepted prophets have a sensible word to say, I repeat, what a joke it would be if the old original sinner should go back and begin corrupting the youth again.

Then suppose you should use a little selective pressure on your student body. You know, some people—excellent people, admirable people—are immune to Pantagruelism. You had some of them here in the old days, like President Wilson and Mr. Newton Baker. They were fine folks, good as gold, most of them, but no good at all for your purposes. Well, suppose when these immune people come around, you tell them after a while that they would probably do better up at Harvard, or maybe Yale. Yes, Yale is the place for them. There is an Institute of Human Relations up there, and these immune people are usually strong on human relations. Did you ever notice that? When Mr. Wilson and Mr. Baker got going on human relations, there was no stopping them. So you might off-load your immune people on Yale, and they could go to the Institute. They would probably find a director there—I mean, a Dean—and plenty of card-indexes and stenographers, and one thing or another like that that are just what you need to study human relations with; and meanwhile you could be getting on with Pantagruelism.

Of course you understand I am not presuming to suggest this to you. That would be most impertinent and I would not think of it. I put it to you only in a vagrant kind of way, as a colossal joke, a piece of grand fun, and perhaps with just a shade of seriousness, as a dream of youth, my own youth. As a youngster, I wished very much to do some of my graduate work here, but for one reason or another it did not come out that way. I knew what I was missing, and now I know it even better. There are youngsters like that now. They would make good Pantagruelists, and they are out of luck; there is no place for them. Maybe you are willing, for a moment, to look at this dream through their eyes. I have been doing it for a good many years now. If you look at it through their eyes, you may see a little touch of beauty in it, beside the fun. I think I do.

This essay was originally given to the Faculty of Medicine at the Johns Hopkins University, on October 28, 1932, on the four hundredth anniversary of the publication of Rabelais's *Pantagruel*. Frank Chodorov printed an edited version in the August 1946 "Nock Memorial Edition" issue of *analysis*. It is published here in its complete version for the first time, taken from the original typescript.

V. THE CULT OF POLITICS

The objection to politics and politicians, the primary indictment against all their works and ways, is that they spoil life. Human life is naturally a lovely, enjoyable, attractive thing. We are all conscious that if we could only be let alone, life would be glorious and desirable and we could do almost anything with it. But the politicians never let us alone; and while we are all busily trying to do our poor best with our lives under such throttling conditions as they put upon us, they are as busily trying to thwart us. —"Pearls Before Swine," the *Freeman,* January 4, 1922

The worst of this ever growing cancer of Statism is its moral effect. The country is rich enough to stand its frightful economic wastage for a long time yet, and still prosper, but it is already so poverty-stricken in its moral resources that the present drain will quickly run them out.

—*Journal of Forgotten Days,* May 28, 1934

In the Vein of Intimacy

The editors of this paper and its publisher appreciate more than they can say, the unlooked-for cordiality shown by the press to its first two issues. Influential daily newspapers throughout the country have held out the hand of kindly hospitality and have given the paper a most prepossessing editorial introduction to their readers. Very courteously, too, have some of the weekly papers come forward with their greeting; and among these is one whose traditions command the utmost respect of all Americans, and whose specific service during the past two years has been immeasurable. Amid a riot of the lowest passions and the most contemptible prejudices, the *Nation* walked worthily. For this it deserves, and as time goes on will increasingly be seen to deserve, the lasting gratitude of all citizens whose loyalty is loyalty to their country rather than to its office-holders; and the *Nation* in its last issue does this paper the honour of generous praise and a cordial welcome into "the field of liberal journalism."

By gratitude, therefore, as well as unusual respect, this paper seems bound to deprecate with all possible delicacy, this recommendation to the *Nation's* readers. The *Freeman* is not a liberal paper; it has no lot or part with liberalism; it has no place in the field of liberal journalism and can not pretend to seek one. That field, indeed, is so competently served by the *Nation* itself and, by the *New Republic* that it would be a superfluity, not to say an impertinence, for the editors of this paper to think of invading it. The *Freeman* is a radical paper; its place is in the virgin field, or better, the long-neglected and fallow field, of American radicalism; its special constituency, if it ever has any, will be what it can find in that field. Hence, readers of the *Nation,* if ever they do this paper the honour of picking it up, must not be misled by Mr. Villard's quick and characteristic generosity in bestowing upon it a distinction to which it has no right.

Radicalism and liberalism, unfortunately, are often used as interchangeable terms; so used, indeed, by whole myriads who, if a free public school-system is half what it is cracked up to be, ought to know better. Really, one is sometimes reminded of the man who told his little boy that ensilage is a kind of mucilage. For present purposes there is no need of contrasting academic and philosophical definitions of the two terms; the dictionary will do that in half the time, and save trouble all round. Some practical distinctions, however—such, for instance, as differentiate a radical from a liberal paper—are perhaps worth mentioning.

In the philosophy of public affairs, the liberal gets at his working theory of the State by the "high *priori* road"; that is to say, by pure conjecture. Confronted with the phenomenon of the State, and required to say where it came from and why it is here, the liberal constructs his answer by the *a priori* method; thus Carey, for example, derived the State from the action of a gang of marauders, Rousseau from a social contract, Sir Robert Filmer from the will of God, and so on. All these solutions of the problem are ingenious and interesting speculations, but nothing more than speculations. The radical gets at his theory of the State by the historical method; by tracing back and examining every appearance of the State, to the most remote examples that history can furnish; segregating the sole invariable factor which he finds to be common throughout, and testing it both positively and negatively as a determining cause.

The result carries the radical to the extreme point of difference from the liberal in his practical attitude towards the State. The liberal believes that the State is essentially social and is all for improving it by political methods so that it may function according to what he believes to be its original intention. Hence, he is interested in politics, takes them seriously, goes at them hopefully, and believes in them as an instrument of social welfare and progress. He is politically-minded, with an incurable interest in reform, putting good men in office, independent administrations, and quite frequently in third-party movements. The liberal forces of the country, for instance, rallied quite conspicuously to Mr. Roosevelt in the good old days of the Progressive party. The liberal believes in the reality and power of political leadership; thus, again, he eagerly took Mr. Wilson on his hands at the last two elections. The radical, on the other hand, believes that the State is fundamentally anti-social and is all for improving it off the face of the earth; not by blowing up office-holders, as Mr. Palmer appears to suppose, but by the historical process of strengthening, consolidating and enlightening economic organization. It is the impetus that Lenin has given to economic organization, and not his army, that makes him a terror to the State. The radical has no substantial interest in politics, and regards all projects of political reform as visionary. He sees, or thinks he sees, quite clearly that the routine of partisan politics is only a more or less elaborate and expensive by-play indulged in for the sake of diverting notice from the primary object of all politics and political government, namely, the economic exploitation of one class by another; and hence all candidates look about alike to him, and their function looks to him only like that of Dupin's pretended lunatic in "The Purloined Letter."

On the side of economics, the practical difference between the radical and the liberal is quite as spacious. The liberal appears to recognize but two factors in the production of wealth, namely, labour and capital; and he occupies himself incessantly with all kinds of devices to adjust relations between them. The radical recognizes a third factor, namely, natural resources; and is absolutely convinced that as long as monopoly-interest in natural resources continues to exist, no adjustment of the relations between labour and capital can possibly be made, and that therefore the excellent devotion of the liberal goes, in the long-run, for nothing. Labour, applied to natural resources, produces wealth; capital is wealth applied to production; so long, therefore, as access to natural resources is monopolized, so long will both labour and capital have to pay tribute to monopoly and so long, in consequence, will their relations be dislocated. The liberal looks with increasing favour upon the socialization of industry, or as it is sometimes called, the democratization of industry. The radical keeps pointing out that while this is all very well in its way, monopoly-values will as inevitably devour socialized industry as they now devour what the liberals call capitalistic industry. What good would possibly come to labour or capital or to the public, from democratizing the coal-mining business, for example, unless and until monopoly-interest in the coal-beds themselves were expropriated? The miners of England have begun to see this and to shape their demands accordingly. What use in democratizing the business of operating railways, as long as the franchise-value of railways remains unconfiscated? What use in democratizing the building industry, so long as economic rent continues to accrue to monopoly? No use whatever, as the radical sees it, except for a very moderate amount of educative value that may probably be held to proceed from the agitation of such projects.

Thus the fundamental differences between the radical and the liberal may be seen, even from this brief sketch, to be considerable; too considerable by far to permit this paper to go under false colours into the hands of any readers of the *Nation*. It has been very distasteful to make the *Nation's* courtesy a text for the drawing-out of these differences; but the dishonourable acceptance, even for a moment, of an honourable distinction, would be much more distasteful.

In the fourth issue of the *Freeman* (March 31, 1920), Nock wrote this unsigned editorial, in which he set out some of the philosophical underpinnings of the magazine by contrasting it with the liberal alternatives of the day.

The Leadership of Ideas

We read attentively the other day in one of the great metropolitan dailies, an uncommonly well written editorial calling resolutely for political leadership. It reminded us that this, too, is the great recurrent cry of our liberal contemporaries. They are never weary of calling attention to the dismal lack of leadership in public affairs, and of pouring forth their deep desire that some great leader should be, miraculously perhaps, raised up. This rather remarkable demand set us wondering, first, what sort of leadership our contemporaries want; and second, why they, instead of calling for leadership and bewailing the lack of leadership, do not themselves furnish a little more of the right kind of leadership than they are in the habit of affording to a nation groping in darkness. To ask for leadership among our politicians at Washington—except as the word is understood in the glossary of party organization—is naïve enough; to intimate that leadership could be exercised among them is still more naïve. Our contemporaries should be aware that the present epoch is one for merely instrumental statesmen, and that none of another type could possibly gain a place in our public life, let alone hold one for forty-eight hours after he had gained it. The instrumental statesman gains his place and holds it upon what Professor Huxley (who knew the breed) wittily called the coach-dog theory of leadership—that of looking sharp which way the coach is going, and then running out in front of it and barking. There is plenty of that sort of leadership, and our system of politics in this epoch has no place for any other kind.

But the epoch is passing. We hope that it will pass without calamity, though we are by no means sure that it will. In the epoch which is now hard at hand, we can foresee a considerable place for another kind of leadership, the leadership of such as can apply thought to politics, of such as live by ideas rather than by clap-trap and dwell habitually in the realm of the idea rather than in the realm of buncombe. We are so sure of this that we venture to bring the prospect to the attention of our liberal friends and to their strange *pro tem.* bedfellow, our powerful daily contemporary. Why might they not even now, indeed, try the experiment of themselves applying a little thought to politics, of themselves venturing occasionally a little way into the realm of the idea, in order to prepare the way of the leader, when the present epoch closes, and make his paths straight? One might draw disagreeable inferences from the conjunction of their unwillingness to do this and their insistence upon leadership, but we do not wish to do anything of the kind. We wish instead to point to an example which our despondent friends who cry for leadership may find practical and suggestive.

It is contained in the writings of Edmund Burke; to be exact, it is among the last words he ever wrote. Burke lived at a time which was in some respects much like our own. He fought the influence of the French Revolution with all the force of utter repugnance and terror. No American banker ever more dreaded the nightmare of bolshevism than Burke dreaded the miasma spread over Europe by the "viper brood of canting egotists" in Paris. Yet in December, 1791, he ends his "Thoughts on French Affairs" with these words:

> The evil is stated, in my opinion, as it exists. The remedy must be where power, wisdom and information, I hope, are more united with good intentions than they can be with me. I have done with this subject, I believe, for ever. It has given me many anxious moments for the last two years.

So much for his sincere convictions about what he regarded as the utter iniquity and madness of the French Revolution. But mark the marvellous words that follow:

> If a great change is to be made in human affairs, the minds of men will be fitted to it; the general opinions and feelings will draw that way. Every fear, every hope, will forward it; and then they who persist in opposing this mighty current in human affairs, will appear rather to resist the decrees of Providence itself than the mere designs of men. They will not be resolute and firm, but perverse and obstinate.

No wonder that Matthew Arnold says that this return which Burke makes upon himself is one of the finest things in any literature.

> That [says Arnold] is what I call living by ideas: when one side of a question has long had your earnest support, when all your feelings are

engaged, when you hear all round you no language but one, when your party talks this language like a steam-engine and can imagine no other—still to be able to think, still to be irresistibly carried, if so it be, by the current of thought to the opposite side of the question, and, like Balaam, to be unable to speak anything *but what the Lord has put in your mouth.*

Yes, that is living by ideas; that sort of thing is what we mean by the application of thought to politics, and its practice will mark political leadership in the next epoch; it would even now mark the only kind of leadership that is worth anything at the present time. But does one hear our great newspapers speak habitually in that vein? Does the *New York Times* speak in any such way of the Russian revolution? Who of our pro-war partisans, without abating one jot of his convictions or his partisanship, ever makes such a return upon himself in the matter of the causes of the war, the participation of America, the terms of the armistice and the peace? Who among all those committed to the support of our political and economic institutions in their present time of trial, can yet close his advocacy of them by saying, "But if a great change is to be made, the minds of men will be fitted to it, and the general opinions and feelings will draw that way—and then those who think as I do, and resist as I do, will not appear resolute and firm, but perverse and obstinate?"

We earnestly suggest to our contemporaries that they cease their importunity for leadership where leadership is neither forthcoming nor possible—that is, in the field of practical politics. We suggest that they themselves begin to apply a little disinterested thought to politics; that they themselves submit with a docility like Burke's to the leadership of ideas, and that by all the power of influence and example they recommend that leadership to others.

This unsigned editorial appeared in the March 15, 1922, issue of the *Freeman*.

The State

I

From all appearances, organized society is tending away from the political theory of government, and towards a theory that may be called purely administrative. The circumstances of the ten years just past have greatly accelerated this tendency, and recognition of it now appears in many quarters where the magnitude of the change involved is perhaps not fully perceived—as, for example, in Principal Jacks's excellent article on the League of Nations, in last February's issue of the *Atlantic Monthly*. It is much to the point, however, to see clearly how great and fundamental this change is. Changes hitherto, throughout the history of humanity's communal life, have been from one mode or form of political government to another. Autocracy has been modified into constitutionalism, and constitutionalism into republicanism, which is generally, also, but quite improperly, identified with democracy. All these modes or forms of government are, however, in their essence, political; a change or development from one to another was merely a modal change, not an essential change. The change now impending is not modal but essential; it is a change in fundamental theory. When completed, it will have divested government of every vestige of political character and function, and will have left it standing only as an administrative agency.

To say that this change is impending is by no means to say that it will soon be reflected in our institutions, or that it will suddenly or violently assert itself or get itself enforced by coarse and indiscriminate methods. Such a thing does not happen. In his last days, Edmund Burke said of the French Revolution, which he so feared and hated, that "if a great change is to take place, the minds of men *will be fitted to it*"; and so it really is, though no one can say precisely how the fitting is done. Formal education and propagandizing have little to do with determining it; indeed, more often than not it goes against these, like the motion of the tide under the waves. The nature of an impending change can be better forecast than from any superficial happenings, by discerning the way the tide is running, the way in which the minds of men are being fitted, the general terms in which they think; and now, apparently, the minds of men are being fitted for the fundamental change above described.

The difference between political and administrative government can not better be made clear than by paraphrasing the first few pages of the treatise called *The State,* by Franz Oppenheimer, professor of political science in the University of Frankfort, now well translated and available in English. Confronted by the problem of the State as a phenomenon of history, English and American writers on the subject have uniformly tried to solve it by the a priori method; or, one may better say, by guesswork. How did the State originate? What circumstances gave rise to it? What was its primary purpose and intention? To these questions, which touch the essence of their problem, English and American writers have invariably replied by conjecture—one even affirming that the State came into being by the will of God; another, that its idea originated in a social instinct; another that it was the development of an early association for the purposes of protection; and so on. The trouble with these theories is that they are insufficiently supported by evidence.

Not long ago, on the Continent, a new method of investigation was set up, whereby the State is examined as far back as its existence can be traced, by a strictly historical method, and its phenomena noted for evidence of its origin and purpose. Among these phenomena, one is invariable. It appears in every form or manifestation of the State, from its earlier and simple type down to its present highly-organized, highly-integrated type. There is no State of which we have record that does not present the phenomenon of two distinct economic classes which have interests directly opposed; a relatively small, owning and exploiting class which lives by appropriating without compensation the labour-products of a relatively large, propertyless and dependent class.

Wherever in history the State appears, it bears this aspect. The State of the primitive herdsmen exhibits it as clearly as our own. How may it be accounted for? It is usually explained as due to the well-known inequalities of natural endowment prevailing among the race. Persons of greater ability soon found themselves, by force of their natural superiority, in a position to command the services of persons who had less ability, and thus the lateral stratification of the State into two classes took place almost at once. We can all remember, by way of illustration, how generally the commercial success of Mr. John D. Rockefeller and Mr. Andrew Carnegie was accounted for in this way.

This assumption is very simple and also very plausible; so naturally it finds ready acceptance. It is nevertheless untenable, and is instantly seen to be untenable when one recalls the fact that this economic exploitation of one class by another could not possibly take place unless all available land were either actually or legally occupied; for no one would submit to exploitation or to working for another for less than he could make by going out upon unoccupied land and working for himself. The Physiocrats, that illustrious body of Frenchmen who, a century and a half ago, founded the science of political economy, saw this. Karl Marx saw it; and it is strange that so clear a thinker should not also have seen all its implications. In his chapter on colonization, after recounting the fruitless experiment of the English colonizer, Mr. Peel, Marx puts it in so many words that the system which he chooses to call capitalism, but which should properly be called economic exploitation, can not be erected as long as land, actually and legally unoccupied, remains available.

It is plain that in no primitive State (wherein, remember, the system of economic exploitation was in full force) was all available land actually occupied; for it is not all actually occupied in any modern State, even those as densely populated as Germany, Belgium or Japan. Therefore it must have been legally occupied; the ruling and exploiting class must have held it out of accessibility by proscription. If not, the exploited majority would have moved out upon it, and the continuance of exploitation would have become impracticable—just as Diaz found that he could not get labourers to work in the Mexican mines unless he first confiscated the communal lands.

The State, then as now, must have been the agency whereby this proscription was made effective and kept effective. It would thus appear that the State, instead of originating according to any of the conjectures made by English and American writers on the subject, originated as a class-weapon of conquest and confiscation, and that its primary function was, and still is, to maintain the stratification of society into the two classes noted.[1]

1. It is worthy of remark that the hunting tribes, with whom conquest and economic

Oppenheimer's conclusion is as follows:

> The State, completely in its genesis, essentially and almost completely during the first stages of its existence, is a social institution forced by a victorious group of men on a defeated group, with the sole purpose of regulating the dominion of the victorious group over the vanquished, and securing itself against revolts from within and attacks from abroad. Teleologically, this dominion had no other purpose than the economic exploitation of the vanquished by the victors.
>
> No primitive State known to history originated in any other manner.

Robertus-Jagetzow also, whom Oppenheimer quotes, says,

> History is unable to demonstrate any one people wherein . . . the division of labour had not developed itself as the subjection of one set under the other.

Thus is derived a conception of the State, or if one prefer a general term that is somewhat simpler, of *political government,* as a purely anti-social organization; indeed, as the archetype and primary pattern of all organization (I can think of no exception whatever) which is now deemed anti-social and as such is reprehended and discouraged by the common conscience of mankind. It will be useful to remark instances— instances known to every one—of the disparity between the social morals of the State and those of the individual, which are in large part enforced upon the individual by the power of the State itself. Upon any other theory of the State, they would be anomalous and inexplicable. If one regard the State, however, as in its origin and by its first intention an anti-social organization—a class-instrument for the perpetuation of economic exploitation—they at once appear normal and logical. Some of these will be discussed in a later paper.

II

Having gone thus far in considering the origin and nature of the State, or political government, it is appropriate just here to examine for a moment the content of the word *political,* as used of government. This

---

exploitation is almost impracticable, on account of the nature of their pursuits, never formed a State; nor yet did the primitive peasants, for the same reason.

can be best done by expanding Franz Oppenheimer's introductory paragraphs, and illustrating them with some examples. Oppenheimer's treatise is extremely brief and compact; the substance of a chapter being often compressed into a paragraph, and that of a paragraph into a sentence. It is therefore a rather hard book to read, and one who approaches the subject for the first time is likely to miss part of its import. These articles are written only for the sake of helping to make its fundamental doctrine, and especially its definitions, clear and easy to be understood.

There are two, and only two, means whereby man can satisfy his needs and desires. These are, first, by labour, by the exchange of labour-products and services; and second, by appropriating without compensation the labour-products and services of others. The former means may be called the *economic means*. It is well understood and needs no illustration, for every exercise of the economic means is easily reducible to the terms of primitive trade and barter. The second, however, needs careful consideration.

This second means whereby man satisfies his needs and desires is obviously robbery. When a person employs this means without sanction of law, as when he breaks a shop or picks a pocket, he is apprehended and punished. When he employs it under sanction of law, as when he uses a tariff to enhance the price of a commodity or uses the monopoly of a natural resource, such as anthracite coal, for instance, to limit production and create an artificial scarcity, with consequent enhancement of prices, he goes unpunished and unquestioned. Yet essentially these acts are robbery; for the enhanced price must be paid, like all prices, out of production, and the enhancement represents no value whatever, but merely represents the privilege conferred upon him by the State through the tariff or the monopoly. By so much, therefore, as the enhanced price is higher than the price determined by free competition in the open market, by so much is he appropriating without compensation the labour-products and services of others. Quite as truly does he do this as though he robbed their shops of labour-products and commanded their services as chattel-slaves.

The State, as we have seen, had its origin in conquest and confiscation, and it has existed ever since as an agency whereby this system of economic exploitation is maintained. It is characterized in every manifestation of which we have record, by this phenomenon of a small exploiting minority and a large exploited majority. Every State, from the earliest to the most modern, is a robber-State. Of its instruments for effecting robbery, the most primitive, and now most costly, are armies and navies. These are used chiefly in safeguarding the economic exploitation of weak alien peoples by the State's beneficiaries at home; as in Morocco by the French State's beneficiaries, or in Haiti, Santo Domingo and Central America by the American State's beneficiaries. The collision of interests, or the prospect of collision, where several sets of beneficiaries are at work in one place, enormously stimulates the growth of armies and navies and the consequent growth of the militarist spirit.

The instruments whereby the State most largely effects robbery of its own citizens are natural-resource monopoly, tariffs, franchises, concessions. These are all delegations of the taxing power. By putting a tariff against the importation, say, of wool, the State permits the domestic wool-producing interests to levy a tax upon consumers of wool to the amount of the excess in price over the price determined by supply and demand in a free competitive market. These interests give the consumer nothing in return for this tax; the State gives them, as beneficiaries, the privilege of levying it, and they accordingly do so.[2]

Similarly, by permitting private monopoly of natural resources, the State delegates to those beneficiaries who are lucky enough to hold such monopoly, the power to levy a tax upon all who desire access to those natural resources for purposes of production. Nothing is given in return for this tax; the beneficiary simply appropriates without compensation so much of the labour-products and services of others as the State permits him to take. In some cases, it is a very large

2. It is rather interesting to observe signs that the true character of tariffs as sheer charters of robbery, is becoming generally known. Formerly there was a good deal of popular argument and discussion of tariff bills, and many pleas in Congress on the ground of "protecting American industries," "protecting the American workingman," etc. There was only a little *pro forma* discussion of our present tariff-law, probably the most outrageous and indefensible in our history, and hardly any pretence that it meant anything but straight theft or that it was passed for any reason but that it could be passed and that its beneficiaries, by making hay while the sun shone, could do quite well out of it in the length of time that must elapse before it can be revised.

amount, e.g., the monopoly of lands in New York City held by the Astor family and by the corporation of Trinity Church. These delegations of the taxing power are called *privileges*.

These are the main devices whereby the State fulfils its primary function of keeping up, in our communal life, the economic exploitation of one class by another. We are now prepared to understand that the second means which man has of satisfying his needs and desires, which is directly opposed to the first or economic means, may be called the *political means*.

It is important to understand these definitions clearly. To gain a livelihood, to satisfy his needs and desires, man can either work or steal; he can use the economic means or the political means. By the economic means, he exchanges labour and labour-products for the labour and labour-products of others. By the political means, he appropriates the labour and labour-products of others, giving neither labour nor labour-products in exchange. Inasmuch as so large a proportion of the State's activity, certainly ninety per cent of it, is spent upon enabling this uncompensated appropriation of labour and labour-products, the State itself is well described by Oppenheimer, in reference to its origin, nature and function, as *the organization of the political means*. "Political government" signifies the same thing; it means the sort of government that has for its primary purpose the maintenance of economic exploitation through privilege.

The reader is now in a position to survey certain aspects of the State which must have impressed him as anomalous. For instance, upon any of the current theories of the State, it is rather remarkable that the right of individual self-expression in politics, which has been rapidly extended and is now wellnigh universal, should have resulted in so much less benefit to the exploited majority than was expected. Republicanism has done little more to make effective the will and the desires of the majority than constitutionalism or autocracy. The war made this clear in a striking and unmistakable way; and even disregarding the revelations made by the war, it is a matter of the commonest knowledge that the interests of the majority are as egregiously disserved in republican France and America as they are in monarchical Britain and Belgium. But if the State is *per se* an anti-social institution, an organization of the political means, then obviously its nature persists under one form as under another, and a change of form or mode counts for nearly nothing. A republic which maintains the integrity of the political means through an army and navy, private monopoly of natural resources, tariffs and franchises, is quite as essentially anti-social as any autocracy that uses the like instruments for the like purpose.

Similarly, in republics and constitutional monarchies where the party-system prevails, a change of party is futile. Party-politics and campaign-promises have quite generally become, in our popular scale of speech, synonyms for falsehood and disreputableness. If the State were a social institution, having its origin in any kind of regard for the general welfare, it is hard to see why this should be as it invariably is. The politically-minded liberal or progressive would be quite justified in his indefeasible optimism, his hopeful belief that a due allowance for human frailty, a little busy tinkering with externals—a change of party, a new platform, a new party, or what not—will help to mend matters. But if the State be the organization of the political means, a device to enable certain persons to live without working, by appropriating the labour and labour-products of other persons, without compensation, his faith and his enterprise are alike devoid of foundation and are mere mischievous absurdity.

Nock wrote a six-part article on the State in five issues of the *Freeman*. Publisher Huebsch described them as "summing up this paper's attitude towards the State." They were also Nock's first sustained attempt to present his views on the State. Parts I and II are included here. They appeared in the June 13 and June 20, 1923, issues of the *Freeman*.

Officialism and Lawlessness

One of our ablest lawyers, Mr. James Coolidge Carter, some years ago raised the question, What is Law? and called attention to its immense difficulty. Mr. Brand Whitlock, then mayor of Toledo, brought it up again about twenty years ago in a little monograph that never got half the attention it deserved, called, *The Administration of Law in Cities.* Both these eminent men gave the question up as unanswerable, and their discussion of the problems involved in it is one of our neglected classics. Perhaps the most useful thing that a publisher could do today, when the subject of law and lawlessness is so much in the public mind, would be to reprint Mr. Carter's lecture and Mr. Whitlock's essay together in a small volume and circulate it.

For when Mr. Hoover, Mr. Taft, Senator Capper, and others of our representative men undertake to reprove us for lawbreaking, their complaints logically run back to this question. The average man's instinct knows that when Mr. Hoover talks about lawbreaking he really means statute-breaking. Anyone can tell offhand what a statute is. It is anything that certain elected persons have written down on a piece of paper, and another elected person has signed. But is a statute *per se* a law? I remember a statute passed in one of our Middle States, I believe, to the effect that two trains approaching an intersection must both come to a full stop, and neither may start again until the other has passed! Is that a law? The instinct of the average man promptly says it is not, and the judgment of instinct is borne out in the fact that no such statute is obeyed, can be obeyed, or has any power to get itself obeyed. But the moment this is acknowledged, the moment it is admitted that private judgment has any play whatever in the premises, that moment there is introduced the whole vast question, *What is law?*

Golden Rule Jones, Mr. Whitlock's predecessor as mayor of Toledo, probably did as well as anyone could with the baffling problem of defining law when he said that "law in the United States is anything that the people will back up." Emerson also observed to the same effect that "The law is only a memorandum." The Constitution is officially, as Mr. Justice Harlan was given so often to declaring it, "the fundamental law of the land." But are the Fourteenth and Fifteenth Amendments actually law? Obviously they are not, and no one would be as much embarrassed by a serious appeal to them as those whose sworn duty it is to enforce them. From the Constitution down to the municipal ordinances of one-horse towns, we have a mass of enactments, many of them practicable enough and some of them rather sensible, that somehow fail of being actual laws; they are not obeyed or enforced or even ever heard of, and they apparently have no power to rescue themselves from this extreme desuetude. Whichever way one looks at it, there seems a most important essential difference between a law and a statute; between a law and an ordinance; even between a law and a Constitutional provision.

Average human instinct, however, without being able to define this difference, is fully aware that it exists; and that is the reason why Mr. Hoover's recent admonitions fell so largely on deaf ears. Mr. Hoover implied that anything good, bad or indifferent, practicable or impracticable that a legislature enacts and that an executive signs is a law; whereas we all know that it may be, and very often is, nothing of the kind. Thomas Jefferson spoke straight from the average man's instinct when he said that the legislative enactments known as the Alien and Sedition Acts had no more effective force of law, and should have no more, "than if Congress had commanded us all to fall down and worship a golden image." We all know furthermore that this instinct, though we may not be able to make a satisfactory intellectual interpretation of it, is logically sound. Once admit Mr. Hoover's theory and, as Jefferson's comparison shows, one is led straight to the acme of absurdity. One need not veer off into any abstract questions concerning the rights of man and the corresponding limitations which those rights put upon lawmaking bodies. It is enough to observe with Jefferson that carrying Mr. Hoover's idea of the nature of law by a short step towards its logical extreme shows it to be utterly preposterous.

Mr. Hoover's pronouncement also, I regret to say, causes him to raise other implications which, while not more culpable than the foregoing, are more directly offensive to large numbers of our citizenry. Those who assume with Mr. Hoover that a statute and a law are one and the same are prone, in their public utterances, to lump all "lawbreakers" together under a general and indiscriminate reprehension, and to regard them as beings who not only ought to be, but who in their hearts really are, ashamed of themselves. Nothing is farther from the truth; and this misapprehension shows how directly intellectual error may lead to a moral error of the first magnitude. If those who thus lecture us for our disregard of law would look into the question of what law is and what it is not, and would study the operation of fundamental human instinct on that question, they would save themselves from doing their fellow-citizens considerable injustice. In the exercise of private judgment against Mr. Hoover's theory of law, average human instinct is conscious not only of its own intellectual integrity but of its moral integrity as well; and no amount of expostulation or abuse—I can call it by no fairer word—will alter its consciousness.

The testimony of instinct comes out negatively, in the degree of respect paid to public servants according as their duties lie mainly with enactments that the common conscience of mankind does not support. Thus the police of London, who are very little occupied with the mere *malum prohibitum,* are more highly respected than those of our cities. Before prohibition everyone thought well of our Coast Guard, but respect for that useful body has decreased notably in the last ten years. The feeling towards agents of the prohibition service amounts to repugnance. One is struck by the way most people take the news that a prohibition agent has been killed in action. They behave at best with indifference; often as if they thought he were well out of the way. Yet when a policeman dies trying to vindicate the law against homicide or burglary the same people admire his heroism.

Human nature can neither be preached nor bullied out of assent to this testimony of instinct, and self-respecting human nature resents the attempt to do either. I confess I cannot understand what has happened to the American people's sense of dignity, that they permit their public servants to address them in the tone that many of these latter have lately chosen to employ. It would seem to me most competent to remind our officials in no uncertain terms that in raising implications against all statute-breakers they are committing an intolerable imper-tinence. We are all statute-breakers, every man, woman, and child in the land; and the discrimination that we instinctively exercise towards enactments which do not command the common conscience of mankind, or concerning which the common conscience is neutral, is not attended by the slightest consciousness of wrong-doing. On the contrary we know that fundamental human instincts are sound and trustworthy, as Thomas Jefferson declared them to be, and that no one has the right to arraign our allegiance to them as immoral.

Does anyone actually presume to intimate that anywhere in the United States a man who walks two miles for pleasure on Sunday, or plays tennis, or buys a newspaper, or kisses his wife is acting from a defective moral sense? If not, just where in the category of prohibited things does the moral sense begin to show defect? One may always use oneself for purposes of illustration in cases where such service might be disagreeable, so I may say I am a statute-breaker and have been one all my life. I have bought cigarettes in Kansas—very bad ones—and in other States where their sale was forbidden. But for the fact that I am no drinker, I dare say I should be evading the inconvenience of prohibition. My path through life is strewn with the wreckage of enactments contemplating not only trivial matters like these but also some that are more serious. But I cannot recall an instance of this kind where my moral sense puts in any testimony against me or where the offense is one that I should hesitate about repeating. In all this I believe I stand with every man-jack of my fellow-citizens. Their offenses may not be the same as mine, but they are of the same order; they are offenses that concern some form of the mere *malum prohibitum,* about which the normal moral sense is silent. Moreover, if all the courts in the country, and all the executives from President to pound-master, should undertake to tell me that my moral sense is defective, their word would make no more impression on me than water on a duck's back; and in this, too, I believe I have every one of my fellow-citizens with me. It is conceivable that even a prohibitionist might be as sincerely impenitent about Sunday golf or ice cream, or failing to declare an extra box of cigars, or about crowding the tax regulations a little as I should be about buying a drink if I wanted one. Somewhere or other we all depart from the strict letter of the law, and so far are we from any sense of crime or sin that in some instances, perhaps, we secretly glory in our shame, and would glory in it openly but for certain practical inconveniences that might ensue.

Such is the force of man's private judgment, and whenever a statute has been set up in opposition to it, the statute has always gone by the board. This sort of thing has been tried for hundreds of years, and never yet has it succeeded. Those who think it should succeed now in the case of prohibition have simply no idea of what it is that they antagonize.

Have our official monitors ever asked themselves where we should all be if we were not what they are pleased to call lawbreakers? What would become of the individual who is trying to live peaceably and decently under a bureaucracy if he were not a lawbreaker? He simply could not get on at all. The average man's instinct prompts him to a just sense of proportion in this matter; the trouble with our monitors is that they speak from the point of view of the doctrinaire or the job holder instead of that of the man in the street who has something to do that is worth doing and wants to get it done. One might say that a bureaucracy exists chiefly for the purpose of impeding a citizen in his legitimate pursuits; and more often than not, the only way of resisting or evading its ignorant and routine-bound exactions is through "lawlessness." The citizen, therefore, takes that way whenever he can, and has the justification of a sound instinct in so doing.

Let me give an illustration or two to make this clear. This morning I undertook to mail the corrected proofs of a book to my publishers in New York, from the head post-office in a French border town. I proposed to send it by registered book-post at third-class rates, as I had every right to do. The clerk demurred, and called in the *controleur,* a sort of first mate of a French post-office, who glanced at the proofs, saw corrections made in handwriting, and said I should have to pay first-class rates, the difference being about a dollar and a quarter. He was an austere and fidgety person who would not listen to any appeal— no doubt he had never seen or heard of a proof-sheet in all his life; so I went back to my hotel, borrowed a copy of the postal regulations, returned to the post-office, looked up the head mogul, and fought the battle out with him to a successful issue. By this time the morning had gone.

Now, the point is that I needed that morning for something more important than a collision with the impenetrable stupidity of a bureaucracy. I needed it for urgent work that could not be delayed. Hence, if there had not been so many people around, I should have dealt with that *controleur* American fashion by quietly slipping him a few francs, and then gone away to resume my work in peace; nor would my conscience have been disturbed by that easy way of settling the matter. Yet I suppose that bribery is as serious a matter in French law as in ours. I could of course have yielded to the extortion and paid first-class postage, but that did not suit me. With me it was a case of millions for baksheesh, but not one sou for bureaucracy. Besides, the whole question of resistance or submission to the incursions of any bureaucracy comes in here. If one does not oppose them somehow, they increase and multiply beyond endurance. If one opposes them personally, it is a ruinous waste of time and energy. It is, therefore, a sound instinct which tells the average man that to exist at all comfortably under a bureaucracy and get anything done, he must on occasions walk after the counsels of the ungodly and stand in the way of sinners.

I remember a story, which may be apocryphal, told of Godkin, the redoubtable editor of the New York *Evening Post* thirty years ago. On his way home one evening he was met at his door by a policeman with some sort of official notice that something was wrong with his frontage; either the snow was not cleared according to rule or the ash-barrels were out of place—some small matter like that. Instead of fooling away a couple of days over red tape, or perhaps appearing in court to answer for violating an ordinance, Godkin cleared up the matter on the spot by making two crimes out of one; he gave the policeman ten dollars, promised it should not happen again, and told him to forget it. Godkin was then engaged in a great newspaper campaign against municipal corruption, so when the story got around, as it somehow did, there was a great laugh over it. Yet according to the average man's instinct, that was the only sensible way to settle the matter. Godkin saved himself a deal of time and trouble, and so was satisfied. The policeman was satisfied. The court was one trivial case short on its crowded docket. The public, in whose interest the ordinance was framed, was satisfied because Godkin straightened up his ash-barrels. The only thing left unsatisfied was the interesting abstraction known as the majesty of the law. There seems no doubt that between Godkin and the policeman, the majesty of the law came off badly. But the average man usually cannot quite settle with himself just what the majesty of the law amounts to. And yet the average man, confirmed and inveterate statute-buster though he be, is law-abiding; he is well-meaning and decent, though from the tone adopted by our moral monitors one might not suspect it. Show him a law that is really a law, something that measurably reflects the common conscience of mankind, and he is quite likely to obey it.

But a bureaucracy will not meet the public half way. Officialism, as Herbert Spencer pointed out years ago, is interested chiefly in strengthening itself, digging itself farther and farther in, and multiplying its encroachments on the rights, liberties, and consciences of the individual citizen. Anything like taking the public into its confidence is obviously inconsistent with this, and cannot be done. Therefore, in their comment on our lawlessness our official servants do not define, do not explain, do not reason: they merely tell us.

The instinct which warns us against this tendency of officialism is wholly sound. It testifies that this tendency should be resisted. A bureaucracy should be put in its place and kept there. The individual, acting alone, cannot do this. All he can do is to ward off from himself the evil incidence of officialism as best and as often as he may; and the only way he can do this is through an occasional discriminating exercise of "lawlessness."

So much for the individual. Now, how can society collectively best withstand progressive incursions of officialism and keep a bureaucracy in its place? We are told, rightly enough, that the first thing, the indispensable thing, is strict attention. Without this nothing can be done. When Thomas Jefferson was representing our Government in Paris, he wrote Edward Carrington that "if once the people become inattentive to the public affairs, you and I and Congress and Assemblies, judges and governors, shall all become wolves. It seems to be the law of our general nature, in spite of individual exceptions." We have a saying which has degenerated into a kind of cliché, but is none the less true, that eternal vigilance is the price of liberty. The mass of our public is supposed to fail in this vigilance and to have become extremely "inattentive to the public affairs," except around election time when the general interest bears something of a sporting character, hardly to be called very serious. This count against our people is probably true, but I do not make a point of it. I mention this commonplace only to bring in a question to which it gives rise.

Mere vigilance is worth very little unless the way is open for immediate
and appropriate action upon the delinquency that vigilance discovers.
What, then, is the use of vigilance against the encroachments of
officialism under a political system which by its fundamental organization makes such action impossible? Here again the average man's
instinct which prompts him to abstain from any political interest, unless
for purposes of profit, seems to me a sound one. The utmost that our
federal system permits is to sack a handful of job holders at the end of
four years or seven years; under the system in other countries they can
be turned out at any time and without notice. Some of our worst
habitual offenders against the liberty and sovereignty of the people,
indeed, are to all intents and purposes irremovable. They may be
impeached, but as far back as Jefferson's time, impeachment, as he said,
was "not even a scarecrow"; and we all know it is no more than that
now. But turning a few job holders out at the end of a fixed term does
nothing against bureaucracy and officialism or against their tendencies;
these go on under the next regime of job holders just as they did under
the last. Meanwhile, too, there is no competent mode of reprehension
that society can collectively apply to a job holder for any insult to the
people's dignity or any injury to their sovereignty. That is to say, there
is none unless society, like the individual, has recourse to lawlessness.

Collective lawlessness interested Mr. Jefferson and gained his calm
and rather naïve approval. "I like a little rebellion now and then," he
wrote one correspondent, and on the occasion of Shays's Rebellion he
expressed his hope that the country would never go twenty years
without one like it. Shays and his malcontents were not altogether
wrong, he thought, but even if they were, the rebellion was probably
a good thing on general principles. It showed that the people were
alive to public concerns, and it also kept the ear of the job holder open
to his master's voice. It is no disparagement to the Founding Fathers
to say that being human, they were not omniscient in their foresight.
Whatever their intentions may have been, they did actually construct
a political system that puts officialism beyond the reach of any remedial
or punitive collective action except violence; and Jefferson was thoroughly aware of it.

While I am entirely of Jefferson's mind in this matter, I am not now
counselling a rebellion on any particular issue, or even counselling

rebellion at all. When the official hue and cry about "lawlessness" started, it led me to contemplate the cancer of officialism in our body politic, and to wonder what could be done about it, first by the individual, and second, by society collectively; and I cannot see but that in both cases "lawlessness" is the only thing that will check its inroads.

I do not intend to speak particularly about the general issues arising out of prohibition, but one special issue serves very well just here for purposes of illustration. I remember my indignation and sense of outrage twenty years ago, in the time of State option, when some officers of a prohibition State boarded a train and cut open the suitcase of an innocent through-passenger, to search it for liquor. It seemed to me then that officialism had reached its limit of affront to the integrity and dignity of the public. Federal agents now, however, seem embarked on the policy—under instructions, mind you, set forth by officialism—of first shooting the suspect out of hand and searching his property afterwards. In a newspaper to-day I see an estimate that these murders run to an average of one every three days.

Now, under these circumstances, what recourse has the community? These assassinations are an immediate concern of the community, and are acutely felt to be such, since no innocent person can know when and under what circumstances he or she will be a victim. The community is as much concerned as it would be with any other mode of brigandage. But, in the premises, just what can it do?

The immediate agents can be indicted and tried; but, in the first place, this hardly suits the average sense of justice. These men are acting under orders and are responsible to their superiors. In the second place, officialism is all on their side, and the trial results in a formal vindication of officialism and not in actual justice. As for implicating their superiors in the issue, the thing is clearly impossible; the attempt would result only in a more spectacular vindication of officialism.

What then? Well, it is possible that the community thus outraged might spread the contagion of its dissent largely through the country. In that case it is again possible that at the end of a term of years we might retire a president to private life, and bounce out a camorra of senators, congressmen, and such. But this measure seems almost ludicrously inadequate and superficial when compared with the amount of effort and expense involved in bringing it about. When it is done, what has the country got? What has it ever got from this procedure? Besides, four years or seven years is a long time to wait for the popular will to become operative. Whether regarded as a measure of retributive justice or as a rebuke to officialism, this procedure seems alike incompetent, and I believe that the natural instinct of the people regards it with extreme dissatisfaction. Yet I know of no other that can be either conceived or applied within the limits of a strict legality.

Although an American citizen, I live much abroad among a people who have their own faults and shortcomings, like the rest of us, and some considerable virtues. One of their virtues is an amazingly quick, passionate, almost vindictive resentment and resistance against the incursions of officialism. Individually and collectively they know their rights and are most jealous of them; otherwise in all their private relations, they are the most tolerant people that I ever had the good fortune to be among. Both these traits seem largely to have been born in them, and the course of their natural history has accidentally been such as to foster both of them very powerfully. For years I have watched the continuous come-out of these traits with a fascinated interest.

Officialism, in a word, is restricted to a degree inconceivable by an American; and it is restricted by the one thing I know of that can restrict it, which is fear. Not fear of losing a job, but fear of losing continuity of the spinal column. Every official from the highest to the lowest, carries on under just that wholesome apprehension. He knows what he may do and may not do; bureaucracy knows how far it may go, and what will happen if it goes farther; and any motion, even the slightest, towards overstepping the line brings out a prompt reminder. A friend of mine who had had large experience in municipal government in America, once told the mayor of the European city I live in that he ought to turn a certain crowded thoroughfare into a one-way street. The mayor threw up his hands and said, "If I did that there would be a revolution!" He was right. That street is a one-way street now, but making it so was a matter of twelve years. The progress of a general traffic-control has been very slow and circumspect, almost block by block, with the people watching every move to decide whether it meant something really for their convenience or was a mere bureaucratic gesture. Whatever failings a critic might observe in this people's type of civilization, it has certainly realized all the advantages that come from never being "inattentive to the public affairs."

Consequently the outrages committed by officialism in America against the dignity and liberties of the public could no more take place here than they could take place in heaven. Supposing the impossible, let us suppose that a woman was shot here under circumstances like those of the prohibitionist raid on a private domicile in Illinois a few months ago. What would happen is that the political equivalents of Mr. Mellon and Mr. Lowman would be immediately eliminated. The people would waste no time on the actual raiders; their sound political instinct would lead them straight to the persons responsible. But nothing like this is ever necessary, because the people watch their job holders like cats and are always ready with some practical application of the principle *obsta principiis* in small matters as well as great. Nothing seems too small and trivial for them to resent, and on occasion the concern of the individual instantly becomes the concern of the community.

Some months ago, for instance, the Communists had been annoying the Socialists by organizing a series of petty strikes; and the mayor of the city that I live in put out a proclamation one morning prohibiting all public meetings and street-processions. The Socialists are politically very strong here, and the Mayor evidently had counted on this to enable him to "get by" with this proclamation so manifestly aimed at the weak Communist faction. But the prohibition lasted just four days. On the morning of the fifth day there was another proclamation posted on the dead-walls, saying it was all off. Meanwhile there seemed to be as many parades and assemblages as usual, with the police maintaining a benevolent neutrality. Undoubtedly what happened was that about the second day, people of every political stripe began to drop into the Mayor's office to tell him that while he was all right as far as he went, they were noticing that the boys seemed to be getting sort of restless, and they were afraid the future looked a little dark for him unless he brisked up and did something.

Some time ago I watched a street fête in the poorest quarter of town until long after midnight, when two men started at fisticuffs in the middle of a side street. A couple of policemen happened along, and for some reason one of them tried to interfere. The men stopped fighting just long enough to set on the policeman, sent him spinning on his head ten feet away, and then at once resumed business. They were quite within their rights, and they knew it. They were not blocking traffic, for there was none; not disturbing anyone, for they were not noisy; not discommoding or injuring anyone, for what few people were around were on the sidewalk. These men were very poor and shabby; in America they would have had no chance at all. They would have been clubbed half to death and then probably "run in" on a charge of resisting an officer; and the bystanders would have let it go at that. Here, however, the incident ended when the policeman got up, brushed himself off, and rejoined his companion, who meanwhile had not stirred. If he had made an issue of it, he would have had to take on the whole population of the district, because, as I say, by every rule of reason and sense, he was "in wrong." If on the other hand he had been in any way justified by reason and sense, the populace would have been just as strongly on his side, as I have often seen it happen.

So it is not only in municipal or local affairs, but in national affairs; this spirit predominates everywhere. About two years ago there was a great demonstration in a northeastern province of the country; thousands of people marched all day, with brass bands, and speech-making of a most inflammatory type. The manifestation was headed by two canons of the cathedral and six university professors. They marched under a foreign flag, advocating the annexation of the province by a neighboring country. Well, by modern American standards, this was sedition of the most flagrant type, but nothing happened. The military were not called out, the ringleaders were not railroaded to Atlanta or maimed on the spot by the police; nothing at all was done about it. After all, if those people felt that way, they had every right to speak up about it. If they could get enough people in the province to feel the same way, and the neighboring country was content they had every right to obtain annexation. The right of secession is inalienable. "When in the course of human events it becomes necessary, etc."—how many times we have heard those noble words! But over here they really believe it and are ready to back up their belief, not only with their lives, their fortunes, and their sacred honor, but with the leg of a chair or whatever first comes handy. In this instance the demonstrators could not make enough people feel their way to carry the issue; but they had absolute and unlimited freedom to try, and so they were satisfied.

The general doctrine that I am describing may be disparaged as terrorism; indeed, it may be very fairly called terrorism, provided one very important condition be kept in mind. It is as true, I believe, as ever Thomas Jefferson thought it was, that the only way the incursions of officialism can be withstood is by keeping the officials in a state of constant fear—not fear for their jobs, but for their skins. I say, *constant* fear, not intermittent or occasional fear. If this be done, as it is in the country where I live, there are never any terroristic consequences, for things simply never get that far. The people among whom I live keep themselves continually framed up to hang somebody, no matter whom, from the head of the general government to the policeman on the beat. Officialism is constantly aware of this, and consequently no one is ever hanged. I never witnessed or heard of a single incident where a few well-chosen words did not immediately and satisfactorily produce results. The officials know the disposition of the people, know it is not to be trifled with, and never trifle with it. Only where the disposition of a people is either complaisant or "inattentive," or both, can officialism make any headway against their liberties.

After all, the thing stands to reason as well as to such experience as is furnished by the country where I live. Suppose Mr. Whalen knew to an absolute certainty that within twenty-four hours after his police had confiscated private medical records the citizenry would descend upon his office, would that peculiarly odious and outrageous raid on Mrs. Sanger's clinic have taken place? Never. Would a single prohibitionist assassination ever take place if Mr. Mellon and Mr. Lowman knew to a certainty that the day when it happened would be their official last? Never. Matters would never come within a thousand miles of such a thing. I am not contemplating occasional and sporadic outbursts of mob-rage caused by some exceptionally flagrant *démarche* of a bureaucracy. Officialism has no fear of those, for it can deal with them. I am speaking of a steady, considered and highly sensitive spirit of repression, which by coming out with promptness and force against the feeblest beginnings of officialism's attempts against the public's welfare and dignity, never needs be called on to resist any of its more daring and flagitious enterprises.

I see no conclusion but that Jeffersonian "lawlessness" affords communal rights and dignity, as well as the rights and dignity of the individual, their only recourse against officialism. Jefferson seems to have thought so, and I see no way whereby one can think otherwise. Moreover, for the community as well as the individual, the determination and delimitation of "lawlessness" runs straight back to the fundamental question, *What is law?*

Americans, searching for available recourse in what seems to me a most trying and humiliating situation, might well broach this fundamental question and demand a plain and thorough discussion of it; and demand especially that it be discussed by those who now so lightly undertake to reprehend them for their lawlessness.

This article originally appeared in the December 1929 issue of *Harper's Magazine*.

The Return of the Patriots

Our current literature, always rich in surprises, has lately provided one that provokes comment. I refer to the sudden change of heart which some of our critics seem to have experienced towards the American scene. One hardly knows what to make of it. Ten years ago, five years, even three years ago, these critics were going very strong indeed against the defects, degradations, weaknesses, stupidities of life in America. If they found any salvage at all in our society, they did not let on. They saw a very dark future for us. The lamp had held out to burn about as long as it was going to, and had already begun to flicker. One felt that under the circumstances any thought of patriotism savoured almost of indelicacy, and that even a sneaking sentimental attachment for one's own land and people was well-nigh inadmissible.

Now, there has been no change in these circumstances in the last ten years, as far as any one can see. Our civilization bears precisely the same general character that it bore ten years ago, its ideals are precisely the same, its institutional, social, and cultural expressions are on precisely the same general level. Everything that these critics found objectionable still remains in full force. There has been no effective growth of public opinion against the imperfections that they dwelt on. If the future that these imperfections portended looked dark ten years ago, or five, or three, it looks just as dark now. If our life was then so unsatisfactory that the best reason and spirit of man had no choice but to pronounce it intolerable, that verdict must still hold.

Yet curiously, though nothing has changed an iota, some of the most articulate and convincing among our critics seem no longer to see these matters in the old light. They still admit that our society is imperfect, but whereas before they were depressed about it, they now regard its imperfections with a gladsome hope, and a faith amounting to certainty. One now infers from their writings—at least it is the only inference I can make—that they think if we merely keep on following our noses, pushing ahead with vigour and congratulating ourselves at the top of our voices on our progress, these imperfections will somehow slough off without our doing anything in particular about them, and leave us as a city set on a hill, a pattern and example unto all peoples, nations, and languages. We may not know where we are going, but we are on our way. To illustrate this remarkable change of heart, or change of front, I recall that one of these critics, only two or three years ago, published this desponding sentence:

> I am wondering, as a personal but practical question, just how and where a man of moderate means who prefers simple living, simple pleasures, and the things of the mind, is going to be able to live any longer in his native country.

This is straightforward, plain, unequivocal, leaving no doubt of what was in the writer's mind. But the same person who wrote this published a book last year, a very good one, a best seller of 1931, out of which I can make nothing but a continuous and affectionate panegyric on the "American Dream." It is the story of a people who, in spite of every appearance to the contrary, have built up a splendid nation, full of strength, hope, and promise, and apparently also—here is the strange thing—full of interest for the intelligent and cultivated citizen. The author ends his book with this rhapsody, a quotation from a woman writer, an adopted citizen whose enthusiasm for America—as is sometimes the way with adopted citizens—has always been notoriously indiscriminate and excessive:

> It is not I that belong to the past, but the past that belongs to me. America is the youngest of the nations and inherits all that went before in history. And I am the youngest of America's children, and into my hands is given all her priceless heritage, to the last white star espied through the telescope, to the last great thought of the philosopher. Mine is the whole majestic past and mine is the shining future.

Would such a civilization as this be interesting? Rather. It would be the most interesting thing in the world. There ought not to be any trouble about living almost anywhere in a country like that. One would think it was made expressly for just such a person as this author declared himself only so short a time ago. "A man of moderate means, who prefers simple living, simple pleasures and the things of the mind"—why, he would find it the very pick of the earth. What one cannot get through one's head, however, is how it happens that this critic did not see the value of America's priceless heritage three years ago; also that he did not see the individual interest accruing to the citizen privileged to live here and look at the last white star through the telescope, and clip coupons on the majestic past and the shining future. If all this gorgeousness were visible three years ago, how could a critic not have noticed it, how could he have helped noticing it? Even a dead critic would notice a display like that.

Again, the ablest and wisest among the muckrakers of twenty years ago has lately published his autobiography, which is also (I think) a best seller, and deservedly, for it is more than a good book, it is a great book, a great study of fundamentals in our public life. If I had on my hands a foreigner who wished to "understand America," this is the first of three books that I should give him for preliminary study, the other two being *The Education of Henry Adams* and Mr. Charles A. Beard's *Rise of American Civilization.* The last few pages of this book, however, are devoted to a loose and hopeful patriotic rhapsodizing that the whole tenor of the book itself shows to be ludicrously devoid of foundation. This does not harm the book, because to a person of any literary experience its naïve sincerity is as manifest as its lack of logical continuity with all that goes before it; yet one is bound to wonder what the vagrant impulse was that made the author end his book in that way.

Again, the puzzled reader must ask himself in some dismay whether Saul is also among the prophets, when he considers the case of one of our younger novelists and a perennial best seller, who made his vogue by the fearful castigations that he has given our society and its culture in book after book for twelve years. This author, on a public occasion not long ago, speaking of our newer crop of writers, came out with this:

> I salute them all with joy as being not yet too far removed from their unconquerable determination to give to the America that has mountains and endless prairies, enormous cities and lost farm cabins, billions of money and tons of faith, the America that is as strange as Russia and as complex as China, a literature worthy of her vastness.

This rhetoric is all very fine, but what about it when brought down into the realm of fact and common sense? What is there to justify taking this tone towards our society at present that did not exist twelve years ago? Clearly, nothing. Well, then, if this tone were justifiable twelve years ago, it seems fair to ask why this novelist has only now begun to take it.

There are other signs, some positive and some negative, that we soon may find ourselves in for another era of pseudo-patriotic flatulence like that which characterized the decades preceding and following the Civil War; and there are signs, even more disturbing, that this era may also resemble those decades in an unreasoning glorification of the Average American Man. Among the positive signs is one that turned up not long ago in the newspapers when James McNeill died in involuntary exile on the French Riviera. James McNeill was an oil magnate who was mixed up in the Teapot Dome affair, and left the country to escape investigation. When he died, the newspapers came out with editorial reflections that might have been written by Edward Eggleston or Edward Everett Hale. They might have been lifted almost bodily out of one of those fine old jingo-nationalistic novels called *A Man without a Country* and *Philip Nolan's Friends; or Show Your Passports*. Poor McNeill had shown the white feather; he had skipped. Now he was dead, a man without a country. Unwept, unhonoured, unsung, he had perished; blind, remorseful, broken-hearted, agonized by the thought that never again might he tread the soil of his dear native land, our great and glorious republic. All this was an interesting throwback, not only in style but in spirit, to the popular literature of what Mr. Lewis Mumford calls the Brown Decades.

Among the negative signs is Mr. Elmer Rice's play called *The Left Bank*, recently put on in New York. Its theme, broadly, is that whereas our voluntary expatriates—at least the young and arty among them—have until recently been loudly vocal, they are now silent. Only a little while ago they were denouncing the United States as a land of money-grubbing, standardization, exploitation, and crass vulgarity. They ostentatiously shook off its dust from their feet, and repaired to the Left Bank, where things were livelier and inspiration free for all. Now they are no longer heard from. Where are they? Why have they ceased to speak up? Can it be that they are home again and have settled down in a chastened reconciliation? Have they discovered that America isn't so dead bad after all? Are they now whispering among themselves that Old Lady Columbia may be pretty raw and spotty, and she may wabble a lot and every now and then blunder like hell, but, dammit, she's ours, and we're here to say she's the best in the world, God bless her!—just give her a little time and she'll make all the rest of creation look like a protested draft.

Mr. Simeon Strunsky has showed an uncanny sense of the psychological moment to bring out his book called *The Rediscovery of Jones.* Mr. Strunsky has long been known as a mighty champion of the social mean, a Philistine of Gath, with six fingers on every hand and on every foot six toes, four-and-twenty in number; and the staff of his spear is like a weaver's beam. He is probably our most conspicuous exponent of the sterling virtues that reside in mediocrity, the most stoutly and philosophically *bürgerlich* of our bourgeois. As a writer for the *New York Times* he would be all this officially, of course, but there can be no doubt that he is so by conviction as well; he is the right man in the right place. He has now come out with a strong defense of Jones, the typical American who turns out to be a sort of shoestring relative of our old friend Mr. Babbitt. Perhaps one should put it that Mr. Strunsky presents Jones as the actual type, of which, in his view, Babbitt is a carefully offensive caricature. Our intellectuals have derided Jones, it seems, without taking the trouble to understand him. Mr. Strunsky now proposes that Jones shall have his day in court and be rehabilitated, and he makes out an excellent case for his client, showing him to be in no respect worse or worse off than the typical *Bürger* of other lands, and in most respects better.

This is all very well, though mostly gratuitous, for one doubts that Jones's good qualities have ever been seriously obscured by any smoke-screen of caricature or contumely. Mr. Strunsky himself says that "the great mass of simple people" are not easily led astray in their estimates of character, which is very true. In Mr. Strunsky's words, they "are not as susceptible as their betters to current fads, fashions, formulas, discoveries and revelations; they obstinately see what they see and hear what they hear." I have often thought that Main Street's own estimate of Babbitt would be likely to hit much nearer the truth about him than the estimate of an outsider. I was born and bred on Main Street myself, so it is natural that I should think so, and perhaps I am wrong.

Certainly, however, I have the right to say that during my residence on Main Street I never ran across any one who struck me as in the least like Babbitt; that is, like him all the time. Some of us, myself included, were like him in some respects some of the time; but not much, really, and not often, and when we were like him we were generally aware of it and none too proud of the resemblance. So I doubt that Jones needs Mr. Strunsky's attorneyship to set him square either with the neighbours or with the world. The neighbours took Jones's measure long ago, and the world is not too captious about accepting him at his face value.

But Mr. Strunsky ends his book with a most dreadful forecast. He says that "a survey of the American scene to-day demands on the part of the observer a new mobilization of courage."

> In the period of insurgency just behind us it required no courage at all to say the most terrifying things about Jones. Everybody was doing it; that is to say, everybody who was anybody. . . . The present hour demands the courage to assert that the Fourth of July orator with his beetling brow and his unterrified cowlick . . . was, and is, in essence right . . . that the clichés, catchwords, stencils, "dope" of the Jefferson Bricks, the Elijah Pograms, the General Cyrus Chokes, had in them, and still have, the sturdy nucleus of truth. . . . In the most unexpected quarters, in the erstwhile citadels of challenge and revolution and devastation, voices are being raised to suggest that perhaps in this respect and in that respect we did not quite do justice to the United States. In a little while these tentative exploratory apologies may have swelled to full choruses of praise.

One has, indeed, an uneasy apprehension that just this may happen; that a license of indiscriminate negation will be followed by a license of indiscriminate affirmation, and nothing more. The newer patriotism will be modelled on the old; it will be turgid, superficial, unintelligent, truculent. Forty years ago, no one saw irony in the practice of reading the Declaration of Independence every Fourth of July to people who knew all about the enormities of the Reconstruction period. The Republican party took "Our Glorious Union" as its watchword for conducting the most flagitious enterprises against the public welfare, in the face of a people who knew just what the party was doing and apparently felt no sense of incongruity. Congressmen brayed about our matchless Constitution before audiences who had lived through the whole régime of Grant-Belknap—Crédit Mobilier—Cooke-Gould-Fisk—Northern Pacific—audiences who had seen Samuel J. Tilden counted out of the Presidency and had felt all the creepy horrors of Black Friday. Everybody glorified his country, right or wrong, and except for an occasional derelict like Henry Adams here and there, everybody was a patriotic American, itching to tell the world all about it. Such was standard American patriotism at the end of the Brown Decades, say ten years after the Civil War. It was identical with the patriotism that Dickens had discovered and assessed at its true value on his visits here, the patriotism of Jefferson Brick, of Colonel Diver, of the Honourable Elijah Pogram, member of Congress—the patriotism, in short, of as fine a set of scoundrels as ever drew breath in any quarter of the globe.

Yet in their innocence, the Babbitt and Jones of the Brown Decades were quite as worthy persons as their spiritual posterity of today. They were mere incurious echoes. The schoolboys who forty years ago declaimed Webster's reply to Hayne, and who pored over the agitating story of Philip Nolan in the pages of the old *Scribner's Magazine,* absorbed this Old Hickory spirit in all innocence. They felt an innocent incurious pride in it as they grew up and heard the Declaration read, and listened while some miserable opportunist praised the Constitution in his campaign for the late Elijah Pogram's seat in Congress. In all sincerity they voted to keep the party of Our Glorious Union in power through one administration after another. There seems to have been something wrong with Babbitt and Jones in those days, yet not with their moral integrity; what they had grown up to believe, they believed, or at least they believed they believed it, and so were quite sincere. Nor perhaps was there much wrong with them in respect of such complaints as our sociologists of the past decade might file against them; Mr. Strunsky might have taken up the cudgels for them as effectively as he does for their posterity today. Yet there seems to have been a little something askew with them, something that both the sociologists and Mr. Strunsky apparently have missed.

The Brown Decades gave place to the Gilded Age, which in turn ushered in the Gay Nineties. The social kaleidoscope revealed Ward McAllister and his Four Hundred in their futile stand against the irruption of crude Western money that broke on New York; it revealed

Mrs. Bradley-Martin's ball and Jennie Jerome's wedding, and Anna Gould's trousseau and the Count de Castallane's pedigree. But meanwhile the old patriotism—the patriotism of Diver, Pogram, and Jefferson Brick—went strong. We were the coming people, and in all the world there was no match for us. The Tyrant and the Despot of effete Europe drew their every breath in uneasy dread of America's indisputable superiority in virtue and valor—had not President Cleveland proved it by his Venezuela message? Freedom, Equality, Democracy, and the crescent glories of Republican Institutions—all these were ours, and by them we took our stand, unconquerable and unafraid.

Then came the Spanish War, and the old patriotism sagged a bit. Embalmed beef, Carnegie armor-plate, and yellow fever helped to take the shine off it, but the whole war-venture was hard to justify; it seemed a scurvy affair, look at it as you would. At this point a little light broke in even on Jones and Babbitt; even to them the old orthodox doctrine seemed to have blow-holes in it, and they were not so sure. Then came the muckraking period, and the light brightened; these were the days of Altgeld, Johnson, Golden Rule Jones, Pingree, and Gaynor in our public life. By 1912 a good many people had taken stock of our patriotic doctrine and decided that it needed revising; it could do with a little less wind and water, and a little more substance. Jones and Babbitt did not object, and even showed themselves somewhat impressed; and for two or three years there were some hopeful signs. Then came the European War and its revelations, about which perhaps the less said, the better. Then the Jazz-and-Paper Decade; then the great squeeze of 1929, followed by a two-year season of repentance; and now, apparently, the best our leaders of thought can do by way of bracer against humiliation and discouragement is to rub up the fustian of Elijah Pogram and the Brown Decades, and pass it out again.

Well, no doubt, this is the easiest way. It is much easier to ladle out this sort of treacle and get Jones to swallow it than it is to find out what really ails Jones and his civilization, and get him interested in that. Yet there seems an odor of shabbiness about it; it is the kind of thing, one might think, that one would just a little rather not do. Jones may now sit at home evenings and be inspired by the American Dream, and be assured that Jefferson Brick and Elijah Pogram were right and that Dickens was full of bile and prunes, and under this dosage he may go to bed as happy and groggy and satisfied as if he had had it straight from the late Coué or out of a demijohn. This is what his forbears did in the Brown Decades, and no doubt they were happy, after a fashion, in their inert romanticism. Still, the fact is writ large in our history that as long as Jones remained thus happily inert, things went from bad to worse, both with him and with the country; and the inference is that to encourage Jones in this attitude was—and is—to use him most unscrupulously.

What really ails Jones is not what the sociologists say. What ails him is that he asks too little of life. He makes too ridiculously few and slight demands on his civilization. Mr. Strunsky presents Jones as an easy-going fellow, and praises his American diffidence in the presence of his self-appointed monitors, his "American good nature and open-mindedness." But that is just the trouble with him. He is too diffident, too easy-going and good-natured, and his mind is open at both ends, so that a great many things run out that it would be to his advantage to detain and ponder over. Chief among these is the importunate suggestion which his civilization holds up to him at every turn—if he could only see it—that he is not getting anything like his money's worth out of life, and that he ought to wake up and raise the devil with a society that denies him more.

Let us consider one or two of the many points at which Jones is gouged. First, the society around him doggedly refuses to regard him as a spiritual being; it keeps insisting that he not only can, but should, live by *things* alone—things that are manufactured, bought, and sold. It insists that his life should be made up exclusively of things, and that without an ever-increasing abundance of things and an ever-increasing appetite for more things, his life would be just no life at all. Hence he should be always doing, in order to be always getting; every little bit added to what he's got makes just a little bit more; and by continuous implication, the effort to *be* or *become*—to become something essentially different from his present self—is a diversion of energy from the main business of life, and should be discouraged.

Second, the whole practical conduct of Jones's civilization is adjusted to the absolute-minimum average. It is everywhere carefully graded to the lowest common denominator. Education, for instance, contemplates only that symbol of mediocrity, "the average student." The literature that Jones reads, the plays he sees, the amusements he takes part in, the social manners he adopts—these aim only at the standard set by the lowest common denominator of intelligence, taste, and character. Thus our society offers Jones no incentive whatever to rise above the level of these average capacities, no matter what his own capacities may be; in fact, it puts upon him a continuous repression and discouragement if ever he shows signs of attempting a breach with normalcy by living up to the full measure of his own capacity in any respect but that of doing and getting.

Third, in consequence of the foregoing, the leading characteristic of Jones's civilization is its hardness, and the penalty that nature puts upon hardness is hideousness. There is nothing of the soft play of life in Jones's society; the sky over the poor fellow's head is of iron and brass. When he seeks surcease from doing and getting, he has only the choice of putting himself at the mercy of raw sensation or of feeling himself uncomfortably alone in the world. He is deprived of the happy sense of co-operation with his fellows except as he finds it in the workaday business of doing and getting, and in such recreations as are addressed directly to pure sensation. Hence in work and play he must live always from a very shallow depth of being; his vocations and avocations, his newspapers, machines, games, domestic and social surroundings, all attest this. They reflect a life that is overspread with the curse of hardness, and therefore overspread with an immense tedium, an immense ennui. Years ago Stendhal, looking over the earlier Jones and Babbitt, remarked that "one is disposed to say that the source of sensibility is dried up in this people. They are just, they are reasonable, but they are essentially not happy." A glance at the later Jones and Babbitt shows that the true line of social criticism begins here, with this observation of Stendhal, and not with the little matters to which the sociologists and Mr. Strunsky give their attention.

For, really, one can not get much worked up over the superficial untowardnesses which engage the sociological mind. In the face of a constitutional disorder, one takes pustules as a matter of course. Middletown is a scandalous place, no doubt; political corruption, racketeering and hijacking are bad, and so are lynchings. Jones's newspapers are contemptible, his radio programs most odious. Certainly Prohibition is a disgusting régime; certainly industrial exploitation is carried to abominable lengths. It is monstrous and shocking that interested persons should be able to find it worth their while to spend nine million dollars to elect some ignorant and servile nincompoop to the Presidency—why, it cost only twenty-five thousand dollars to elect old Jim Buchanan, who was, at that, a man of ability and a gentleman, far and away ahead of any Presidential timber in our present public life. All these things are bad, certainly they are bad, but the question, after all, is, What else can you expect? Obviously nothing else can be expected until our society transforms itself; and until Jones transforms himself and demands his natural rights, this will never happen.

Probably Jones will take the easiest way with the newer patriotism, as he did with the earlier. Probably he will accept the American Dream and all the rest of it, as convenient to believe; after all, he has a good deal on his mind, what with a business to run, a wife to support, a lot of gadgets to take up his spare time, bridge to play, a car, a radio— yes, probably the American Dream will do well enough to justify the spiritual destitution in which he spends his life. How animating it would be, though, if instead of this, Jones should suddenly say to the fuglemen of the newer patriotism, "Before I take stock in that high-pressure Americanism of yours, I will have to be shown. Society must take a different tone towards me. I am sick of being treated as if work and money, grub and gadgets, were all there is to life. I am something more than a well-conditioned animal. Take notice, I was created in the image of God, by thunder, a spiritual being, and before I believe what you say, America has got to show some discernment and respect for the things of the spirit—not patronage, you understand, but deep and humble respect. I don't know much about those things myself, but I have a right to know them better and to make them mine, and say what you please, a society that wet-blankets me out of that right is simply not a civilized society. So put that in your pipe and smoke it."

If Jones should transform himself to the point of firing off a few broadsides like that, our society would not be long about transforming itself and finding itself several steps nearer the realization of an American dream that is really worth dreaming. The ghost of Stendhal would take a look at Jones's face, and decide that the "source of sensibility," the well-spring of human happiness, so long dried up, had begun to flow in a surprising fashion. But, for the reasons given, this is too much to expect of Jones; he is too cluttered and dishevelled. The most that can be expected of him now—and in his circumstances it is a great deal, it is enough—is that as he sits by his fireside and reads our newer perfectionist-patriotic literature, he will recall Governor Smith's shrewd atticism, and gently murmur, *"Boloney!"*

This article originally appeared in the April 1932 issue of the *Virginia Quarterly Review.*

'A Little Conserva-tive'

I often think it's comical
How Nature always does contrive
That every boy and every gal
That's born into the world alive
Is either a little Liber-al
Or else a little Conserva-tive.
—W. S. Gilbert, *Iolanthe*

Gilbert's lines recall Professor Huxley's pungent observation on the disadvantages of going about the world unlabeled. Early in life, he says, he perceived that society regards an unlabeled person as a potential menace, somewhat as the police regard an unmuzzled dog. Therefore, not finding any existing label to suit him, he took thought and invented one. The main difference between himself and other people, as he saw it, was that they seemed to be quite sure of a number of things about which he not only was not sure, but also suspected that he never could be sure. Their minds ran in the wake of the first-century Gnostic sects, while his did not. Hence the term *agnostic* suggested itself to him as descriptive of this difference, and he accordingly adopted it as a label.

The great weight of Huxley's authority forced the term into common currency, where ignorance promptly twisted it into a sense exactly contrary to its philology, and contrary to the original intention which Huxley gave it. To-day when a person says he is an agnostic, it is ten to one he means that he knows the thing at issue is not so. If he says, for instance, as one of my acquaintances did the other day, that he is a thoroughgoing agnostic concerning the existence of God and the persistence of consciousness after death, he means that he is sure there is no God and that consciousness does not persist. The term is so regularly used to imply a negative certainty that its value as a label, a distinguishing mark, is false and misleading. It is like the hotel labels which unscrupulous tourists in Paris buy by the dozen and stick on their luggage as evidence that they have visited places where they have never been, and put up at hotels which they have never seen.

Something like this appears to be the common destiny of labels. It brings to mind the fine saying of Homer which I have so often quoted, that "the range of words is wide; words may tend this way or that way." There are few more interesting pursuits than that of examining the common popular connotation of labels, and observing how regularly it runs the full course from sense to nonsense, or from infamy to respectability, and back again. For example, our voting population is divided into two major groups, Republicans and Democrats; how many of them know anything about the history of their labels? How many could describe the differentiations that the significance of these labels indicates, or could attach any actual significance whatever to them, except in wholly irrelevant terms, usually in terms which in the last analysis turn out to mean habit, money, or jobs?

The Republicans went into the pangs of parturition at Cleveland last summer, and brought forth a sorry mouse. As one of my friends put it, about the only thing their platform did not do was to give the Democratic Administration a formal endorsement. As far as one can see, all their pledges amount to is a promise to do what the Democrats have been doing, but to do it better.

Similarly the new Russian constitution seems to show merely that Stalin thinks it is easier to run things the way Mark Hanna used to run them than the way they have been run in Russia hitherto. No doubt he is right about that; but meanwhile one wonders what the word *bolshevik* will mean to the average Russian fifty years from now, and how many voters in holy Russia will know the history of the word, or even know that it has a history.

Reflections like these make one quite doubtful about Huxley's position concerning the balance of advantage and disadvantage in the matter of labels. His misfortune was in his honesty; he invented a label that precisely described him, and he could hardly have fared worse if he had worn none, for on the one hand ignorance at once invested it with an alien meaning, while on the other hand prejudice converted it into a term of reproach. I have had a curious experience lately which has caused me to ponder afresh upon these matters, and which I am now tempted to relate.

For more than a quarter of a century I have been known, in so far as I was known at all, as a radical. It came about in this way: I was always interested in the *rerum cognoscere causas,* liking to get down below the surface of things and examine their roots. This was purely a natural disposition, reflecting no credit whatever on me, for I was born with it. Any success I had in its indulgence brought me the happiness that Lucretius observed as attaching to such pursuits, and I indulged it only for that reason, never seeking, and indeed never getting, any other reward. Therefore when the time came for me to describe myself by some convenient label, I took one which marked the quality that I thought chiefly differentiated me from most of the people I saw around me. They habitually gave themselves a superficial account of things, which was all very well if it suited them to do so, but I preferred always to give myself a root-account of things, if I could get it. Therefore, by way of a general designation, it seemed appropriate to label myself a radical. Likewise, also, when occasion required that I should label myself with reference to particular social theories or doctrines, the same decent respect for accuracy led me to describe myself as an anarchist, an individualist, and a single-taxer.

On the positive side, my anarchism came mainly as a corollary to the estimate of human capacity for self-improvement which I had picked up from Mr. Jefferson. His fundamental idea appeared to be that everyone answering to the zoölogical classification of *homo sapiens* is a human being, and therefore is indefinitely improvable. The essence of it is that *homo sapiens* in his natural state really wishes and means to be as decent towards his fellow-beings as he can, and under favorable conditions will progress in decency. He shares this trait with the rest of the animal world.

> *Indica tigris agit rabida cum tigride pacem*
> *Perpetuam; sævis inter se convenit ursis,*

—so long, that is, as irritating interferences, such as hunger, lust, jealousy or trespass, are kept at a minimum. Man's moral superiority over the animal consists in an indefinitely cultivable capacity and will to deal with these interferences intelligently from the long-time point of view, and thus gradually immunize himself against their irritant influence.

Granting this premise, the anarchist position appeared logical to me, as it did to Prince Kropotkin and Bakunin. Putting it roughly, if all men are human, if all bipeds classifiable as *homo sapiens* are human beings, social harmony and a general progress in civilization will be far better brought about by methods of free agreement and voluntary association than by constraint, whether directly under force, or under the menace of force which is always implicit in obedience to law.

The negative argument for anarchism seemed quite as cogent as the positive argument. The whole institution of government, wherever found and in whatever form, appeared to me so vicious and depraving that I could not even regard it with Paine as "at its best a necessary evil." The State stood, and had stood in history as far back as I could trace its existence, as little else but an instrument of economic exploitation, a mere mechanism, as Voltaire said, "for taking money out of one set of pockets and putting it into another." The activities of its administrators and beneficiaries appeared to me as they did to Voltaire, as no more or less than those of a professional-criminal class. As Nietzsche calls it, "the coldest of all cold monsters," the State's character was so completely evil, its conduct so invariably and deliberately flagitious, that I did not see how society could possibly be worse off without it than with it, let the alternative condition be what it might.

My individualism was a logical extension of the anarchist principle beyond its narrow application to one particular form or mode of constraint upon the individual. The thing that interested me, as it interested Emerson and Whitman, was a general philosophy of life which regards human personality as the greatest and most respectworthy object in the world, and as a complete end-in-itself; a philosophy, therefore, which disallows its subversion or submergence, whether by force of law or by any other coercive force. I was convinced that human beings do better and are happier when they have the largest possible margin of existence to regulate and dispose of as they please; and hence I believed that society should so manage itself as to leave the individual a maximum of free choice and action, even at a considerable risk of results which from the short-time point of view would be pronounced dangerous. I suppose it may be seen how remote this is from the bogus affair of dollars and cents which is touted under the name of individualism, and which, as I showed in last February's issue of this magazine, is not individualism in any sense.

The single tax impressed me as the most equitable and convenient way of paying the cost of such matters as can be done better collectively than individually. As a matter of natural right it seemed to me that as individually created values should belong to the individual, so socially created values should belong to society, and that the single tax was the best method of securing both the individual and society in the full enjoyment of their respective rights. To the best of my knowledge these two propositions have never been successfully controverted. There were other considerations, too, which made the single tax seem the best of all fiscal systems, but it is unnecessary to recount them here.

Probably I ought to add that I never entered on any crusade for these beliefs or sought to persuade anyone into accepting them. Education is as much a matter of time as of anything else, perhaps more, and I was well aware that anything like a general realization of this philosophy is a matter of very long time indeed. All experience of what Frederick the Great called "this damned human race" shows beyond peradventure that it is impossible to tell anyone anything unless in a very real sense he knows it already; and therefore a premature and pertinacious evangelism is at best the most fruitless of all human enterprises, and at worst the most vicious. Society never takes the right course until after it has painfully explored all the wrong ones, and it is vain to try to argue, cajole, or force society out of these set sequences of experimentation. Over and above the impassioned outpourings of the propagandist for an untried way of salvation, however straight and clear that way may be, one can always hear old Frederick saying, "Ach, mein lieber Sacher, er kennt nicht diese verdammte Rasse."

But while I have never engaged in any controversy or public discussion of these matters, or even in any private advocacy of them, I have spoken my mind about them so freely and so often that it would seem impossible for anyone to mistake my attitude towards them. Only last year, in fact, I published by far the most radical critique of public affairs that has as yet been brought out here. Hence I was mildly astonished to hear the other day that a person very much in the public eye, and one who would seem likely to know something of what I have been up to during all these years, had described me as "one of the most intelligent conservatives in the country."

It was a kind and complimentary thing to say, and I was pleased to hear it, but it struck me nevertheless as a rather vivid commentary on the value and the fate of labels. Twenty, or ten, or even three years ago, no one in his right mind would have dreamed of tagging me with that designation. Why then, at this particular juncture, should it occur to a presumably well-informed person to call me a conservative, when my whole philosophy of life is openly and notoriously the same that it has been for twenty-five years?[1] In itself the question is probably worth little discussion, but as leading into the larger question of what a conservative is, and what the qualities are that go to make him one, it is worth much more.

It seems that the reason for so amiably labeling me a conservative in this instance was that I am indisposed to the present Administration. This also appears to be one reason why Mr. Sokolsky labels himself a conservative, as he did in the very able and cogent paper which he published in the August issue of the *Atlantic*. But really, in my case this is no reason at all, for my objections to the Administration's behavior rest no more logically on the grounds of either conservatism or radicalism than on those of atheism or homœopathy. They rest on the grounds of common sense and, I regret to say, common honesty. I resent the works and ways of the Administration because in my opinion such of them as are not peculiarly and dangerously silly are peculiarly and dangerously dishonest, and most of them are both. No doubt a person who wears the conservative label may hold this opinion and speak his mind accordingly, but so may a radical, so may anyone; the expression of it does not place him in either category, or in any category of the kind. They mark him merely as a person who is interested in having public affairs conducted wisely and honestly, and who resents their being conducted foolishly and dishonestly.

1. Mr. Ralph Adams Cram's theory is that the human being is a distinct species, and that the immense majority of *homo sapiens* is not human, but is merely the raw material out of which the occasional human being is produced. I have already discussed this theory in the *Atlantic* of April 1935, in an essay called "The Quest of the Missing Link." If this be true, the anarchist position would give way to the position of Spencer, that government should exist, but should abstain from any positive interventions upon the individual, confining itself strictly to negative interventions. I find myself inclining more and more towards Mr. Cram's view, and shall probably embrace it, but not having as yet done so, I must still call myself an anarchist.

With regard to Mr. Sokolsky, I may not, and do not, presume to doubt him when he says he is a conservative. All I may say is that I cannot well see how his paper makes him out to be one. If, now, he had said *reactionary,* I should have no trouble whatever about getting his drift, for my understanding is that he is in favor of a reaction from one distinct line of general State principle and policy back to another which has been abandoned. This is an eminently respectable position, and *reactionary,* which precisely describes it, is a most respectable term; but I cannot make it appear that this position is dictated by conservatism, or that holding this position justifies a person in calling himself a conservative.

Philology is a considerable help in these matters, but in guiding ourselves by its aid we must make an important discrimination which is set by the presence or absence of a moral factor. It is a commonplace of a language's growth that the significance of certain terms, like certain interpretations of music, becomes deformed and coarsened by tradition. I once heard a performance of the *Messiah* in Brussels, and was amazed at finding it almost a new composition, so far away it was from the English traditional interpretation, which was the only one I knew. Similarly there is no doubt that terms like *grace, truth, faith,* held very different connotations for Christians of the first century and for those of the fourth and again for those of the sixteenth, while for those of the twentieth they seem voided of all significance that is relevant to their philology, much as our formula, *my dear sir,* means only that a letter is begun, and *yours sincerely* means only that it is ended.

In instances like these there is no moral quality discernible in a term's passage from one meaning to another which has less philological relevancy, or to one which has none. There is no evidence of any interested management of its progress. In instances where this progress has been deliberately managed, however, the case is different. The term then becomes what Jeremy Bentham calls an *impostor-term,* because it has thus purposefully been converted into an instrument of deception, usually in the service of some base and knavish design.

It is notorious that a managed glossary is of the essence of politics, like a managed currency, and it is highly probable that the debasement of language necessary to successful political practice promotes far more varied and corrupting immoralities than any other infection proceeding from that prolific source. Thus terms like *conservative, progressive, radical, reactionary,* as they stand in the managed glossary of politics, are made to mean whatever the disreputable exigencies of the moment require them to mean. The term *radical,* for example, stands to account for anything from bomb-throwing to a demand for better wages. Again, we all remember Mr. Roosevelt's culpable debasement of the term *tory* to further an electioneering enterprise; and the manhandling of the term *liberal* into an avouchment for the most flagrantly illiberal measures of coercion, spoliation, and surveillance is surely well enough known.

The term *conservative,* which in the course of the campaign this summer we have heard applied to a curious medley made up of all sorts and conditions of men, suffers the same abuse. On the one hand, Mr. Smith is a conservative, and so is Mr. Raskob, Mr. Owen Young, the denizens of Wall Street, and the whole du Pont family; while, on the other hand, so is a majority of the Supreme Court, so is Mr. Newton Baker, Mr. Wolman, Mr. Lewis Douglas, and so, it seems, am I! What an extraordinary conjunction of names! On the day I wrote this I saw a headline which said that 53 per cent of the persons polled in a questionnaire or straw-vote conducted by some publication reported themselves as "conservative." I read further, and found that when all comes to all, this means that they are against the Administration, and that their difference with the Administration is over the distribution of money.

In the glossary of politics and journalism, the commonest, nay, the invariable connotation of "conservatism" is in terms of money; a "conservative policy" is one by which a larger flow of money can be turned towards one set of beneficiaries rather than towards another, while a "radical" or "progressive" policy is one which tends more or less to divert that flow. According to this scale of speech, the policies of Mr. Hoover and Mr. Mellon, which turned a great flow of money towards a political pressure-group of stockjobbers, speculators, shavers, were eminently conservative; while those of Mr. Roosevelt and his associates, which largely divert that flow towards a rival pressure-group of job-holders, hangers-on, single-crop farmers, unemployed persons, bonus-seekers, hoboes, are eminently radical. The designation follows the dollar. Even Mr. Sokolsky, whose valiant stand against the Administration I so much admire and so cordially approve, seems to associate his idea of conservatism rather over-closely with "prosperity"; that is to say, with money.

So one can imagine Mr. Justice McReynolds, for instance, surveying the rank and file of his fellow-conservatives with some dismay while he wonders, like the hero of French comedy, what he is doing in that particular galley. The thought suggests that it might be a good thing all around if we who are so indiscriminately labeled as conservatives should stand for a time on the windward side of ourselves while we examine this label and see whether or not we can properly take title to wear it. What is a conservative, and what is the quality, if any, that definitely marks him out as such?

This question can best be got at by considering an incident in the career of an extraordinary personage, about whom history, unfortunately, has had all too little to say. In a lifetime of only thirty-three years, Lucius Cary, Viscount Falkland, managed to make himself a most conspicuous example of every virtue and every grace of mind and manner; and this was the more remarkable because in the whole period through which he lived—the period leading up to the Civil War—the public affairs of England were an open playground for envy, hatred, malice, and all uncharitableness. The date of his birth is uncertain; probably it was at some time in the year 1610; and he was killed in the battle of Newbury, September 20, 1643, while fighting on the royalist side.

Falkland had a seat in the Long Parliament, which was divided on the specious issue of presbyterianism against episcopacy in the Church of England. When a bill was brought in to deprive the bishops of their seats in the House of Lords, Falkland voted for it. He was all for puncturing the bishops' pretension to "divine right," and for putting a stop to the abuses which grew out of that pretension. The presbyterian party, however, emboldened by success, presently brought in another bill to abolish episcopacy, root and branch, and Falkland voted against it.

Hampden, in a bitter speech, promptly taunted him with inconsistency. In reply, Falkland said he could see nothing essentially wrong with an episcopal polity. "Mr. Speaker," he said, "I do not believe the bishops to be *jure divino;* nay, I believe them not to be *jure divino;* but neither do I believe them to be *injuriâ humanâ.*" This polity had been in force a long time, it had worked fairly well, the people were used to it, the correction of its abuses was fully provided for in the first bill, so why "root up this ancient tree," when all it needed was a severe pruning of its wayward branches, which had already been done, and for which he had voted? He could not see that there was any inconsistency in his attitude. He then went on to lay down a great general principle in the ever-memorable formula, "Mr. Speaker, when it is not *necessary* to change, it is necessary *not* to change."

Here we get on track of what conservatism is. We must carefully observe the strength of Falkland's language. He does not say that when it is not necessary to change, it is expedient or advisable not to change; he says it is *necessary* not to change. Very well, then, the differentiation of conservatism rests on the estimate of necessity in any given case. Thus conservatism is purely an *ad hoc* affair; its findings vary with conditions, and are good for this day and train only. Conservatism is not a body of opinion, it has no set platform or creed, and hence, strictly speaking, there is no such thing as a hundred-per-cent conservative group or party—Mr. Justice McReynolds and Mr. Baker may stand at ease. Nor is conservatism an attitude of sentiment. Dickens's fine old unintelligent characters who "kept up the barrier, sir, against modern innovations" were not conservatives. They were sentimental obstructionists, probably also obscurantists, but not conservatives.

Nor yet is conservatism the antithesis of radicalism; the antithesis of *radical* is *superficial.* Falkland was a great radical; he was never for a moment caught by the superficial aspect of things. A person may be as radical as you please, and still may make an extremely conservative estimate of the force of necessity exhibited by a given set of conditions. A radical, for example, may think we should get on a great deal better if we had an entirely different system of government, and yet, at this time and under conditions now existing, he may take a strongly conservative view of the necessity for pitching out our system, neck and crop, and replacing it with another. He may think our fiscal system is iniquitous in theory and monstrous in practice, and be ever so sure he could propose a better one, but if on consideration of all the circumstances he finds that it is not *necessary* to change that system, he is capable of maintaining stoutly that it is necessary *not* to change it. The conservative is a person who considers very closely every chance, even the longest, of "throwing out the baby with the bath-water," as the German proverb puts it, and who determines his conduct accordingly.

And so we see that the term *conservative* has little value as a label; in fact, one might say that its label-value varies inversely with one's right to wear it. Conservatism is a habit of mind which does not generalize beyond the facts of the case in point. It considers those facts carefully, makes sure that as far as possible it has them all in hand, and the course of action which the balance of fact *in that case* indicates as necessary will be the one it follows; and the course indicated as unnecessary it not only will not follow, but will oppose without compromise or concession.

As a label, then, the word seems unserviceable. It covers so much that looks like mere capriciousness and inconsistency that one gets little positive good out of wearing it; and because of its elasticity it is so easily weaseled into an impostor-term or a term of reproach, or again into one of derision, as implying complete stagnation of mind, that it is likely to do one more harm than it is worth. Probably Huxley was wrong, for while it may be that society regards an unlabeled person with more or less uneasy suspicion, there is no doubt that it looks with active distrust upon the person who wears an equivocal and dubious label; and equally so whether one puts the label on oneself, as Huxley did, or whether it is put on by interested persons for the purpose of creating a confusion which they can turn to their own profit.

This is true of all the terms that we have been considering, and therefore it would seem the sensible thing simply to cease using them and to cease paying attention to them when used by others. When we hear talk of men or policies as conservative, radical, progressive or what not, the term really tells us nothing, for ten to one it is used either ignorantly or with intent to deceive; and hence one can best clear and stabilize one's mind by letting it go unheeded. It is notoriously characteristic of a child's mentality to fix undue attention on the names of things, and in firmly declining to be caught and held by names one brings oneself somewhat nearer the stature of maturity.

By this, moreover, one puts oneself in the way of doing something to mature and moralize our civilization. Every now and then some prophet, like another Solomon Eagle, warns us that our civilization is at the point of collapse. We may regard these predictions as far-fetched, or we may say with Emerson, when an Adventist told him the world was coming to an end, that if so it were no great loss; or again, we may feel towards our civilization as Bishop Warburton felt towards the Church of England.[2] But however much or little we may think our civilization worth saving, and however we may interpret its prospects of impending dissolution, we may hardly hope that it can keep going indefinitely unless it breaks its bondage to its present political ideas and ideals.

We must observe, too, that it is held in this ignoble bondage largely, perhaps chiefly, by the power of words; that is to say, by the managed glossary of politics. Mr. Hoover and Mr. Mellon, for example, will be long in living down the scandalously misapplied term *conservative,* if indeed they ever do; and there is a vicious irony in the fact that Mr. Roosevelt and his associates will always be known as radicals or liberals, according as it is meant to hold them up either to blame or to praise.

The main business of a politician, as Edmund Burke said, is "still further to contract the narrowness of men's ideas, to confirm inveterate prejudices, to inflame vulgar passions, and to abet all sorts of popular absurdities"; and a managed glossary is the most powerful implement that he applies to this base enterprise. We hear a good deal about inflation at the moment, and inflation is indeed a formidable thing. Our people have no idea of what it means, and I, for one, distinctly do not care to be around when they find out what it means, for I have seen it in action elsewhere, and have seen enough. But dreadful as it is, a far worse form of inflation, the most destructive that politicians and journalists can devise, is inflation of the public mind by pumping it full of claptrap.

The words we have been discussing are standard terms in the politician's managed glossary. By recognizing them as such, and

2. William Warburton, bishop of Gloucester, 1760–1779. He said, "The Church, like the Ark of Noah, is worth saving; not for the sake of the unclean beasts that almost filled it, and probably made most noise and clamour in it, but for the little corner of rationality that was as much distressed by the stink within as by the tempest without."

resolutely disregarding them, we should disarm the politician and journalist of much, perhaps most, of their power for evil, and thus give our civilization the one service of which it especially stands in need. If we are looking for an example of wisdom, insight, and integrity in their application to public affairs, let us find it in Falkland. Instead of permitting our attention to be caught and held by recommendations of person, party, or policy as conservative, liberal, radical, progressive, let us rather employ it in rigorously determining what the actual needs of the situation are, and then permit it to come to rest upon the simple and sufficient formula: "Mr. Speaker, when it is not *necessary* to change, it is necessary *not* to change."

This article originally appeared in the October 1936 issue of the *Atlantic Monthly*.

The Criminality of the State

As well as I can judge, the general attitude of Americans who are at all interested in foreign affairs is one of astonishment, coupled with distaste, displeasure, or horror, according to the individual observer's capacity for emotional excitement. Perhaps I ought to shade this statement a little in order to keep on the safe side, and say that this is the most generally-expressed attitude.

All our institutional voices—the press, pulpit, forum—are pitched to the note of amazed indignation at one or another phase of the current goings-on in Europe and Asia. This leads me to believe that our people generally are viewing with wonder as well as repugnance certain conspicuous actions of various foreign States; for instance, the barbarous behavior of the German State towards some of its own citizens; the merciless despotism of the Soviet Russian State; the ruthless imperialism of the Italian State; the murders and executions of the Spanish Red State; the bombings of civilians by the Spanish Fascist State; the "betrayal of Czecho-Slovakia" by the British and French States; the savagery of the Japanese State; the brutishness of the Chinese State's mercenaries; and so on, here or there, all over the globe—this sort of thing is showing itself to be against our people's grain, and they are speaking out about it in wrathful surprise.

I am cordially with them on every point but one. I am with them in repugnance, horror, indignation, disgust, but not in astonishment. The history of the State being what it is, and its testimony being as invariable and eloquent as it is, I am obliged to say that the naïve tone of surprise wherewith our people complain of these matters strikes me as a pretty sad reflection on their intelligence. Suppose someone were impolite enough to ask them the gruff question, "Well, what do you expect?"— what rational answer could they give? I know of none.

Polite or impolite, that is just the question which ought to be put every time a story of State villainy appears in the news. It ought to be thrown at our public day after day, from every newspaper, periodical, lecture-platform, and radio-station in the land; and it ought to be backed up by a simple appeal to history, a simple invitation to look at the record. The British State has sold the Czech State down the river by a despicable trick; very well, be as disgusted and angry as you like, but don't be astonished; what would you expect?—just take a look at the British State's record! The German State is persecuting great masses of its people, the Russian State is holding a purge, the Italian State is grabbing territory, the Japanese State is buccaneering all along the Asiatic Coast; horrible, yes, but for Heaven's sake don't lose your head over it, for what would you expect?—look at the record!

That is how every public presentation of these facts ought to run if Americans are ever going to grow up into an adult attitude towards them. Also, in order to keep down the great American sin of self-righteousness, every public presentation ought to draw the deadly parallel with the record of the American State. The German State is persecuting a minority, just as the American State did after 1776; the Italian State breaks into Ethiopia, just as the American State broke into Mexico; the Japanese State kills off the Manchurian tribes in wholesale lots, just as the American State did the Indian tribes; the British State practices large-scale carpet-baggery, like the American State after 1864; the imperialist French State massacres native civilians on their own soil, as the American State did in pursuit of its imperialistic policies in the Pacific; and so on.

In this way, perhaps, our people might get into their heads some glimmering of the fact that the State's criminality is nothing new and nothing to be wondered at. It began when the first predatory group of men clustered together and formed the State, and it will continue as long as the State exists in the world, because the State is fundamentally an anti-social institution, fundamentally criminal. The idea that the State originated to serve any kind of social purpose is completely unhistorical. It originated in conquest and confiscation—that is to say, in crime. It originated for the purpose of maintaining the division of society into an owning-and-exploiting class and a propertyless dependent class—that is, for a criminal purpose.

No State known to history originated in any other manner, or for any other purpose. Like all predatory or parasitic institutions, its first instinct is that of self-preservation. All its enterprises are directed first towards preserving its own life, and, second, towards increasing its own power and enlarging the scope of its own activity. For the sake of this it will, and regularly does, commit any crime which circumstances make expedient. In the last analysis, what is the German, Italian, French, or British State now actually doing? It is ruining its own people in order to preserve itself, to enhance its own power and prestige, and extend its own authority; and the American State is doing the same thing to the utmost of its opportunities.

What, then, is a little matter like a treaty to the French or British State? Merely a scrap of paper—Bethmann-Hollweg described it exactly. Why be astonished when the German or Russian State murders its citizens? The American State would do the same thing under the same circumstances. In fact, eighty years ago it did murder a great many of them for no other crime in the world but that they did not wish to live under its rule any longer; and if that is a crime, then the colonists led by G. Washington were hardened criminals and the Fourth of July is nothing but a cutthroat's holiday.

The weaker the State is, the less power it has to commit crime. Where in Europe today does the State have the best criminal record? Where it is weakest: in Switzerland, Holland, Denmark, Norway, Luxemburg, Sweden, Monaco, Andorra. Yet when the Dutch State, for instance, was strong, its criminality was appalling; in Java it massacred 9000 persons in one morning, which is considerably ahead of Hitler's record or Stalin's. It would not do the like today, for it could not; the Dutch people do not give it that much power, and would not stand for such conduct. When the Swedish State was a great empire, its record, say from 1660 to 1670, was fearful. What does all this mean but that if you do not want the State to act like a criminal, you must disarm it as you would a criminal; you must keep it weak. The State will always be criminal in proportion to its strength; a weak State will always be as criminal as it can be, or dare be, but if it is kept down to the proper limit of weakness— which, by the way, is a vast deal lower limit than people are led to believe—its criminality may be safely got on with.

So it strikes me that instead of sweating blood over the iniquity of foreign States, my fellow-citizens would do a great deal better by themselves to make sure that the American State is not strong enough to carry out the like iniquities here. The stronger the American State is allowed to grow, the higher its record of criminality will grow, according to its opportunities and temptations. If, then, instead of devoting energy, time, and money to warding off wholly imaginary and fanciful dangers from criminals thousands of miles away, our people turn their patriotic fervor loose on the only source from which danger can proceed, they will be doing their full duty by their country.

Two able and sensible American publicists—Isabel Paterson, of the New York *Herald Tribune,* and W. J. Cameron, of the Ford Motor Company—have lately called our public's attention to the great truth that if you give the State power to do something *for* you, you give it an exact equivalent of power to do something *to* you. I wish every editor, publicist, teacher, preacher, and lecturer would keep hammering that truth into American heads until they get it nailed fast there, never to come loose. The State was organized in this country with power to do all kinds of things *for* the people, and the people in their short-sighted stupidity, have' been adding to that power ever since. After 1789, John Adams said that, so far from being a democracy or a democratic republic, the political organization of the country was that of "a monarchical republic, or, if you will, a limited monarchy"; the powers of its President were far greater than those of "an avoyer, a consul, a podesta, a doge, a stadtholder; nay, than a king of Poland; nay, than a king of Sparta." If all that was true in 1789—and it was true—what is to be said of the American State at the present time, after a century and a half of steady centralization and continuous increments of power?

Power, for instance, to "help business" by auctioning off concessions, subsidies, tariffs, land-grants, franchises; power to help business by ever-encroaching regulations, supervisions, various forms of control. All this power was freely given; it all carried with it the equivalent power to do things *to* business; and see what a banditti of sharking political careerists are doing to business now! Power to afford "relief" to proletarians; and see what the State has done to those proletarians now in the way of systematic debauchery of whatever self-respect and self-reliance they may have had! Power this way, power that way; and all ultimately used *against* the interests of the people who surrendered that power on the pretext that it was to be used *for* those interests.

Many now believe that with the rise of the "totalitarian" State the world has entered upon a new era of barbarism. It has not. The totalitarian State is only the State; the kind of thing it does is only what the State has always done with unfailing regularity, if it had the power to do it, wherever and whenever its own aggrandizement made that kind of thing expedient. Give any State like power hereafter, and put it in like circumstances, and it will do precisely the same kind of thing. The State will unfailingly aggrandize itself, if only it has the power, first at the expense of its own citizens, and then at the expense of anyone else in sight. It has always done so, and always will.

The idea that the State is a social institution, and that with a fine upright man like Mr. Chamberlain at the head of it, or a charming person like Mr. Roosevelt, there can be no question about its being honorably and nobly managed—all this is just so much sticky fly-paper. Men in that position usually make a good deal of their honor, and some of them indeed may have some (though if they had any I cannot understand their letting themselves be put in that position) but the machine they are running will run on rails which are laid only one way, which is from crime to crime. In the old days, the partition of Czecho-Slovakia or the taking-over of Austria would have been arranged by rigamarole among a few highly polished gentlemen in stiff shirts ornamented with fine ribbons. Hitler simply arranged it the way old Frederick arranged his share in the first partition of Poland; he arranged the annexation of Austria the way Louis XIV arranged that of Alsace. There is more or less of a fashion, perhaps, in the way these things are done, but the point is that they always come out exactly the same in the end.

Furthermore, the idea that the procedure of the "democratic" State is any less criminal than that of the State under any other fancy name, is rubbish. The country is now being surfeited with journalistic garbage about our great sister-democracy, England, its fine democratic government, its vast beneficent gift for ruling subject peoples, and so on; but does anyone ever look up the criminal record of the British State? The bombardment of Copenhagen; the Boer war; the Sepoy Rebellion; the starvation of Germans by the post-Armistice blockade; the massacre of natives in India, Afghanistan, Jamaica; the employment of Hessians to kill off American colonists. What is the difference, moral or actual, between Kitchener's democratic concentration-camps and the totalitarian concentration-camps maintained by Herr Hitler? The totalitarian general Badoglio is a pretty hard-boiled brother, if you like, but how about the democratic general O'Dwyer and Governor Eyre? Any of the three stands up pretty well beside our own democratic virtuoso, Hell-roaring Jake Smith, in his treatment of the Filipinos; and you can't say fairer than that.

As for the British State's talent for a kindly and generous colonial administration, I shall not rake up old scores by citing the bill of particulars set forth in the Declaration of Independence; I shall consider India only, not even going into matters like the Kaffir war or the Wairau incident in New Zealand. Our democratic British cousins in India in the Eighteenth Century must have learned their trade from Pizarro and Cortez. Edmund Burke called them "birds of prey and passage." Even the directors of the East India Company admitted that "the vast fortunes acquired in the inland trade have been obtained by a scene of the most tyrannical and oppressive conduct that was ever known in any age or country." Describing a journey, Warren Hastings wrote that "most of the petty towns and *serais* were deserted at our approach"; the people ran off into the woods at the mere sight of a white man. There was the iniquitous salt-monopoly; there was extortion everywhere, practiced by enterprising rascals in league with a corrupt police; there was taxation which confiscated almost half the products of the soil.

If it be said that Britain was not a sister-democracy in those days, and has since reformed, one might well ask how much of the reformation is due to circumstances, and how much to a change of heart. Besides, the Black-and-Tans were in our day; so was the post-Armistice blockade; General O'Dwyer's massacre was not more than a dozen years ago; and there are plenty alive who remember Kitchener's concentration-camps.

No, "democratic" State practice is nothing more or less than State practice. It does not differ from Marxist State practice, Fascist State practice, or any other.

Here is the Golden Rule of sound citizenship, the first and greatest lesson in the study of politics: *you get the same order of criminality from any State to which you give power to exercise it; and whatever power you give the State to do things* for *you carries with it the equivalent power to do things* to *you.* A citizenry which has learned that one short lesson has but little more left to learn. Stripping the American State of the enormous power it has acquired is a full-time job for our citizens and a stirring one; and if they attend to it properly they will have no energy to spare for fighting communism, or for hating Hitler, or for worrying about South America or Spain, or for anything whatever, except what goes on right here in the United States.

_____

This essay appeared in the March 1939 issue of the *American Mercury,* in Nock's column, "The State of the Union."

Liberalism, Properly So Called

I understand that what you want is not a publishable article but merely a conspectus or brief, which will aid the comprehension of two remarkable historical phenomena.

First, why is it that Liberalism is now motivated by principles exactly opposite to those which originally motivated it, and how did this change come about? Second, why has the spirit and temper of Liberals undergone a corresponding change, and how did this change come about?

The facts are clearly apparent. We now see on all sides the extraordinary spectacle of Liberals doing their best to destroy the cardinal freedoms and immunities which Liberals formerly defended, while all the forces which are historically and traditionally known as Tory or Conservative are arrayed in defense of those freedoms. Furthermore we see Liberals vehemently vilifying those who hold to the original basic principles of Liberalism, denouncing them as enemies of society, and doing all they can to discredit and disable them. These two are probably the strangest anomalies that recent history presents.

To understand them it is necessary to consider Liberalism's origin and rise in Britain, since it is only in this perspective that American Liberalism can be clearly seen and correctly assessed. British political Liberalism was a continuator of Whiggism, which as far back as the time of Charles II proposed to subordinate the royal power to the power of Parliament. Toryism, on the contrary held to the "divine right" theory of monarchy, with all its implications. Put in terms of general principle, the Tory held that obedience to established authority is *unconditional;* the Whig held that it is *conditional.* It is of the utmost importance to keep these two primary principles constantly in mind.

Toryism therefore contemplated a type of society organised around a system of compulsory cooperation. This system is best illustrated by the example of a conscript army. The individual soldier has no option about joining or leaving the service; nor has he any say about his duties, his maintenance or his pay. In all ranks throughout the service obedience is unconditional, and is enforced under coercion. The final intention is thus to bring and keep the many under rule of the few;

and the service's rules and regulations are devised with a view to strengthening a highly centralised coercive military power over the many, and making them more easily manageable. This is the point to be kept in mind when considering the structure of civil society as Toryism would have it, and for some time did have it. As the Army, not the individual soldier, is the unit of ultimate value, so the civil structure with its system of fixed ascending subordinations, and not the individual member, was Toryism's ultimate criterion; and hence the regulatory laws, edicts, mandates, which Toryism set up were devised with a view to strengthening a highly centralised coercive civil power over the many, and making them more easily manageable.

Liberalism, on the contrary, contemplated a type of society organised around a system of voluntary cooperation; a system of original contract, free contract. This system is best illustrated by the example of an industrial concern like the Standard Oil Company. The individual need not work for Standard Oil unless he wishes to do so; he is not conscripted. His acceptance of the Company's rules is a matter of free contract; he is not coerced; he may leave if he does not like them. His wages, hours and conditions of labor are fixed by consent; if they do not suit him as proposed, he is free to refuse them. Under this system the individual is regarded as the unit of ultimate value. The logic of this position was that society as a whole would gain more from the aggregate initiative and enterprise of groups pursuing various ends in free association and by such means as of free choice should seem best to them, than it would from the efforts of groups pursuing prescribed ends under coercion.

Consequently the political design of Tory measures was uniformly to increase the coercive power of the government over the individual and enlarge its range of action. The design of Whig measures, and subsequently Liberal measures, was uniformly to decrease the govern-ment's coercive power and to reduce its range of action. This must be kept clearly in mind, for it is the fundamental distinction between Toryism in practice and Liberalism in practice. It furnishes the one and only test by which to determine whether a specific political measure should be classified as Tory or Liberal. No matter what political label the measure bears; no matter whether its direct object may be desirable or undesirable; its mark of identification is found only by addressing these questions to it: Does this measure tend to diminish or to increase the government's coercive power over the individual? Does it tend to narrow the range of the government's coercive power, or to widen it? Does it tend to diminish compulsory cooperation or to increase it? Does it tend to enlarge the area of conduct in which the individual is free to do as he pleases, or does it enlarge the area in which he must do as governmental agents please? If these questions can be answered by the one affirmative, then the measure is a Liberal measure, properly so called; and if by the other, it is a Tory measure; and it must be repeated that neither the desirability *per se* of the immediate end which the measure is designed to serve, nor its lack of desirability, has any bearing whatever on this decision.

Liberalism held that society's work should be carried on, its responsibilities met, and its difficulties dealt with, by the application of social power, not governmental power; social power meaning the power generated and exercised by individuals and groups of individuals working in an economy which is free of governmental interference—an economy of free contract. This follows logically from the conception of government inherited from Whiggism in opposition to Toryism's conception of it. Toryism held that the ruler derived his authority from God and distributed that authority to his agents in various degrees according to their function; therefore the agents exercised power by divine right *ad hoc,* responsible only to the ruler, who in turn was responsible only to God. Whiggism, on the contrary, regarded rulership as purely a civil institution established by the nation for the benefit of all its members, with no inherent power of its own, and responsible only to the nation.

The early Liberals inherited from the Whigs this conception of government as an agency set up by the nation and responsible to it, with no power of its own, but with certain coercive powers granted to it for exercise in sharply defined directions and in none other. They contemplated a government whose interventions on the individual should be purely negative in character. It should attend to national defense, safeguard the individual in his civil rights, maintain outward order and decency, enforce the obligations of contract, punish crimes belonging in the order of *malum in se,* and make justice cheap and easily accessible. Beyond these negative interventions it should not go; it should have no coercive power to enforce any positive interventions whatever upon the individual.

When the Whigs came into power they kept all the foregoing tenets in mind, and so did the early Liberals who succeeded them. They worked steadily towards curbing the government's coercive power over the individual; and with such effect, as historians testify, that by the middle of the eighteenth century Englishmen had simply forgotten that there was ever a time when the full "liberty of the subject" was not theirs to enjoy. In this connexion the thing to be remarked is that the Whigs proceeded by the negative method of repealing existing laws, not by the positive method of making new ones. They combed the Statute-book, and when they found a statute which bore against "the liberty of the subject" they simply repealed it and left the page blank. This purgation ran up into the thousands. In 1873 the secretary of the Law Society estimated that out of the 18,110 Acts which had been passed since the reign of Henry III, four-fifths had been wholly or partially repealed. The thing to be observed here is that this negative method of simple repeal left free scope for the sanative processes of natural law in dealing with all manner of social dislocations and disabilities. These processes are slow and usually painful, and impatience with them leads to popular demand that the government should step in and anticipate them by positive statutory intervention when anything goes wrong. The Liberals were aware that no one, least of all the "practical" politician, can foresee the ultimate effects, or even all the collateral effects, of such interventions, or can calculate the force of their political momentum. Thus it regularly happens that they bring about ultimate evils which are not only far more serious than the specific evils which they were meant to remedy, but are also wholly unexpected. American legislative history in the last two decades shows any number of conspicuous instances where the political short-cut of positive intervention has been taken towards remedying a present evil at the most reckless expense of future good. The Prohibition Amendment is perhaps the most conspicuous of these instances.

Towards the middle of the nineteenth century British Liberals turned their backs upon their historical principles and gave support to a series of coercive measures, continuously increasing both in number and particularity, from the poor-laws, the Factory Acts, and the subvention of school-house building in the 'thirties, down to the proposals set forth in the Beveridge Report of last year. It is hardly possible to conceive of a more complete *volte-face* on fundamental doctrine. Three circumstances bearing on this change may be noticed.

First, the period from the third quarter of the eighteenth century to the second of the nineteenth was one of wars; and as always in a war period, it was one of savage governmental coercions of all kinds. As always, again, the general structure of society reverted from the more advanced type contemplated by Liberalism, the type marked by voluntary cooperation, to the more primitive type contemplated by Toryism, the type marked by enforced cooperation. The normal development of a society is always from the primitive closely-organised militant type towards the loosely-organised industrial type; that is to say, from organisation in mass to organisation in group. Hence this mutation of type was a retrogression; and in consequence, as invariably happens, the mind and spirit of the people underwent a considerable readjustment. From their adjustment to the terms of pre-war "liberty of the subject," they became largely readjusted to the terms of a slave-status.

Second, as is usually the case, the period almost immediately succeeding the period of war was one of great general distress and serious civil disturbances. "The Hungry 'Forties" was on its way to become a byword. This state of things brought heavy pressure on the government; and the pressure for positive interventions of one kind and another was much increased by the readjustment just now mentioned. To understand the attitude of Liberals in these premises, one must keep clearly in mind the fact that nothing is more natural than to regard a remedied evil as an accomplished good, and to forget entirely the all-important differentiation of the means by which the good was accomplished; and therefore to conclude that the thing to be aimed at is the direct accomplishment of a present good, or what it presumed to be a good, rather than the consistent employment of a means contemplating far larger measures of ultimate good.

Thus it was natural for Liberals to say, "The government intervened to accomplish *that* great good, and *that* and *that;* why should it not intervene to accomplish *this* and *this?*" The cardinal fact that in the one case the intervention was *negative* while in the other it must be *positive,* was lost sight of or disregarded. The questions of principle which early Liberalism would address to any proposal of intervention were no longer put; the only questions now put were those of expediency and practicability. In this way the later Liberalism progressively abetted the lapse of British society into a mode of State-servitude quite as rigid and unconditional as the mode contemplated by Toryism, and marked by far greater particularity.

Third, the later Liberalism was confirmed in its digression by the spread of a new doctrine of society fathered by Bentham in England and on the Continent by Comte. This doctrine made a slight side-approach to Toryism in holding that society is the unit of ultimate value; rather than the individual, as early Liberalism had held; hence "the greatest good to the greatest number" is the thing to be aimed at, for the individual will find his greatest advantage and happiness in a society controlled by this principle. The consequent justification of expediency is obvious; and the extent to which the later Liberalism has been affected by Benthamite doctrine is well known.

Passing now to consideration of Liberalism and Liberals in the United States, there is hardly anything to be said which is not clearly implicit in the foregoing. We once had a short-lived political party led by Henry Clay and known as Whigs, but it had nothing in common with British Whiggism. It was formed in opposition to Jackson's stand on the National Bank and on nullification, and took the name of Whig only as an anti-Roosevelt party today might do. It came into power in 1840 for four years, and went to pieces some ten years later.

Liberalism in this country never had a political organisation, nor has it ever had anything in common with earlier British Liberalism. It was never formulated in definite terms, even according to the broad original British formula which defined a Liberal as "one who advocates greater freedom from restraint, especially in political institutions." Thus it has had no tradition, unless one might say that it has perhaps come more or less into the degenerate British Liberal tradition of Benthamite and Comtist expediency; but this is no doubt a matter of coincidence rather than design.

Hence we see that those who call themselves Liberals proceed on no fixed principles whatever, and their action in any given premises is notoriously unpredictable. Their title is usually self-chosen, in virtue of an interest in some one special enfranchising or humanitarian cause like freeing slaves, universal suffrage, "social security," improving the conditions of labour, raising the status of Negroes. This interest is often exclusive; the absence of fixed principle is apparent in the Liberal's active opposition to other causes which stand on a logical footing with the cause he favours; as when, for example, many Liberals were rabidly against withholding the suffrage from Negroes and equally against giving it to women.

But the determining factor in the honest Liberal's attitude is his indifference towards the essential nature of the means employed to further the cause in which he is interested. There is here no implication against the honest Liberal's moral character. Nor is there an implied charge that he is acting in black ignorance of history; the charge is only one of stark incompetence with history. Having all history to guide him, he nevertheless fails to look beyond the immediate effect producible by a measure bearing on his cause, and thus fails to see that the ultimate sum-total of effect may be to produce a much worse state of things than the one which it was meant to remedy, and perhaps did remedy.

I have purposely refrained from illustration, since any one with ordinary knowledge of history can readily supply a dozen for every point I have raised. I shall make one here, however, partly to clear the point of the last paragraph, and partly as in a general way typical.

Twelve years ago, when a government made up of professing Liberals proposed a large-scale positive bureaucratic intervention to relieve distress, and by use of the taxing-power brought all citizens into enforced cooperation with it, Liberals were in favour of it. They regarded only the immediate end—the relief of distress—and not at all the nature of the means; and the means did actually serve that end, though in a most disorderly and wasteful fashion.

The true Liberal, the Liberal of the eighteenth century, would at once have looked beyond that end and asked the great primary question which finally judges, or should judge, all political action: "What type of social structure does this measure tend to produce? Does it tend to improve and reinforce the existing type, or to bring about a reversion to the primary militant type? Does it tend towards advance or retrogression, towards progress in civilisation or towards re-barbarisation?" Let us take the measure apart, and see.

The subordinate questions would then follow: "Will this measure increase the government's coercive power over the individual and widen its scope?" Clearly so. "Will it, through taxation, confiscate social power and convert it into State power?" Yes, to an incalculable extent. "Will it diminish voluntary cooperation and increase compulsory cooperation?" Yes, greatly. "Are the directions and the driving force of this measure's political momentum at all determinable?" No, not even a conjecture is worth making.

If the true Liberal had subjected the proposed relief-measure to these tests twelve years ago, he would have said at once, "This is in no sense a Liberal measure. There is not a suggestion of Liberalism anywhere in it. On the contrary, it exactly meets every specification laid down by the most hide-bound Toryism, and for that reason I oppose it."

This illustration brings us in sight of reasons why the self-styled Liberal of the present day vehemently defames the representatives of historic Liberalism. But we should make a distinction here by leaving out of account those who are Liberals for revenue only; those of the rice-Christian kind, who take this title with a view to personal gain, as a convenience for getting political jobs, prestige as journalists, essayists, commentators, prestige in one-or-another order of society, or for acquiring some other modicum of advancement or distinction. Such as these meet opposition by the political method technically known as smearing; that is, by applying terms which are irrelevant to the matter in hand, and which are therefore neither descriptive nor meant to be so, but are merely terms of opprobrium. Terms such as *Fascist, Naziist, economic royalist, anti-Semite,* are now conspicuously the property of persons who call themselves Liberals for the sake of personal profit, as *nigger-trader* and *nigger-lover* were a century ago, and as *bolshevik* was in the days following the Russian revolution. Such persons obviously stand outside any serious discussion of Liberalism.

Another order of persons, quite in the majority, style themselves Liberals in all good faith, but being ignorant of Liberalism's principles and history, they understand neither what they say nor whereof they affirm. They conceive of themselves as on the side of progress, enlightenment, a larger measure of welfare and happiness all round, and they regard the content of Liberalism as made up of whatever matters seem compatible with this view. Whether or not they are actually compatible with Liberalism can be determined only by analysis, which they do not attempt to make. To them, whatever social or political end attracts their allegiance is a Liberal desideratum; and whatever means will attain it is, by consequence, a Liberal means.

These usually, and in quite good faith, meet opposition by attributing to the opponent opinions which he does not hold; opinions perhaps which he has often openly disavowed. In my own case, for example, an old friend, a member of the Administration and a self-styled Liberal (but of this second order) describes me as an anarchist because I hold to the theory of government maintained by the eighteenth-century British Liberals, by Mr. Jefferson and Thomas Paine. Nothing could be in more violent contrast with the spirit and temper of the early Liberals. They and the Tories each at least knew what the other's opinions and principles were, and could state them in specific terms. My friend, I regret to say, is wholly ignorant of both.

Again, this ignorance sometimes leads to conclusions prejudicial to an opponent's character; and in a time of popular excitement it quite regularly does so; and I repeat, in all good faith. Here also I may take my own case by way of example. When I questioned the policy of governmental poor-relief twelve years ago, on sound Liberal principles, I was met with the question, "But would you let Americans starve?"; and as it happened, the question was pressed hardest on me by persons who called themselves Liberals. As professing Liberals, it meant nothing to them that the exigency clearly called for the application of social power, not governmental power; that there was plenty of social power available, and plenty of social agencies available for its distribution; and that a Liberal government's duty was to stimulate and encourage this application, but not in any way to supplant or supplement it.

I think that now, in the main, the anomalies which are the subject of this inquiry have been accounted for. Enough has been said to show how and why it is that persons calling themselves Liberals are now, many in good faith, some in despicably bad faith, advocating a coercive totalitarian type of government, a recession from the advanced type to the primitive, from the more nearly civilised to the more nearly barbarous; and are also denouncing as reactionary and anti-social those who adhere to the historical principles of Liberalism.

This essay comes from an unpublished manuscript, apparently prepared for the National Economic Council around 1943 or 1944, the time Nock was editing the *Economic Council Review of Books*. A typescript of this essay was prepared and distributed to members of the Nockian Society by Edmund A. Opitz in 1968.

VI. MISCELLANY

Metternich's work has crumbled to nothing, and Talleyrand's, Richelieu's, Bismarck's, and innumerable others. But not Bach's, Shakespeare's, Homer's, Rembrandt's, Dante's, and the work of many more whose names stand in their glorious company. Does not this fact of itself show that side of life upon which we should bear lightly and that upon which we should rest with our whole weight?

—"Miscellany," the *Freeman*, February 27, 1924

Culture and Freedom

Many of our correspondents are unsympathetic towards Mr. Harold Stearns's frank discussion in our columns a few weeks ago, of the difficulties besetting the spirit which finds itself alien to our civilization. Some think it is the alien's duty to remain here and strive to make his views of life and demands on life prevail over the too, too solid flesh of contemporary hundred-per-cent Americanism. Others, like Miss Chown, whose letter we printed 25 August, without raising the point of duty, think that America presents an exhilarating opportunity for this exercise of the evangelistic impulse and that one should accept it as a kind of sporting proposition, apparently. The former view is undoubtedly specious; and the latter also should be sifted rather carefully before one gives it unqualified acceptance.

A good case could be made out for the thesis that the interests of general culture are better served intensively, by strengthening the centres of culture than by scattering one's energies about its hinterland; just as it is debatable whether, in a single nation, the best and most generally profitable fruits of culture do not accrue from the high culture of certain classes, rather than from a policy of greater extension. Four, at least, of the best critical minds of the last century maintained an affirmative view of these questions—Renan, Goethe, Arnold and Niebuhr—and comparing France or Italy with the United States, for example, culture certainly seems to stand better in those countries where this view has been traditional. Possibly, therefore, the American friends of culture might in the long-run do more for the future of culture in America itself by emigrating to strengthen the centres of culture elsewhere than by leading a forlorn hope here; they might thus show themselves wiser and more efficient missionaries than if they followed Miss Chown's advice and carried on a single-handed struggle to make culture prevail as it were vi et armis against an inimical environment.

We said what we had to say about this aspect of the matter, in our last issue. There is another question, however, which all our correspondents seem to have overlooked; and that is the question of taste involved in advising the alien to stay in a civilization which has no more interest in him than he has in it. To us it seems highly dubious. We are individualists and democrats, believing in absolute freedom, and we have always objected strongly to the doctrine that man is in any sense his brother's keeper. We feel as much bound to object to it when it is proposed in our favour as when it is proposed to our prejudice. We are therefore thrown back strongly on the *noblesse oblige* when, for example, one of our correspondents asks "how America will ever be a better place to live in" if those who believe in culture and desire to make all their works and ways promote the interests of culture, fall in with Mr. Stearns's implied suggestion, and emigrate. How can one be quite sure that America ought to be a better place to live in? For the time being, at any rate, America's culture apparently satisfies immense numbers of people who live here, and not only satisfies but delights them. They are always praising it and saying how much better it is than anything to be had elsewhere, and they continually bear about with them an almost savage jealousy of its superiority. Do not the newspapers take up their parable after them?—and read any of our war-literature, strike into it anywhere, and you will find a tone of almost aggressive complacency.

In view of this immense majority-opinion, does not our correspondent really mean that America should be a better place *for us* to live in—for him and for ourselves? He must mean something like that; and his question therefore carries a savour of the essential prohibitionist temper. Let us be quite explicit about this. We know the "dismal home towns" that Mr. Mark Sullivan and Mr. Stearns refer to; and to us their dismalness and hideousness is indeed appalling. Yet when our correspondent, Mr. Coon, whose letter we published in our issue of 25 August, speaks of "regenerating some of these towns, giving them some art, music, drama, intellectual life and so on," we could not help thinking—if Mr. Coon will forgive us for saying so—of the social survey, of the uplifter, of a whole depressing apparatus of charts and dockets for plotting the status of the submerged tenth; and above all, we could not help wondering what the townspeople themselves would think of Mr. Coon's intentions. We mean no disparagement; but culture works differently. For really, dismal and illiberal as the life of those towns may be, it is the collective life of those who live there, it is their chosen mode of collective self-expression, they are satisfied with it, and we can not see why they should not rest undisturbed in their satisfaction. Their representative men, such as Mr. William Allen White and Mr. Meredith Nicholson, glorify that life; politicians do their obeisance to it—do not our presidential candidates themselves come from Marion and Dayton?—and when the Rotary Clubs and Chambers of Commerce hold their recurrent powwows, their speakers quote Mr. White and Mr. Nicholson, and are all of their way of thinking, and everyone present is aglow with pride and contentment.

Why, then, should we, or why should our correspondents, propose to infringe upon the sensibilities of this majority, and go about making a nuisance of ourselves and trying their patience? When they impose their views of life upon us, as characteristically they are always endeavouring to do—this is the essence of Mr. Stearns's complaint, and it is wholly justifiable—we, for our part, deeply resent it. The *New Republic* on 18 August published a story called "The Bruised Patriots," the story of some Americans returning from Europe, Americans who typically represented the civilization we have been speaking of, the civilization of Mr. White and Mr. Nicholson. It is well worth reading. Suppose, now, that such a deputation should invade Weimar or Rome or Vienna, where Mr. Stearns and his friends and our correspondents and ourselves were all happily busy with the kind of cultural life that satisfies us; suppose they should, out of a pure missionary spirit, wish to extend upon us the blessings of their own culture and regenerate us into the civilization of the motor-car, the movie and the land-deal, the civilization of Mr. White and Mr. Nicholson! We should all be desperately annoyed and would soon be saying roundly to each other that they were ignorant, vulgar dogs who had no business there, and hoping that lightning would strike them. So far would we be from gratitude for their good intentions; and we should be quite right. During Mr. Palmer's brief heyday, the saying was much in vogue that "if the alien does not like our ways, he should go back where he came from." We could never see anything wrong with this; we hold it even more true of the alien in spirit than of the alien by mere accident of birth, and it is as true of the alien in Emporia or Indianapolis as of the alien in Weimar or Vienna.

But it may be said that there is a more nearly absolute standard in such matters; that the best reason and judgment of mankind, the self-preserving instinct of humanity itself, is on the side of our culture and against that of the "dismal home towns." This is true. The forces of nature are on our side, the stars in their courses fight against Mr. White and Mr. Nicholson; but by so much as this is true, by so much there is no play for the proselytizing spirit in behalf of culture—which is fortunate, because culture is nothing to be deliberately imposed or propagated or institutionalized. Its ideal is that of a Messiah who shall not strive nor cry, neither shall any man hear his voice in the streets. Culture makes its way by its invincible power of attraction, its amiability and amenity, and not by the stark violence of any evangelistic mission; and nothing can finally withstand it. Mr. White and Mr. Nicholson can withstand it for the moment, but their grandchildren will capitulate in their cradles. Mr. Coon may spare himself the effort to regenerate the civilization of the dismal home town through the imposition of what he may regard as culture; posterity of the townspeople will wear a pathway to his door, *Mansueti possidebunt terram,* the Psalmist said— the *amiable* shall possess the earth—and so, if you but give them time enough, they do; and it is the *amiability* of culture, its sheer loveliness and desirableness, that will win its way ultimately even upon the civilization of the motor-car, the movie and the land-deal, the civilization of Mr. White and Mr. Nicholson. Meanwhile, those whom Mr. Stearns speaks of as under collateral obligations to remain here, can permit their alien culture to fulfil the law of its being like a wild flower of the woods in spring, so that if there should pass that way some one who notices and desires it, it may be freely his. This is all that they can do, and it is much. But those who have no such commitments, will, we think, do far better service to general culture, and thereby also to America's own final share in general culture, by throwing in their powers to strengthen the centres of culture which at present lie elsewhere.

This unsigned article appeared in the September 8, 1920, issue of the *Freeman.*

Miscellany

Seeing Mr. Cyril Maude in his excellent new comedy, "Aren't We All?" gives one a hint of the distance that we have already gone towards civilizing our conception of marriage. The play is most happily devoid of "moral purpose," but I have not seen anything in years which brings about a better *rapport* between the moral sense of an audience and that of a playwright. By far the most interesting feature of the evening is the quick and intelligent response of the audience to certain lines which in the bad old days of my youth—Mrs. Wharton's "age of innocence"— would, I am sure, have been received in pensive and embittered silence. The moral of the play—for though it is free from any pestiferous moralities, it has a moral, and a sound one—is that the best insurance of happiness in such a delicate and difficult relation as marriage, is freedom. Even this the audience caught and approved at once, which I thought quite remarkable because it has long seemed to me that any such thing as faith in freedom had long ago disappeared from among us.

Of all things that human beings fear (and they are a timorous race) the one that strikes them with abject and utterly demoralizing terror is freedom. They are so afraid of it for other people that almost simultaneously they come to dread it for themselves. So they devise systems of checks and balances, restraints, moral sanctions, conventions and moral mass-expectations of one kind and another; they are willing to go to the most fantastic lengths in restriction and repression; but the one thing that they never yet have shown the courage to try is simple freedom, which some day they will have the happy surprise of discovering to be the only thing that really works. Pending this general discovery, each person can, in a much larger way than he thinks possible, discover it for himself, and thereby put himself in the way of a great deal of solid satisfaction and happiness. If one puts no expectation whatever, of any kind, upon any person, no matter how intimate one's association with him, the returns that one gets are marvellous. This does not mean making no demands upon him, but really, in one's inmost heart, not expecting anything of him, not *wishing* to make any demands upon him. Few are able to do this, fewer still are wise enough to wish to do it, and almost no one dares do it.

These considerations of course go far beyond their application to the very special and limited question of "how to be happy though married," which is the basis of Mr. Maude's new play. They apply to all relations of life, collective as well as individual, public as well as private. One of the things that will interest the historian of civilization in the United States is the progress of the principle of liberty since the Colonial period, to show what its actual practical applications have been, what their limitations were, and how the popular understanding and acceptance of the doctrine itself have become modified in consequence. But all this is a long way from Mr. Maude's comedy, which shows merely that liberty—not a formal and factitious liberty, but liberty *ex animo*—is the indispensable condition of successful and happy love. The whole philosophy of success in this delicate and easily-marred relation was put strikingly in the remark of Philina to Wilhelm in Goethe's novel, "If I love you, what business is that of yours?"

The very advantages which American women enjoy, which lead foreigners to say we spoil them, really work against their interests where companionship with men is concerned, whether in marriage or out of it. The American girl has, relatively, a pretty wide range of experience and cultivation, and she has unusual opportunities for developing what cleverness she has, so that she rather tends to outstrip her male associates. If she picks the exceptional man for companionship, she finds him hard to live with, as such men notoriously are; if she picks the commonplace man, who is the most amiable soul on earth to live with, and who pampers her shockingly, she finds him really, in the long run, pretty dull. Adjustment either way is therefore much harder for her than for her European sisters. While Englishmen and Europeans are always very keen to tell us how badly the American woman has been brought up, I notice that they get mightily interested in her in very short order, and that they remain interested as long as she is around.

American life is a little easier on a young woman's willingness to become civilized than it is on a young man's. It may not be said to encourage her intellectual curiosity and her aspirations after culture, but it does not, perhaps, so expressly and truculently discourage them. Hence one may put it broadly that there are not enough relatively first-rate men to go around among the relatively first-rate women. This has a bearing, insufficiently recognized, upon divorce, and upon the alienations and miserable misunderstandings that beset the maintenance of an arbitrary monogamy. Some one has said (I think it was Mr. George Shaw, though I may be unconsciously slandering him) that a first-rate woman would rather have a part-interest in a first-rate man than all of a second-rate man. This is quite natural, too, for men as for women, I think; that is, when they have come to the time, as Mr. Maude says in his comedy, "when humour takes the place of jealousy and when tolerance takes the place of indignation."

The stoppage of the newspapers puts me in mind again of the odd neurasthenic people who seem to live in fear of what they call the "collapse of civilization," if, for instance, the League of Nations dies of inanition or some conference of pitiful rascals breaks down in disagreement over political trades and deals. I wonder what they mean by that. Do they not mean having fewer newspapers, motor-cars, trains, telephones, banks, finance-companies, domestic servants, and the like? In Europe I have seen "civilization," in this point of view, on the verge of collapse for a long time now, and I can not feel that matters would be significantly worse if it collapsed altogether.

The question is easily tested. Civilization is the progressive humanization of men in society; and this can not be measured by the number of newspapers and the conveniences of transportation and communication. Civilization is the outward and visible sign of an inward and spiritual development. So far only as the abundance of banks, servants, railways and the like conduces to this development, has it any significance for civilization. These things do not necessarily humanize mankind; conceivably, indeed, they may work the other way. My own belief is that if they all tumbled into chaos, the processes of actual civilization would not miss them half as much as some seem to think. Civilization certainly got on without them for many ages, and in some ages exceedingly well; and I think it might manage to do so again.

Seeing what the self-styled "practical men," the monopolists and politicians, have made of the world, does it ever occur to any one to wonder what the poets and artists might make of it if the débris were turned over to them?

The "Miscellany" column of the *Freeman* was signed "Journeyman" and was often written by Nock. This one, from the October 3, 1923, issue, is an excellent example of the type. Incidental paragraphs on the events and manners of the times are loosely related by a common thread. Portions of this column were reprinted in *The Freeman Book.*

The Oxometer

Glancing at Mr. Coolidge's daily syndicated colyum, I am reminded of what to me is one of the most vivid and pleasing expressions in our vivid American vernacular, viz., "throwing the bull," or "shooting the bull." I wonder where it came from and how it originated. Some day I must look it up, for it always charms me, especially since I heard the other day of an invention that my friend Bill M. said he is working on and hopes soon to make commercially practicable. He calls it the oxometer. It is a device to be installed wherever there is conversation or oratory going on, and the idea is that it automatically separates the bull from the solid substance of the discourse, leaving the latter as a residuum. There is an immense field for this ingenious mechanism. The halls of Congress and our State legislative assemblies alone represent a good potential market. Then there are the public dinners, the meetings of our innumerable societies for the promotion of this-or-that, and the international "conferences." If the naval conference at London had installed an oxometer, the residuum left after all the bull was racked off would have been nil. Bill thinks the radio will be an enormous help to him. He is very sanguine about that. He expects that in a couple of years or so after his invention goes on the market, every purchaser of a radio set will buy an oxometer without any pressure of advertising.

The trouble with Bill's oxometer is that it meets only half of a great public need. It won't work on the printed page, and as everyone knows, the printed page is most in need of this great device. Even counting the radio, there is much more bull disseminated by type than by word of mouth. Bill says he has thought of that. He intends to work out a new type of oxometer that shall combine sight and sound, like the talking pictures. He will patent the complete instrument, and hold it for a while until the market for the simple sound-device shows signs of saturation. Bill is a good business man. Just incidentally, while my mind was occupied with thoughts of this great invention, a newspaper-man happened to mention that the telegraph-English used by newspapers for their cable-dispatches often performs a function like that of the oxometer. He quoted a line from some Australian politician's speech that had come in over the cable the day before: "Smith outpoints path duty leads heights glory." The word "outpoints" is code-English for "points out." When the elided words are filled in, the sentence reads just like Mr. Coolidge or Mr. Hoover on dress-parade. Leaving them out, however, does seem somehow to clarify the bull.

This piece originally appeared as part of the "Miscellany" column of the *new Freeman* in the July 30, 1930, issue. Nock later included it in *The Book of Journeyman*. He returned to this topic in a longer article of the same name in the September 1937 *Atlantic Monthly*.

Sinclair Lewis

And so I see to my great delight that my old friend Sinclair Lewis has walked away with the Nobel prize. I call him Sinkler nowadays, out of deference to his habit of hobnobbing with the British literati, for I am told they pronounce his name that way. Sinkler's victory in the great free-for-all has stirred up a deal of talk in the country's little literary clans, cliques, camps and cubicles; so I understand at least, though I have not heard much of it, being only a hanger-on in literary circles here, and living on their extreme fringes. I suppose the sum and substance of it all is that we can not tell how an American product looks to Swedes, any more than they can tell how a Swedish product looks to us. I hear that Ibañez is no great shakes in Spain. I remember, too, when I was in Russia nearly twenty years ago, a highly cultivated young girl, the daughter of one of the provincial governors, told me that nobody could understand why Pavlova made such a tremendous hit abroad; they had plenty of dancers as good as Pavlova, and some much better; she would show them to me any evening, and I could judge for myself. Many reputations thus consolidate their makings abroad. "It's an old saying, but a true one," said Abe Potash to his partner, "that there's no profit for a feller in his own country."

This is not the case with Sinkler, of course, for his reputation was made here and he has a great vogue. My notion is that the Swedes accepted him as an interpreter, and that the award is, in its essence, a left-handed compliment to the quality of our civilization. In such parts of Europe as I am acquainted with, the representative American is for one reason or another regarded as an incomprehensible sort of fellow, uninteresting and rather odious. Sinkler represents him as such; he represents him and his whole *entourage* as something that Netherlanders, Italians, Frenchmen, would not find quite congenial. Possibly the Swedes share this view; and so, naturally, when they find an American author who reflects this view, they do not put the same estimate on him that a native critic might. Even if the native critic had an equally unfavorable view of the run-of-mine American and his social and

institutional *entourage,* it would not be the same view. He would be in
a position to show what the proper reservations were, and how to make
them, and how much to allow for them in the sum-total of his estimate.
My impression is that Sinkler's books measured up pretty closely to
the prevailing *Svensk* estimate of the Yankee and Yankeedom, and that
this had a good deal to do with the award.

But I, as a native critic, though a most obscure and unconsidered
one, would nevertheless have come pretty near giving Sinkler the
award—not quite, but pretty near—and this on grounds that I
think very few would suspect. I speak of this because it falls
in so well with what I said last week about the curious limitation
put upon the practice of the literary art in America, whereby
books are used and judged purely according to their content and
with no regard whatever to the literary workmanship that they
display. For twelve years now, Sinkler and I have had a frank
and joyous understanding. I know he would rather throw over
the Nobel prize than read one of my books from cover to cover,
and he knows that I have had desperately up-hill work with his.
When we meet, alas, so infrequently nowadays it is—*eheu fugaces
labuntur anni!*—I tell him that as a literary workman he is most
exceeding rotten, and that he ought to be ashamed of himself.
He then points with pride to his 'steen-millionth edition of something
or other, tells me that I am just an ignorant old man who ought
to be chloroformed and mummified, and then we both say how
thankful we are that those matters all lie miles below the plane
of affection and respect.

But in the words of the prophet, Sinkler put one over on me lately,
just as I knew some day he would. When he was going his strongest,
he quietly slipped a real book off the bottom of the deck, a very little
book but an exhibit of good high-grade literary art. It is a model of
first-class sensitive editorial judgment, accurate character-portrayal with
no approach to caricature, judicial temper, effortless and continuous
superiority to its subject with never a lapse into snobbism, unkindness
or savagery. All the social criticism set forth in Sinkler's other books
is there, and it is expressed in the most effective way, by artless and
unconscious self-revelation. When you read this book you know what
our civilization is like, its good points and its bad points, you see just
where it is heading in and why, and you see all this without having it

pointedly and servigerously editorialized for you; it all simply unfolds and tells its own story. I have often wondered whether Sinkler did not write this book mostly for the sake of showing a few of us old-fogy academic critics that he could do it. This small example of excellent literary art is entitled *The Man Who Knew Coolidge*.

This book was relatively little read, and I imagine that about all the reading it ever got was on the strength of Sinkler's reputation. That brings me to my point, which is this: If Sinkler had had an intelligent public, if he could have written for people who read with a cultivated and sensitive imagination, and who knew good workmanship, his artist's instinct would have led him to write this sort of book a dozen years ago and let it go at that. It would have rocked the country, and there would have been no demand whatever for the books on which Sinkler's reputation now rests. Who would have read *Main Street*? Why, I was born and bred on Main Street and know it from end to end and everybody on it, as Sinkler certainly does not. His Main Streeter is no more like a real one than a zebra. He is somewhat like him part of the time, but not twenty-four hours a day, seven days a week. No intelligent public would have stood having Main Street rubbed in by Babbitt, Babbitt by Gantry, Gantry by Dodsworth, and so on. All these are summed up in just the right proportions and with exactly the right implications, in *The Man Who Knew Coolidge*. He tells the whole story of our civilization in a hundred pages, tells it himself, with no idea that he is telling it, and much more convincingly than the most talented reporter can tell it for him in a dozen volumes.

It all comes back to the quality of one's reading public. The question of how far an artist is justified in shaping his work to suit that quality is perhaps open. Certainly Sinkler could not have captured his public if he had not landed on them as he did; certainly, if I am any judge, in so doing he let every consideration of good art go to pot. Whether such a public is worth capturing or not is another matter; frankly, I would not turn my hand over for it if I were ever so able to do so. But all this is by the way; the thing to be noticed is, as I remarked last week, the peculiar and I think crippling limitation laid upon literary practice in this country—a limitation which no amount of mass-education, book-boosting and progress in literacy has in the least tended to loosen, but quite the contrary. Since I think Sinkler's career conspicuously establishes this contention—especially since I have seen his excellent tribute to good art and seen the sort of recognition it got—I am not so sure but that the Swedes could make out a pretty plausible case in favor of their award.

This piece originally appeared as the "Miscellany" column of the *new Freeman* in the December 3, 1930, issue. Nock later included it in *The Book of Journeyman*.

Thoughts from Abroad

The currents of Chance lately washed me up on the shores of a little-visited European country which I soon found to be in some respects perhaps the most interesting in the world, at the moment. I can be more at ease in writing about it if I give it the thin disguise of a pseudonym, so let me call it Amenia. It deserves this name not only because it is a very beautiful land, but also because its inhabitants are so uncommonly amiable and gracious to strangers; I find that they have an international reputation throughout all Europe for this trait. They will take no offense, I am sure, at my masking their country under a fanciful name, for I am merely following an old-fashioned convention which has its root in delicacy, like the convention that governs the British House of Commons, where one member may pretty well say what he likes about another member, provided he do not name him.

What made Amenia so interesting to me, as a visitor fresh from America, can be summed up in a sentence. From our point of view, nearly everything in Amenia is wrong, and yet the country manages to get on remarkably well. By every rule of the game, Amenia ought not to get on at all, but it somehow does. Its politics are frightfully wrong, its economics are wrong, its views of a proper constitution of human society are practically all wrong; yet there the wretched country is, impenitently racking along, quite as if its fundamental theories of collective human life were as sound as ours.

I submit that to a student of civilization this is an interesting state of things, and doubly so at the moment. For example, Amenia is solvent, as I hear few countries are; certainly those I see and read about seem mostly busted. The *publice egestas, privatim opulentia,* which Sallust puts into the mouth of Cato as evidence of a nation's decline, is visible everywhere. I notice in a London paper to-day the statement that our own national debt now amounts to twenty-two and a quarter billion dollars; also that Britain's national debt is eleven times as much as it was in 1913. My notion is that it would take a bit of scratching to get that amount of money together in either country. Amenia has only a trifle of debt, which worries nobody, and which she could clean up on short notice without overstraining herself. Amenia, moreover, pays as she goes. Amidst the general fiscal dilapidation of the last four years, Amenia has balanced her budget each year. I was told that in the good days when our bankers were dusting money around Europe all so freely, some of them urged a loan on Amenia, but the government said no, much obliged, they thought they would try to squeeze along on their own. Again, business in Amenia is very fair—nothing startling, but probably up to Sam Weller's standard of normality—while in other countries it is apparently slack. Again, Amenia seems to have no unwieldy labour-surplus. Everyone able to work has some sort of job which perhaps will not make his everlasting fortune, but which manages to keep him going; and in this respect, too, other countries are not so well off, according to all I hear.

In drawing comparisons between Amenia and other countries, however, I have not the least idea of advertising Amenia as a happy hunting-ground for American visitors, and making it out so attractive that everyone will wish to go there. Not at all. On the contrary, I think that for many reasons the average run of our tourists would do better elsewhere; Amenia, I should say, is probably not quite their kind of thing. Still less would I suggest that we ought to copy Amenia's ways and views and ideals. Amenia did not impress me in this stark fashion, either as bait for the vagrant impulse to "go places and do things," or as an institutional model. It impressed me only as an incentive to a study of absolutes. What I saw there turned my mind back on itself, and made me reëxamine a number of matters which we tend to put down as absolute; absolutely Good, absolutely Bad, absolutely True or False, absolutely Right or Wrong. What my conclusions were, or whether I came to any, is of no importance. The only thing I wish to dwell on is the sheer pleasure of being in a situation that moves one strongly to review the *chose jugée,* to reopen questions that mere use-and-wont has led us to regard as definitively closed, and let one's consciousness play over them freely. There are few exercises more exhilarating than this, and Amenia is one of the few spots left in a highly uninteresting world that stimulate one to pursue it.

I shall put down my impressions at haphazard as they occur to me, with no special care for arrangement. In the first place, I found that

there is a great deal of illiteracy in Amenia; and by the way, I was led
to this discovery by the conspicuous and delightful absence of roadside
advertising-signs. I was told that the Amenians are fifty per cent
illiterate; some put it higher. Having no passion for statistics, I did not
take the trouble to look up the official figures; it was enough for my
purposes to know that most of the people I saw about me were unable
to read or write.

In our view, this is of course wrong. It is an absolute of our social
faith that illiteracy is Bad. This is one of the very few points, indeed I
think the only one, at which Mr. Jefferson succeeded in striking his
belief deeply into the American consciousness. He put literacy as a
condition of good citizenship, and the people accepted his view; which
was in itself, perhaps, an indication that the matter would stand a little
sifting. No one now, I imagine, has any doubt that general literacy is
a Good-in-Itself—that is to say, an absolute. This belief is a republican
heirloom, passed on in complete integrity, and unexamined, from the
casket of eighteenth-century political theory to its present place in
Columbia's shining crown.

Just so. I noticed, however, that the capital of Amenia is remarkable
for its bookstores; it has relatively more and better bookstores, I believe,
than any city in the world. In fact, the only commercial exhibits there
that strike a stranger's eye are the bookstores and jewellery stores; the
rest are unimpressive. Leaving aside all questions of comparative quality,
I tried to estimate how many bookstores New York would have in the
same ratio, first, to its actual population, and second, to its proportion
of literacy; but the figures were so incredibly fantastic that I did not
think it worth while even to make a note of them.

These premises seemed to warrant the inference that Amenia has a
small but serious reading public; one that owns its books and reads
them, and that in general may be thought to regard a book as an
instrument of culture rather than as a stopgap for idle time. This
inference is borne out by a French authority, who says that Amenia
has *une petite élite extrêmement brillante et cultivée.* My mind then went
back to the immense masses of garbage shot daily from the press of
more literate lands, and I wondered just what the net gain—understand
me clearly, the *net* gain—of a general and indiscriminate literacy really
is. Our republicanism assumes that there is a net gain, and so indeed
there may be, but just what is it? With all our devotion to "research,"

I do not think that our institutions of learning have ever entertained this question; yet I submit that it is worth attention.

In the eighteenth century, before Western society had been penetrated by the minor commonplaces of republicanism, Bishop Butler—almost a contemporary of Mr. Jefferson—remarked that the great majority of people are far more handy at passing things through their minds than they are at thinking about them; and therefore, considering the kind of thing they usually read, very little of their time is more idly spent than the time spent in reading. This fact is more noticeable now by far than it was in Bishop Butler's day; and when set off against Amenia's condition, it is bound to make one wonder what, precisely, this particular absolute of our republicanism amounts to. What, precisely, would the civilization of Amenia gain by a more general spread of literacy? What, precisely, would ours lose by a shrinkage of literacy to Amenia's level? Does the indiscriminate spread of literacy encounter an unsuspected moral equivalent of Gresham's law, that "bad money drives out good"? Does it encounter a moral equivalent of the law of diminishing returns?

The whole question is rather a pretty one, and as far as I know, our doctrinaire republicanism has hitherto had no better answer for it than the "plain argument" which Lord Peter applies to the doubts of his brothers, in the Tale of a Tub; and this, while in a sense perhaps effective, is hardly satisfactory.[1]

One can not go to and fro among the Amenians for any length of time without perceiving that their theory of business is wrong. Their idea is that supply should follow demand, and that the purchaser should seek the vendor; whereas the Right Idea, as we all know, is that supply should precede demand, and that the vendor should hound and bedevil

---

1. Satirizing the doctrine of transubstantiation, Swift brings in Lord Peter at dinner, carving slices of bread for his brothers, Jack and Martin (i.e., Calvin and Luther), assuring them that it is mutton, and becoming very angry when they express their doubts. " 'Look ye, gentlemen,' cries Peter, in a rage: 'to convince you what a couple of blind, positive, ignorant, wilful puppies you are, I will use but this plain argument: by God, it is true, good, natural mutton as any in Leadenhall market; and God confound you both eternally if you offer to believe otherwise.' Such a thundering proof as this left no farther room for objection." Tale of a Tub, section 4.

the purchaser with all kinds of importunities, in order to keep demand going at its maximum speed. Thus the ideal development of a nation's business is a joyous game of what in our youthful days we used to call "outrunning the constable"; and hence, to an American eye, nothing is more unnatural and shocking than the stringency with which Amenia's business is kept down to the level of solid requirement. Hardly anything is done deliberately to increase consumption. The Amenians have only the vaguest and most uncertain notion of "creating a market," or of splitting up purchasing-power among a dozen or more competing varieties of what is actually the same thing. Yet, as I said, somehow or other business manages to do very well under these conditions, and it is perhaps equally remarkable that the visiting stranger who comes here quite unaccustomed to these peculiar ideas of business soon finds that he too is doing very well, even though he sees the line pretty sharply drawn between amenities, comforts and conveniences, on the one hand, and mere gadgets on the other. Perhaps his contentment tends to show that human beings are highly adaptable and very easily corrupted. I argue nothing from it, but offer the fact merely as an object of interesting speculation.

The Amenians have not even learned the art of sophisticating their products. Their excellent staples, such as flour, olive-oil, wine, come to you pretty much, one might say, as the Lord made them. Nor have these interesting people learned to sophisticate their workmanship. Amenia reckons its money in écus or *escudos* (pronounced *scoots*), worth at the moment about four cents apiece. You can buy an excellent suit of clothes, custom-made of domestic wool, for five or six hundred scoots, and the workmanship will be as good as the fabric; that suit will stand hard wear, and thrive on it. Shoes, too, that one buys handmade for something like two hundred scoots, show no sign of the familiar devices to "make people shoe-conscious," and thereby increase consumption; and the same may be said for the workmanship put into everything one uses, as far as my observation goes.

These practices seem to spring from the root-idea that things should be made to use rather than to sell; a distinction first drawn in literature by Canning, I believe, in the rhymed fable of Hodge's razor. Moreover, the Amenians do not appear to believe that the "pursuit of happiness" contemplated by Mr. Jefferson's great document means only the accumulation and use of purchasable things. Yet, in spite of this handicap, not only does business manage to drag on, but also most of the Amenians whom I saw seemed a great deal happier than under the circumstances they should be.

For example, I spent three weeks at one of Amenia's principal health-resorts, which is in a most beautiful mountainous region, with no settlement of any size near by. I never saw a place where one was thrown more heavily on one's own resources. One could not buy anything more interesting than postage-stamps. One could take delight-ful walks, and enjoy the air, birds, trees and flowers, but there was no golf, tennis, squash, ping-pong, cinema, radio or gramophone; the hotel had only an utterly impracticable billiard-table and a decrepit upright piano of French make, much out of tune. There was not even the usual job-lot of abandoned books lying about the lobby; not a book on the premises save what one brought for oneself.

The guests were a good cross-section of Amenian society. The four learned professions were there, some royal blood and hereditary high-life, some *arriviste* or Brummagem high-life, some industry and trade. The average age of the company ran unusually young, and on that account I was all the more curious to see what they would do with themselves. I soon remarked that no one was at all afraid of being left alone with his own thoughts; and this, if not absolutely Bad, is seriously irregular, for if a person is alone and thinking, he is not doing anything to increase consumption. There was no great "get-together" movement organized to insure one against the chance of a moment's solitude. No one seemed in such desperate need of company; on the contrary, the guests kept contentedly each one to himself pretty much all day, except for casual meetings. There was a very pleasant cordiality all round; if someone came along, well and good, but if not, well and good. No one was bored; with nothing whatever to "do," and no apparatus to help fight off boredom, everybody seemed quite unreasonably and perversely happy. Again, in the evenings I remarked how the whole company showed itself capable of immense enthusiasm over the simplest parlour-games, peasant-dances, peasant-songs. Royalty, high-life and all grades of bourgeois rollicked through boisterous and exhausting dances with bursts of uproarious laughter, and seemed to be having the best time in the world, up to half-past ten or so, when all hands went quietly to bed.

St. John's Eve came on while I was there, and the thing to do on St.

John's Eve, apparently, is to make brush-bonfires of eucalyptus, rosemary and other aromatic twigs, and leap across them through the flames. It seems a very moderate sort of diversion; I do not know what the significance of it is, nor could anyone tell me. However, everybody went in for it with immense energy and gusto, and got no end of fun out of it, though some of the ladies singed their legs a bit, and only missed setting their skirts afire by the closest kind of shave.

Three weeks of this sort of thing is bound to set one's mind going over the assumption which, though tacit, amounts to an absolute— that happiness is built up of purchasable things. These people were not poor, yet they were not only capable of being happy as lords without a dollar's worth of apparatus to help them, but also they did not appear to care whether they had any apparatus or not. The sum of their activities for three whole weeks did not increase consumption, or assist the development of mass-demand, to the amount of a punched nickel; yet they were quite happy. I could not help recalling the contrasting observation of Stendhal, on a visit to the United States, where there is such an immense amount of the apparatus of happiness available everywhere, that "the springs of happiness seem to be dried up in this people," and the amazing statement of Edison, eighty years old, when a reporter asked him what human happiness consisted in, "I am not acquainted with anyone who is happy." Perhaps the visitor to Amenia might be a little put to it to say offhand precisely what human happiness does consist in, but the question is forced on him by such incidents as the ones I have just cited.

Indirectly, too, it is forced on him by observation of the instinct for the *ne quid nimis,* the instinct for the level of real requirement, that he sees coming out everywhere. In the matter of transportation, for instance, Amenia's railways are cheap, safe, clean and good, but that is all one can say, and all one is supposed to say; they do not pretend to lure you into taking them merely for the fun of the thing. The same is true of the motor-roads; they are excellent, plenty good enough for anybody who has to use them, but they are not a standing temptation to the canine love of joy-riding. I remember once, when my charming friend Cassandre was standing up stoutly for France, she said there was great hope that the French would remain a civilized people, for they had not yet put down any cement roads; when a nation begins to lay cement roads, she said, it is gone, past any hope of reform or redemption.

There would seem to be something in this from the Amenian point of view, which regards a road primarily as a thing of use rather than of pleasure. I took a two-hour walk between four and six o'clock of a beautiful afternoon, on a main road out of one of Amenia's largest towns—her fourth in population, I believe—and in that time I saw only one motor-vehicle, a truck.

In three months, during which I covered Amenia pretty thoroughly from end to end, I did not see a single tractor, reaper or binder. I saw grain being reaped with sickles—only twice did I see scythes in use— and threshed with flails. I saw irrigation carried on in pre-Mosaic fashion by boy-power on vertical treading-wheels, and by donkey-power on horizontal pumps. By all accepted rules, these practices are wrong and bad, yet really—really, now—just how dogmatic may one be about erecting their wrongness into an absolute? They got results— there is no question about that—and as to their effect on the sum of human happiness, it is difficult, very difficult indeed, to assure oneself one way or the other. On the evidence available, I am by no means sure that the net sum of happiness in Amenia would be increased by further mechanization of these processes. It might be; I am simply not sure. On the evidence attested by Edison and Stendhal, I am not sure that the net sum of happiness in the United States would be reduced by demechanization to the level of Amenia. Again, it might be, but I am not sure; I can only say that I found the question a very powerful solvent of dogmatism, and as such I recommend it.

Amenia's population is most improperly distributed, for two-thirds of it is rural. Agriculture is the country's chief industry, and it is carried on mostly by small independent holdings. In urban growth, Amenia is far behind other European countries. One notes with surprise and disapproval that the huge industrial proletarian agglomerations which are perhaps the most conspicuous characteristic of true prosperity— though William Cobbett gruffly called them *Hell-holes*—do not exist. Amenia does relatively little in the manufacturing way, and hardly any processing. Almost one might think that the Physiocrats had come to life there, and were spreading their detestable doctrine of the *produit net.* It is here, perhaps, that one sees Amenia's most egregious departure from the Right Way. Surely by this time Amenia should have learned that the chief end of man in his collective capacity is to industrialize himself as completely as possible, remove the land from competition with industry in the labour-market in order to force down wages by creating a standing labour-surplus, and then go in for a strong policy of economic nationalism; that is to say, a policy of selling everything one can to everybody, and not buying anything from anybody.

Amenia is well off for natural resources, especially in minerals and water-power, but there is unanimous testimony that the Amenians are extremely lackadaisical about exploiting them; and if anything can be absolutely Wrong, this is. The Right Way with natural resources is to turn them over wholesale to private enterprise, to be looted as rapidly and thoroughly as possible. All precedents point to this as of the essence of prosperity. Yet it would appear that the Amenians are merely pecking at their minerals, and realizing on only about eight per cent of their available hydroelectric power. A Scots engineer who has been twenty years in Amenia told me that a couple of foreign prospectors had struck gold there lately, but nobody seemed to be properly worked up about it. The general sentiment was that the gold would stay put; it would not run away, and there was no occasion to get into a great sweat over digging it out. There seemed to be enough gold around already to go on with, so why not let it lie awhile? This Scotsman told me that the Amenians had always taken this easy attitude towards "development," and hence they still have pretty nearly everything that nature gave them to start with.

This may be put down to lack of enterprise, and properly so in a sense, no doubt; it depends on what one's notion of enterprise is. But there is a little more to it than that, I think. It may be, in part at least, the outcome of a sense of moderation, for the Amenian struck me as being by nature the most consistently temperate person I ever saw. Once led to look for this trait, I kept an eye out for it continually, and saw it exhibited everywhere, whether in small matters or great. To take one instance, rather unimportant in itself, but bearing on a question that has lately been a good deal discussed in the United States, a wine-merchant who took me over his property showed me certain casks to which his work-people were free to resort at any time, for as much as they cared to drink; and he told me that in the whole history of the firm, which ran considerably over a hundred years, there had never been a tipsy person on the premises.

With its colonial resources Amenia follows the same easy policy as with its domestic resources. Though one of the smallest countries of Europe, its colonial holdings are enormous, exceeded only by those of England and France. One is rather surprised by the fact that whereas about fifty-five million of the earth's people speak French, about seventy million speak Amenian; and the Amenian tongue is perhaps the most widely diffused language in the world, except our own. Amenia's colonies are very rich; a really capable and energetic administration, such as the English or French or old Leopold's Belgians or we ourselves know how to furnish, could get simply no end of profit out of them.

Yet Amenia bears the white man's burden very lightly. It gets some return out of its colonies, but nothing like what it might get. A young and progressive Amenian told me sadly that the colonies had for years been "virtually abandoned." Amenian colonial policy does not, in our expressive phrase, crowd the mourners. It seems to be not unlike the policy of "salutary neglect" which farsighted Englishmen advocated in the days of Pitt. It neither exploits the native peoples in an economic way, nor does it essay to moralize either their private convictions and habits or their social customs and practices; it does not tell them what they should eat or drink, or wherewithal they should be clothed. Hence the colonies are contented under Amenian rule, I am told, and are not all the time raising disturbances and insurrections. "The Amenians don't try to civilize their colonies," an Englishman said to me, with a touch of irony in his tone; "consequently they've still got them. We bossed ours around and tried to make them do our way, and so we lost them."

All this again may be put down to mere shiftlessness, but once more I suggest that the innate sense of moderation may account for something; and perhaps the extraordinary spirit of tolerance and courtesy, for which, as I have said, the Amenians are internationally noted, also accounts for something. If one gets a moderate yield out of one's colonies, well, enough is enough, and why jeopardize peace and good feeling by squeezing them? Meanwhile, if the heathen in his blindness bows down to wood and stone, why bother him about it? Why not look the other way and let him bow? If he would rather go naked than wear Amenian textiles, it is bad for business, no doubt, but why force him all at once to accept a strictly cash-registral evaluation of life and its amenities, even though it be orthodox? Why not break the glad news to him a little gently and give it a reasonable time to sink in? If a widow sets out with pomp and ceremony to burn herself alive on her late husband's funeral pyre, why not conclude that there is probably something in it from her point of view, and let it go at that?

Amenia's government is a simon-pure military despotism; it governs by general orders. Yet up to date it has been extremely disinterested, able and efficient; the best and cheapest government, I should say, that is to be found anywhere. Doubtless it will not remain so, for that would be contrary to all human experience with any kind of government, but such is its record at the moment. It went through the motions of submitting itself to a popular mandate the other day, and was approved by a large majority. I do not know how far this election was "on the level," or how sincere the government was minded to be about abiding by it. One's general knowledge of government makes one skeptical; Herbert Spencer cites with approval the generalization that "wherever government is, there is villainy," and it seems to be, on the whole, a sound one. Nevertheless, for all I actually know or have heard, this election may have been honestly undertaken and scrupulously conducted.

I suppose the sight of a military dictatorship should have set me thinking of Spartacus, Masaniello, Jack Cade, Daniel Shays, the Whiskey Boys and all the other great liberators, until I was ready to turn my back on Amenia in disgust. What it did instead, however, was to set me thinking about some of the absolutes of eighteenth-century political theory, and wondering what basis they have in actual human experience. Representative government; the parliamentary system; universal suffrage; "checks and balances"; a responsible executive—Amenia has thrown all these overboard, and yet is governed well and cheaply. The question is not whether other countries would do well to throw them overboard, but whether the quality of government is as much a matter of systems and institutions as we think it is. Rival systems are now everywhere competing for the world's attention to the colour of their several shirts—well, just what is the necessary and inevitable effect of *any* system upon the quality of government?

America had great students of government in its early days; it is a pity that they are now so much more read about than read. One of them was William Penn. The sight of Amenia's contribution to the great current rivalry of systems brought to my mind this paragraph from the preface which Penn wrote for Pennsylvania's original "frame of government":

> When all is said, there is hardly any frame of government so ill designed by its first founders that in good hands would not do well enough; and story tells us the best, in ill ones, can do nothing that is great or good. . . . Governments, like clocks, go from the motion men give them; and as governments are made and moved by men, so by them they are ruined too. Wherefore governments rather depend upon men than men upon governments.

Against its background of competing systems, moreover, Amenia's autocracy suggests what is no doubt the most pressing public question of our time, namely: whether eighteenth-century republican doctrine has not put upon the mass-man a burden greater than he can bear. Heretofore the question has not been so much with the mass-man's actual capacity as with the advisability, for purely collateral reasons, of letting him have anything like a free hand in shaping social and political institutions. The rapid spread of republicanism, however, has given us of the present day an uncommonly good chance to appraise the type of social ideal towards which the enfranchised mass-man chooses to move. Therefore, quite aside from all considerations of sincerity, integrity and good will, the question now is whether the mass-man is able, or will ever be able, to direct the development of society in accordance with his own ultimate best interest. Has he the force of intellect to perceive clearly what that interest is, and the force of character to pursue it steadfastly? Do his present performances encourage the belief that he will ever have them? Has republican doctrine, in short, any basis either in actual experience or in reasonable hope?

We have, too, an uncommonly good chance to observe the kind of leadership which at present succeeds in imposing itself on the mass-man's allegiance, and to remark its conformity to a historical type. At almost every turn of the world's affairs nowadays, one is most sharply and painfully reminded of the French revolutionist's saying, "I *must* follow the mob, because I lead them." Finally, aside from the light it throws on the possible unsoundness of republican doctrine and the possibly dubious character of republican mass-leadership, Amenia's condition makes one wonder whether political nationalism has not gone over the margin of diminishing returns. Economic nationalism seems clearly to have done so; may not its political counterpart have done so too? Amenia is small and isolated, and it is possible for a one-man government to maintain political nationalism there at something like reasonable expense. Elsewhere, however, people are uneasy about the rapidly growing cost of Statism, centralization and bureaucracy, and well they may be; in the United States, for example, people are extremely uneasy about it, and with reason. Is it not possible that political nationalism, like a business which is economically overgrown, has begun to cost more than it takes in? Or, to cite the comparison attributed to Lincoln, has it become like the tugboat that stopped running whenever the whistle blew, because it had a four-foot boiler and a six-foot whistle? Is political nationalism any longer commercially practicable (if I may so put it) over an area of much more than township size? It is an interesting question and a serious one; one which, from present appearances, the larger and more highly integrated political units will soon be obliged by circumstances to entertain.

Probably Amenia will not long remain as I found it, for there are the beginnings of a lively onset towards "development" and "progress." I heard these words often; they seemed to mean a closer approach to the condition of other nations. Well, improvement is always possible, and the study of other people's ways is always useful. "They measuring themselves by themselves," the Apostle says, "and comparing themselves among themselves, are not wise." One energetic young Amenian assured me that "we shall be a civilized country in ten years." A visiting friend may not presume to give advice to his hosts, but he may perhaps be permitted to observe in a general way that when one is examining other countries one is likely to find that the most valuable testimony they bear to the nature of true civilization is often of a negative kind; and that this is particularly true of civilization's higher and finer concerns. A friend, too, may without impropriety, I think, venture in all gratitude to express the hope that the "civilized" Amenia of ten years hence will be in all respects as charming and captivating to the cultivated spirit, as interesting and thought-provoking, as the Amenia which I have had the good fortune to visit.

This essay was published in the December 1933 issue of the *Atlantic Monthly* and reprinted in *Free Speech and Plain Language*.

VII. CULTIVATING A SINGLE GARDEN

The trouble with the "Western civilization" that we are so proud of and boast so much about, is that it makes such limited demands on the human spirit; such limited demands on the qualities that are distinctly and properly humane, the qualities that distinguish the human being from the robot on the one hand and the brute on the other.
—"An Idealess World," the *new Freeman*,
September 17, 1930

The abbey of Theleme is a portrayal of all that human society might be if only human beings were free to become as good, kind, enlightened, gentle, generous, as they know they can be, and really wish to be. There was no discipline in the abbey but such as was self-imposed; every arrangement was based upon individual responsibility—needless to say, therefore, the reverse of actual practice then or now, which leaves but little scope for individual responsibility.
—*Francis Rabelais: The Man and His Work*

On Doing the Right Thing

For my sins I had to spend a good deal of time in London lately, while an east wind was blowing; and under these depressing circumstances I had some notion of showing cause why the much-touted understanding between the English people and ours can never really exist. In spite of the Sulgrave Foundation, and of all the perfervid buncombe fired off at Pilgrims' dinners about cousinship, hands across the sea, common tradition, common ideals, and what Mr. Dooley called "th' common impulse f'r th' same money"—only that, I believe, is never mentioned— the two peoples will never understand each other as long as the world stands. There are many obscure, unregarded, and potent reasons against it; of which, for example, language is one. An American can make sounds to which an Englishman will attach approximately the same meaning that the American does, and hence each assumes that they have a common language, when actually they have nothing of the kind; that is to say, language does not enable a true understanding of each other, but rather the contrary. Indeed, I believe that they would come nearer a real understanding if each had to learn a new language to get on with. There are many other reasons; and the reasons proceeding from recondite and apparently insignificant differences in training, habit, social and institutional procedure, and in the ordinary technique of living, account for more, I think, than those arising from weightier matters. As I said, I had the vagrant thought of tracing out and expounding some of these, but indolence interfered so persistently that it never was done and now, probably, never will be. One item on the list, however, recurs to me at the moment as worth salvaging for another purpose.

The English are addicted to a curious practice which is apprehended by an American only with great difficulty, and to which they give the rather conventional and indefinite name of "doing the Right Thing." The name at once brings to mind the late Sir Harry Johnston's fine novel; the best novel in that genre that has been written in our language since *The Way of All Flesh*. As far as I have been able to discover, the addiction to this practice pervades all classes of English society. The lower and middle classes do a good deal of it. The upper orders do not do as much with it as formerly, but they still do something; and even the official class does not quite escape. It is not a rationalised process, apparently, but on the contrary, one would perhaps say that it amounts to a kind of ritual. Given a certain set of circumstances, that is, an Englishman may be trusted to take a certain course of conduct, and to take it with energy, resolution and courage, for no reason in particular except to satisfy some inward sense of obligation. He may not, usually does not, have much light on the subject; doing the Right Thing may be far enough, indeed, from doing right. In other circumstances, too, where the inner sense is quiescent, he may do something much worse; but in *those* circumstances he is sure to carry through with a darkened and instinctive allegiance to what he believes to be the Right Thing.

Aside from the apparently irrational character of this addiction, what strikes the American as odd is that casuistry has no place in it. When an Englishman is bitten by a sense of the Right Thing, it seems never to occur to him, for instance, to raise the question whether the Right Thing, after it is done, will have enough practical importance to be worth doing. Again, it seems never to occur to him to put a mere personal desire, however strong, in competition with the Right Thing, and then to cast about him for plausible ways of justifying himself in following his desire. This uncommonly useful faculty seems largely left out of the individual Englishman, though collectively they show more of it than any other nation—a curious anomaly. The great French scholar, M. Nisard, once complimented Matthew Arnold on belonging to a nation that had the *savoir se gêner,* that did not take a mere powerful desire to do something as a sufficient reason for doing it, but could, if need be, bottle up the desire and cork it down and go steadily on doing something quite different. A dozen times a day one will hear Englishmen mutter in an apologetic tone, "Beastly bore, you know!— oh, dev'lish bore!—but then, you know, one really must do the Right Thing, mustn't one?" The formula and the intonation never seem to vary, whether the matter at issue be utterly trivial or so important as to redetermine the whole course of a life.

I have always been interested in this trait of the English because of the connection which it immediately established in my mind with the principle of liberty. The theory of freedom rests on the doctrine of natural rights, and I have always held with the Declaration of Independence that this doctrine is a sound one, that mankind is endowed by its Creator with certain inalienable rights, and that one of them is liberty. But the world is fast going away from old-fashioned people of my kind, and I am told that this doctrine is debatable and now quite out of style; that nowadays almost no one believes that mankind has any natural rights at all, but that all the rights it enjoys are legal and conventional, and therefore properly subject to abridgement or suppression by the authority that confers them. Aside from theory and principle, however, this matter of freedom has a practical side which is undebatable, and about which, for some reason, very little is said; and this curious trait of the English serves admirably to bring it out.

A comparison drawn between the English and ourselves in the matter of devotion to the Right Thing seems at first sight unfavourable to Americans; and so, to some extent, it is. But the great point is that an Englishman keeps up his susceptibility to the Right Thing very largely because he is free to do so; because, that is, he is free to regulate so large a portion of his life in such way as he sees fit. In respect of control, the whole general area of human conduct may be laid off into three regions. First, there is the region in which conduct is controlled by law, *i.e.,* by force, by some form of outside compulsion. A man, for instance, may not murder or steal, because an organized power outside himself will withstand him before the fact, if possible, and make trouble for him after the fact. Second, there is the region of indifferent choice, where, for instance, a man may use one kind of soap or safety-razor rather than another. Third, there is the region where conduct is controlled by unenforced, self-imposed allegiance to moral or social considerations. In this region, for instance, one follows the rule of "women and children first," takes a long risk to get somebody out of a burning house, or, like Sir Philip Sidney, refuses to slake one's own thirst when there is not water enough to go round.

Now, for whatever reason and however it came about, the Englishman's first region, the region of compulsion, is relatively small. He has not many laws to obey, and most of these relate to property; and what few of them bear on personal conduct are quite obviously bottomed on reason and good sense. He has too many laws, of course, and the present tendency over there, as everywhere, unhappily, is to multiply them; his situation is not ideal; but as compared with the American, he lives in an anarchist's paradise. Moreover, his second region, the region of indifferent choice, is relatively large because there is no great pressure of unintelligent and meddlesome public opinion to reduce it. Hence life in England is an affair of much more individual responsibility than here. With so little law and so much choice, the sense of things "up to" the individual is correspondingly quickened. Therefore the third region of conduct, the region controlled by allegiance to the Right Thing, is less trespassed upon and does not tend to shrink, but on the contrary, should normally tend to enlarge by the progressive transference of items from the first and second regions.

One is really astonished by the magnitude of the part that this sense of individual responsibility plays in the ordinary routine of living. Let me give two examples, one at each end of the scale of social importance. One Sunday morning in May, on the top deck of a Piccadilly bus, I saw a superb old specimen of sixty-five or so, looking precisely like du Maurier's cartoon of Sir Digby de Rigby. He wore a white plug hat with a two-inch black band, and a long shadbelly black coat, a purple-and-gold figured waistcoat, a high collar of antique design—something like a stock—a red tie, red socks, russet shoes and a pair of black-and-white checked pants such as no American has seen, I dare say, since the days of Christie's minstrels. Exclusive of jewelry, I estimated the whole layout at something like five hundred dollars; there was not a shoddy thread in it. He had a couple of ladies with him, and his conversation was entertaining and delightful; and as they disembarked opposite St. James's, I judged they were headed for church, the time being right for it. The thing to be remarked is that no one commented on all this gorgeousness or paid any attention to it. If the old chap liked to dress that way, why, that was the way he liked to dress, and since he was not actually annoying anybody, it was up to him—why not? Anywhere in America, on the other hand, a man who got himself up like that to go to church would have attracted a charmed and enthusiastic rabble from the moment he put his nose out of doors.

So much for a small matter. At the other end of the scale of social importance, it is noteworthy that in England fornication is not a crime.[1] An unmarried couple may set up housekeeping in London and remain undisturbed by the law as long as they live, and if anyone else disturbs them the law will protect them; for English law protects those against whom it has no stated grievance, even though their conduct may not be exactly praiseworthy or popular. They may register at an hotel under their several names, and the law will not only leave them at peace but will protect their peace. English law interferes in sex relations only in the case of minors, to safeguard immaturity; and in the case of adultery, to safeguard a property-interest, or the vestiges of one. Other cases are put over into the third region of conduct and left subject to the individual sense of the Right Thing.

In America, on the other hand, the first region of conduct is egregiously expanded. I remember seeing recently a calculation that the poor American is staggering along under a burden of some two million laws; and obviously, where there are so many laws, it is hardly possible to conceive of any items of conduct escaping contact with one or more of them. Thus, the region where conduct is controlled by law so far encroaches upon the region of free choice and the region where conduct is controlled by a sense of the Right Thing, that there is precious little left of either. What is left, moreover, is still further attenuated by the pressure of a public opinion whose energy and zeal are in direct ratio to its meddlesomeness and ignorance. The complaint of critics against what they call our "standardisation" is a complaint against this pressure; and it is so just, and its ground so obvious, that it needs no reiteration here. The only thing I wish to remark is the serious and debilitating deterioration of individual responsibility under this state of affairs. In this respect, living in America is like serving in the army; ninety per cent of conduct is prescribed by law and the remaining ten per cent by the *esprit du corps,* with the consequence that opportunity for free choice in conduct is practically abolished. This falls in very well with the indolent disposition of human nature to regard responsibility as onerous and to dodge it when possible; but it is debilitating, and a

1. I am told, to my astonishment, that neither is it a crime in the State of Maryland!

civilisation organised upon this absence of responsibility is pulpy and unsound.

Indeed, a vague sense of this unsoundness has lately been pervading our people; but it has expressed itself, so far, only in a panicky hospitality to political nostrums of the "liberal and progressive" type, whose tendency is all to aggravate the complaint that they are advertised to remedy. To get a correct measure of our Liberals and Progressives, all one need do is to observe that they contemplate a further enlargement of the first region of conduct; they would have us even more closely controlled by law than we already are! They are more for this, more for indulging an ignorant and licentious zeal for law-mongering than even the hide-bound Tories. As well as I can make out, Chief Justice Taft or Mr. Coolidge or even Mr. Hughes would organize far less trespass on the second and third regions of conduct, if they had their way, than would the late Mr. Roosevelt or the late Senator La Follette; and certainly, of all men I ever knew, the Liberals of my acquaintance have the greatest nervous horror of freedom, the most inveterate and pusillanimous dread of contemplating the ideal picture of mankind existing in free and voluntary association. From such as these, then, nothing may be expected but an exacerbation of the social trouble whereof they seem able to contemplate nothing but the symptoms.

It is not to the point to protest, for example, that Mr. Roosevelt's laws or Senator La Follette's would all be good laws, that their enlargements of the first region of conduct would all be for our own good. The point is that *any* enlargement, good or bad, reduces the scope of individual responsibility, and thus retards and cripples the education which can be a product of nothing but the free exercise of moral judgment. Like the discipline of the army, again, any such enlargement, good or bad, depraves this education into a mere routine of mechanical assent. The profound instinct against being "done for our own good" even by an Aristides—the instinct so miserably misinterpreted by our Liberals and Progressives—is wholly sound. Men are aware of the need of this moral experience as a condition of growth, and they are aware, too, that anything tending to ease it off from them, even for their own good, is to be profoundly distrusted.

The practical reason for freedom, then, is that freedom seems to be the only condition under which any kind of substantial moral fibre can be developed. Everything else has been tried, world without end. Going dead against reason and experience, we have tried law, compulsion and authoritarianism of various kinds, and the result is nothing to be proud of. Americans have many virtues of their own, which I would be the last to belittle or disparage, but the power of quick and independent moral judgment is not one of them. In suggesting that we try freedom, therefore, the anarchist and individualist has a strictly practical aim. He aims at the production of a race of responsible beings. He wants more room for the *savoir se gêner,* more scope for the *noblesse oblige,* a larger place for the sense of the Right Thing. If our legalists and authoritarians could once get this well through their heads, they would save themselves a vast deal of silly insistence on a half-truth and upon the *suppressio veri,* which is the meanest and lowest form of misrepresentation. Freedom, for example, as they keep insisting, undoubtedly means freedom to drink oneself to death. The anarchist grants this at once; but at the same time he points out that it also means freedom to say with the gravedigger in *Les Misérables,* "I have studied, I have graduated; I never drink." It unquestionably means freedom to go on without any code of morals at all; but it also means freedom to rationalise, construct and adhere to a code of one's own. The anarchist presses the point invariably overlooked, that freedom to do the one without correlative freedom to do the other is impossible; and that just here comes in the moral education which legalism and authoritarianism, with their denial of freedom, can never furnish.

The anarchist is not interested in any narrower or more personal view of human conduct. Believing, for example, that man should be wholly free to be sober or to be a sot, his eye is not caught and exclusively engaged by the spectacle of sots, but instead he points to those who are responsibly sober, sober by a self-imposed standard of conduct, and asserts his conviction that the future belongs to them rather than to the sots. He believes in absolute freedom in sex-relations; yet when the emancipated man or woman goes simply on the loose, to wallow along at the mercy of raw sensation from one squalid little *Schweinerei* to another, he is not interested in their panegyrics upon freedom. Instead, he is bored and annoyed, and sometimes casts hankering glances towards the trusty fowling-piece, vainly wishing he could convince himself that a low rake or a dirty drab is worth the price of a dozen buckshot. Then he turns to contemplate those men and women who are responsibly decent, decent by a strong, fine, self-sprung consciousness of the Right Thing, and he declares his conviction that the future lies with them.

The anarchist, moreover, does not believe that any considerable proportion of human beings will promptly turn into rogues and adventuresses, sots and strumpets, as soon as they find themselves free to do so; but quite the contrary. It seems to be a fond notion with the legalists and authoritarians that the vast majority of mankind would at once begin to thieve and murder and generally misconduct itself if the restraints of law and authority were removed. The anarchist, whose opportunities to view mankind in its natural state are perhaps as good as the legalist's, regards this belief as devoid of foundation. Seeing how much evil-doing is directly chargeable to economic pressure alone, the anarchist maintains that the legalists and authoritarians have no proper means of estimating natural human goodness until they postulate it as functioning in a state of economic freedom. They have no proper estimate of the common run of moral sensitiveness, strictness, and scrupulousness until they postulate the moral sense as functioning in a state of social and political freedom based upon economic freedom. Indeed, considering the disabilities put upon this sense, and the incessant organised efforts to deform and weaken it, the anarchist makes bold to marvel that it functions as well as it does.

But I have no intention of digressing into a syllabus of anarchist philosophy. I have thought it worth while to write out the foregoing thoughts, however, merely to make clear that there is a practical side to this philosophy, as well as a theoretical side, and one which is not perhaps wholly unworthy of consideration. The anarchist does not want economic freedom for the sake of shifting a dollar or two from one man's pocket to another's; or social freedom for the sake of rollicking in detestable license; or political freedom for the sake of a mere rash and restless experimentation in system-making. His desire for freedom has but the one practical object, *i.e.,* that men may become as good and decent, as elevated and noble, as they might be and really wish to be. Reason, experience and observation lead him to the conviction that under absolute and unqualified freedom they can, and rather promptly will, educate themselves to this desirable end; but that so long as they are to the least degree dominated by legalism and authoritarianism, they never can.

This essay originally appeared in the *American Mercury* of November 1924 and became the title essay in Nock's collection, *On Doing the Right Thing*.

Index

Absolutism, antithesis of democracy, 178
Acquiescence of age, 53
Adams, Henry, 250
Adams, James Truslow, 175
Adams, John, 14, 24, 45, 272
Adams, Henry Brooks, 99
Administration of Law in the Cities, The
  (Whitlock), 230
Administrative theory of government,
  222–229
Aeschylus, 33
Aging, 52–53
Agnosticism, 256
Albert I, 100–101
Aldrich, Nelson, 146
Alexander I, 192
Alfonso of Castile, Prince, 56
Alien and Sedition Acts, 231
Alpena, MI, xvi, 24–25, 28–29
Altgeld, John Peter, 37, 251
Amenia (fictitious), 301–314
American Association for the Advance-
  ment of Colored People, 142–143
American Dream, 254
American Magazine, xvii
American Mercury, xx, xxii
Americans, civilization of, xiii
Amos Judd (Mitchell), 192
Anarchism
  vs. institution of government, 259
  and Nock, xiv, xxii, 34–51, 258–259
  understanding of freedom, 323–324
Anderson, Sherwood, 115
Angell, Norman, 113
Anti-Armament Society, 68
Anti-Saloon League, 116–117
Apollonides, 58
Aristotle, 21, 200

Arnold, Matthew, 97, 287
  biography of, 8–9
  on Burke and living by ideas, 220–221
  Désiré Nisard on, 318
  essays by, 14
  on Greek and Latin literature, 20
  on John Keats, 112
  "Artemus Ward" (Nock), 32
Astor family, 228
Atlantic Monthly, xx, 28, 32, 149, 151,
  222
Aurelius, Marcus, 61
  and culture, 105
  and daemons, 197
  on masses, 127–128
  reign of, 125
Ausonius, 131
Austria, annexation of, 273
Autobiography
  of Nock, xxii–xxiii, 23–33
  purpose of, 5, 9–10
  of Nikolai Rimsky-Korsakov, 10–13
  of Oswald Villard, 9–10, 14, 117
Autocracy, 222, 312

Babbitt (*Babbitt,* Lewis), 248, 250, 299
Babson, Roger, 67
Bach, Johann Sebastian, 33, 285
Badoglio, Pietro, 274
Bagehot, Walter, 14
Baker, Newton, 115, 211, 263, 265
Bakunin, Mikhail, 258
Balaam, 192, 194
Balakirev, Mily, 13
Baldwinsville, Artemus Ward on, 113
Balfour, Arthur, 78
Barker, Granville, 202
Beard, Charles A., 47n, 96, 246

Being and becoming, 175, 181–182
Jones and, 252
Belgium, 86
culture in, 97–98
schools in, 175–176
Belknap, William, 250
Bell, Bernard Iddings, xi-n
Benda, Julian, xxiv
Bentham, Jeremy, 262, 281
Berlioz, Hector, 33
Bethmann-Hollweg, Theobold von, 271
Beveridge Report (Social Insurance and
Allied Services), 279
Beyle, Marie-Henri [pseud. Stendhal],
253, 254, 307, 308
Bicknell, Thomas, 44
Big Stick doctrine, 67
Biographies, 5–15, 104
Bismarck, Otto von, 28, 285
Blair, Montgomery, 114
Blue Monday, derivation of, 204
Blunt, Wilfrid Scawen (My Diaries,
1888–1914), 14
Bolkonsky, Prince Andrey (War and
Peace, Tolstoy), 193, 198
Bonaparte, Napoleon, 8, 51
Artemus Ward on, 183
and Mihail Kutusov-Smolensky,
188–192
Boni, Albert, 107
Bonn, university at, 175
Book of Journeyman, The, xx
Borodin, Aleksandr Porfirevich, 11, 13
Bottomley, Horatio, 87
Bounderby, Josiah, 74, 156
Bourne, Randolph, xviii
Bowers, Claude, 96
Bribery, 235
Brick, Jefferson, 249, 250, 251
Bright, John
on politicians, 41–42
on Artemus Ward, 114, 197
Brooklyn, NY, xvi, 34
Brooks, Van Wyck, 14

Brown, John, 117–118
Brown Decades, the, 247, 250–252
Browne, Charles Farrar [pseud. Artemus
Ward], 109–120
Bright on, 114, 197
as critic, 112–113
on critics, xxiv
on Napoleon, 183
Nock essay on, 32
"Bruised Patriots, The" (Stearns), 289
Brussels, 100
university at, 175–176, 178
Buchanan, James, 254
Bull detector. See Oxometer
Bureaucracies
controlling, through fear, 239–243
and law, 234–236
Burke, Edmund
on great changes, 50, 222
on colonialists, 274
on the English, 88
on French Revolution, 220
on manners, 149
on politicians, 267
Burns, William J., 143
Business
in Amenia, 304–306
as anti-culture, 101–102
overemphasis on, 208
State conspiracy with, 272
Butler, Joseph, 9, 33, 304
Butler, Judge, 142, 144
Butler, Nicholas Murray, 71, 116
Byron, Lord George Gordon, 186

Calvin, John, 205
Cameron, W. J., 272
Canby, Henry, 7
Canning, George, 305
Capper, Arthur, 150, 230
Carey, Henry C., 216
Carleton, George W., 109
Carnegie, Andrew, 67, 71, 73, 74, 224
Carrington, Edward, 236

This book is set in Berkeley Oldstyle Medium, a typeface based on University of California Old Style, designed in 1938 by Frederic W. Goudy at the request of the university for its Press. It was first used two years later in Goudy's own Typologia, *published by the Press.*

Editorial services by BooksCraft, Inc., Indianapolis, Indiana
Book design by Madelaine Cooke, Athens, Georgia
Typography by Monotype Composition Company, Inc., Baltimore, Maryland
Printed and bound by Edwards Brothers, Inc., Ann Arbor, Michigan